MODERN BRITAIN 1700–1983

MODERN BRITAIN 1700-1983

A Domestic History

Geoffrey Alderman

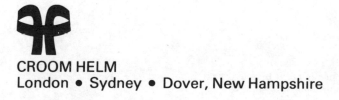

CROOM HELM
London • Sydney • Dover, New Hampshire

© Geoffrey Alderman 1986
Croom Helm Ltd, Provident House, Burrell Row,
Beckenham, Kent BR3 1AT
Croom Helm Australia Pty Ltd, Suite 4, 6th Floor,
64–76 Kippax Street, Surry Hills, NSW 2010, Australia

British Library Cataloguing in Publication Data
Alderman, Geoffrey
  Modern Britain 1700–1983: a domestic history.
  1. Great Britain——History——18th century
  2. Great Britain——History——19th century
  3. Great Britain——History——20th century
  I. Title
  941.07   DA470

  ISBN 0–7099–0537–8
  ISBN 0–7099–0582–3 Pbk

Croom Helm, 51 Washington Street, Dover,
New Hampshire 03820, USA

Library of Congress Cataloging in Publication Data applied for

ISBN 0–7099–0537–8
ISBN 0–7099–0582–3 (Pbk)

Printed and bound in Great Britain
by Billing & Sons Limited, Worcester.

CONTENTS

LIST OF TABLES

For Marion Joan

PREFACE

There are on the market today a number of substantial textbooks covering the political and social development of modern Britain. My purpose in writing the present volume is not to add to them, but rather to present an interpretation of major trends in the domestic history of the United Kingdom since the beginning of the eighteenth century, illustrating my arguments by reference to original source material. My choice of themes is blatantly subjective but not — I hope — outrageously so. I have, in general, omitted any detailed treatment of foreign and colonial policy, partly out of considerations of space but also from a sense of professional inadequacy; I am happy to leave diplomacy to the diplomatic historians.

A work such as this must, perforce, lean heavily upon the researches of others; the works referred to in the Guide to Further Reading comprise those I have found most helpful and their citation will, I trust, serve as an acknowledgement of my debt in this respect.

I should like to place on record my thanks to Richard Stoneman, my editor at Croom Helm, for his patient handling of my drafts, and to Royal Holloway and Bedford College for having granted me a period of sabbatical leave during which I was able to write unencumbered by teaching and administrative duties. Rex Pope read through the entire text, and has saved me from many errors of fact and interpretation; I alone am responsible for any which remain.

Dr Geoffrey Alderman,
Royal Holloway and Bedford New College,
University of London

1 FOUNDATIONS OF THE MODERN BRITISH STATE

The roots of modern British society lie embedded in the eighteenth century. To make this assertion is not to deny that some features of present-day Britain have their origins in earlier periods of history. The obsession with colonies may be traced to the sixteenth century, while the modern tragedy of Irish entanglement began to be written in the seventeenth. However, even these historical developments were given significant new impulses during the Hanoverian period. More importantly, the major social and political formations of modern Britain have grown directly or indirectly out of the Hanoverian age: industrialisation, urbanisation, mass communications, constitutional monarchy, the rule of parliamentary law, and many others. Although, therefore, the bulk of this work is concerned with the nineteenth and twentieth centuries, its examination of modern Britain begins a century earlier, when the upheavals of civil war and palace revolution had indeed demonstrated that absolute monarchy had had its day, and when the War of the Spanish Succession had indeed shown that Britain had a role to play in Europe. But it was also a period when the precise relationship between monarch and legislature was still unclear, and when the advisability and extent of British involvement in the affairs of continental Europe was still a matter of hot dispute.

Britain in the eighteenth century was a sparsely populated and largely agricultural country. The first national census was not undertaken until 1801, when the population of England was found to be just over 8.6 millions. The best available estimates suggest that at the beginning of the eighteenth century the total population of England was about 5.0 millions, with another half million or so living in Wales and Scotland. But this growth in population was not uniform throughout the century. There appears to have been a rapid rise in population in the first two decades, a decline in the 1720s followed by a modest rise until 1760, and a much accelerated growth of population thereafter, averaging nearly 1 per cent per annum in the closing decades of the century.

It is easier to account for the check in population growth in the

1720s (a decade marked by smallpox and influenza epidemics) than to explain the rise at other times. It is highly improbable that the rise was due, to any significant extent, to immigration. The increase appears to have stemmed from natural causes, a combination of declining mortality and rising fertility. The proportion of deaths per thousand live births was high at the beginning of the century. Even among the aristocracy the figure was about 170 per thousand; not one of Queen Anne's children survived into adulthood. Among the humbler classes the infant death-rate was truly appalling. Today, in Britain, the death of a child is a rare event: in 1980 there were only 11.2 deaths per thousand live births. In 1715 a parliamentary inquiry into the deaths of babies put into the care of the parochial authorities of St Martin in the Fields, in London, found that three out of every four babies in the care of the parish died shortly after birth. The average life expectancy at birth was only about 35 years. There can be no doubt that these rates of infant mortality fell by the end of the eighteenth century. We know that by the last quarter of the century the mortality rate of abandoned children — 'foundlings' — in London appeared to have fallen to about one in four, and that by 1838 the death-rate of children under one year old per thousand live births, in England and Wales, was only 151 — that is, about one in seven.

The death-rate was also affected by an improvement in medical standards. In 1700 there were only four general hospitals in England and Wales: two in London, one in Bath and one in Rochester. By 1760 there were at least twenty, of which London had six. The incidence of some diseases lessened. Bubonic plague was not known in England after 1667. Inoculation against smallpox was introduced in England about 1720, and was widespread by mid- century; but smallpox had by then ceased to be a killer-disease. After mid-century, epidemics of influenza and typhus also appear to have waned, and quinine and bark were successfully used to treat malaria ('ague').

After 1750 it is likely that rising fertility was much more significant than declining mortality as a cause of population increase. The proportion of the population never marrying fell from 15 per cent to 7 per cent, and the average age at which women first married fell from 26.5 to 23.5 years. Because more women married, and married earlier, the number of births per marriage increased. Contemporary observers themselves agreed that this was so; the economist Thomas Malthus argued that over-population could be corrected by postponing the age of marriage.

Now marriage was as expensive an undertaking in the eighteenth century as in the twentieth. Couples, once married, were expected to lead financially independent lives. So it was prudent to defer marriage until some resources had been built up. Expanding economic opportunities after mid-century thus encouraged earlier marriages. It is significant that fertility was higher in industrial areas than in the countryside; most of the increase in population in the 1740s and 1750s took place in counties such as Lancashire, Warwickshire and the West Riding of Yorkshire, all areas in which there was growing industrial activity. Moreover, in some industries, such as textiles, children could be sent to work early in life to boost the family income. The more children, the greater was the income derived from them. This greater income could be used to buy better food and fuel. Although, therefore, environmental conditions in towns undoubtedly deteriorated towards the end of the eighteenth century, the people living in them enjoyed — paradoxically — higher standards of living than their forebears. In addition, there was almost certainly a rise, in the second half of the century, in the numbers of children born out of wedlock. We should note, in this connection, that public attitudes towards pre-marital sex became less harsh, and that it was common for unmarried but established couples, bringing children into the world, to be regarded as married *de facto*. Until the passage of Lord Hardwicke's Marriage Act (1753), which made a church wedding the test of a proper marriage, even clergymen had been inclined to regard the children of established but unwed couples as legitimate.

In the mid-eighteenth century over three quarters of the population of Britain lived in the rural areas of the country, in village communities so scattered that the population density of most of England was less than 100 persons per square mile (in 1980 the population density of England was over 900 per square mile). In 1750 there were few large towns. London was in a class of its own; with a population of around 700,000 it was not merely the largest town in Britain, but the largest in Europe, and its population grew with such speed that by 1801 it exceeded one million, having doubled its size in the space of a hundred years. Most of the other 800 or so 'towns' were in reality large villages or townships with populations of one or two thousand each. Norwich had a population of nearly 30,000; Bristol about 20,000; and Colchester, Exeter, Newcastle-upon-Tyne, Yarmouth and York each had between 10,000 and 15,000. Birmingham, Hull, Leeds, Liverpool and Manchester were clearly recognisable as growing commercial and industrial centres even at the beginning of the century, but each had a population restricted to between 5,000 and 10,000. Even by mid-century there were only 14 towns with over 10,000 inhabitants in England and Wales, only two (Glasgow and Edinburgh) in Scotland and only one (Dublin) in Ireland.

London was the centre of the nation's political system, with the monarchy at its head. It was also the centre of England's legal and economic systems, and of the worlds of fashion, arts and science. It was the financial centre of Britain, housing not merely the Bank of England (founded 1694) but also Lloyds (which originated about 1683 in Edward Lloyd's coffee house), where marine insurance could be arranged, and even a number of more general insurance houses, such as the Phoenix (founded 1680) and the Sun Fire (1708), both of which pioneered fire insurance in the capital. When, at the bequest of Sir Hans Sloane, the British Museum was opened in 1759, London boasted the first publicly owned free-entrance museum in Europe; it already possessed a considerable number of pleasure-gardens and commercial theatres. The capital was also the centre of a growing newspaper industry; by 1790 there were 14 London morning newspapers, and one in the evening.

London possessed a geographically located social structure. The fashionable and well-to-do congregated in Westminster (where a third of the inhabitants were domestic servants); 'the City' (the term was already in common usage) was the commercial and business centre, where bankers and financiers had their headquarters; merchants, shipbuilders and the professional classes inhabited the newer 'suburban' areas in the East End, such as Deptford and Islington; and the humbler classes, such as dockyard workers, dwelt along the banks of the Thames, at Wapping and Rotherhithe. Even the artists and craftsmen of the metropolis congregated together: watchmakers in Clerkenwell, mercers and drapers in Lombard Street, shoemakers in Shoemaker Row, brewers and dyers in Southwark. But London was not in the eighteenth century, as it is now, a city of government employees. The most important departments of state — the admiralty, the treasury, and the offices of the two secretaries of state — were located in Whitehall, close by St James's and Kensington palaces, but they were exceedingly small establishments; in 1726 the staff of the secretaries' offices numbered no more than 24, while the royal household itself only accounted for about 1,000 people, including peers and others performing purely formal or honorary functions.

London was also the greatest centre of consumption in Britain. The nonconformist journalist Daniel Defoe, in his *Tour through the whole Island of Great Britain*, published between 1724 and 1726, argued that in addition to local markets and regional economies the country enjoyed a national economy which originated with and was sustained by the demands of London for consumer goods. 'This whole kingdom', he explained, 'as well as the people, as the land, and even the sea, in every part of it, are employed to furnish something, and I may add, the best of everything, to supply the city of London with provisions.' Corn was imported into the capital along the Thames from Oxfordshire; cattle and sheep were driven to Smithfield on the hoof from the Midlands, Wales and Scotland; vegetables came from Kent; cheese and salt from Cheshire; fish from Devon and Sussex; poultry from Suffolk. Seventy per cent of all Tyneside coal was sent, by coaster, from Newcastle to London. All this activity generated a sub-economy of its own: credit had to be given, bills of exchange negotiated, and long-distance accounts settled by wholesale butchers, corn factors and the like.

Yet the student of eighteenth-century British society would do well not to be mesmerised by London. If it was true that over half the town-dwellers of Hanoverian Britain lived in London, it was also true that London was, spatially and in human terms, far distant from the bulk of the country's population. Turnpike building around London had started in Stuart times, but elsehwere the roads were in a generally poor state, rutted by heavily laden ox-wagons and livestock. The journey by stage-coach from Newcastle to London took nine days, and six from Chester to London. By 1740, turnpikes had been built on the route northwards from London only as far as Grantham; the journey to Edinburgh could still take a fortnight in winter. By mid-century the major trunk roads connecting London with Manchester, Bristol, Birmingham, York and Dover had all been turnpiked, so that by 1770 some 500 turnpike trusts looked after 15,000 miles of road.

Turnpikes certainly improved travelling times. The journey time from Norwich to London was cut from 50 hours, in 1700, to 40 by 1750 and to 19 by 1800; the journey from Manchester to London took 90 hours in 1700 but only 65 by 1750. Leicester acquired a coach service to London in 1753; by 1765 a 'flying machine' could travel the distance in one day. But road travel was both expensive and hazardous. For an 'outside' passage on the Leicester-London coach the fare (1765) was 12s 6d; the price 'inside' was doubled. Even a petty bourgeois family, on a very solid income of, say, £100 per annum, would have found travel at this price something of a luxury, and it was, of course, quite beyond the means of an ordinary wage-earner supporting a family on £40 a year. For those who could afford the fare, a journey by road was often an unpleasant experience. The agencies of law enforcement were few and far between; the wise traveller carried a firearm for protection. At his trial in 1725 Jonathan Wild was accused of being 'a confederate with great numbers of highwaymen, pickpockets, house-breakers, shoplifters and other thieves'. Nor were the gentlemen of the road any respecters of rank. In 1774 the Prime Minister, Lord North, recorded 'I was robbed last night as I expected . . . at the end of Gunnersbury Lane'.

Although there was a great deal of internal migration, most of it was local, from one village to the next or from villages into nearby towns. The greater part of the population of Britain lived in villages with, at most, a few thousand inhabitants; they worked upon and lived off the land. But they did not own it. Land- ownership in eighteenth-century Britain was a complex mosaic. The peerage accounted for only just over half the 400 great landlords with incomes in excess of £3,000 a year; the rest comprised the ranks of the wealthier gentry — the rich baronets, knights, esquires and gentlemen whose importance in eighteenth-century society had already been recognised in the work of the statistician and civil servant Gregory King at the end of the previous century. The remainder of the gentry, comprising perhaps 20,000 families, enjoyed annual incomes ranging from £300 to £3,000, and there were, in addition, about 150,000 freeholders with incomes under £100. In 1688 King had estimated that there were 150,000 tenant farmers and 364,000 'labouring people and out-servants'; these particular figures (based not merely upon King's own researchers, but also upon the Hearth Tax returns to which he had access as secretary to the Commissioners for the Public Accounts) are remarkably close to the estimates made by Joseph Massie in 1759–60, though Massie indicated a growth in the number of labourers to about 400,000 outside London.

Although the most intensive phase of the enclosure movement did not occur until the end of the eighteenth century, land enclosure was common throughout the century and went hand-in-hand with improvements in agricultural techniques. According to Gregory King's calculations a quarter (10 million acres) of the total land area of the country was uncultivated in 1688; in 1795 the Board of Agriculture estimated that eight million acres were still uncultivated. Judged by the number of enclosure awards sanctioned by Parliament (over 1,000 Acts were passed between 1760 and 1800) the enclosure movement did not gather momentum until the reign of George III. Before 1760 only 130 parliamentary enclosure awards had been passed, encompassing about 337,000 acres. But enclosure by statute was only one of a number of methods by which land enclosure could be carried out; other methods included common agreement, and private agreements enrolled in Chancery. It is probable that, prior to 1760, much more land was enclosed through the Chancery procedure than through statute law, particularly in the Midlands and southern England.

The economic effects of enclosure should not be exaggerated. The mere replacement of a strip system by a field enclosed by a fence or ditch did not itself amount to an agricultural 'revolution'; not every enclosure resulted in technical improvements; and experiments with new crops and rotations could and did take place in unenclosed parishes. But it was widely acknowledged that the strip system enshrined traditional farming methods and dignified the standards of the most inefficient cultivators. Innovation, whether in land use or in animal breeding, could only come with great difficulty; the innovator had to obtain the agreement of those much more conservative in farming techniques. The importance of enclosure lay in the fact that it made possible a far greater degree of innovation in a far shorter space of time.

During the eighteenth century the pressure for agricultural innovation derived largely from the need of landowners to meet interest charges and generally increasing expenditure. The period 1690–1715 had seen land taxation rise to four shillings in the pound (it later fell by half) to meet the cost of foreign wars. This squeezed the profits of the smaller and less efficient estates. Between 1730 and 1750 there was a fall in agricultural prices, leading to arrears of rent. The legal device of strict entail prevented the head of a landed family from selling part of his estate; capital assets (i.e. land) could not be sold to pay debts, except as a whole. The wealthier landed families therefore tended to buy up the smaller estates. But parallel with this development was the relentless desire of the merchants and businessmen to buy themselves into the landed classes, either by purchasing bankrupt estates or by marrying their daughters (suitably provided with fulsome dowries) to the sons of landowners fallen upon hard times. Daniel Defoe observed that in the home counties there were 'several very considerable estates purchased and now enjoyed by citizens of London, merchants and tradesmen', and he noted that 'the present increase of wealth in the City of London spreads itself into the country, and plants families and fortunes who in another age will equal the families of the ancient gentry'. The purchase of landed estates in this way afforded security as well as status; investment in land — particularly if the land was improved, so raising its capital value and the rent it could command — was relatively safe.

But the injection of commercial instincts and habits into farming activities fuelled the search for ever more efficient methods of husbandry. Land might be 'improved' in a variety of ways, perhaps by exploiting the minerals found underneath it, perhaps by building turnpikes or canals and deriving income thereby, perhaps by using it for urban expansion. However, agricultural improvement usually meant indulging in more intensive methods of farming and adopting the techniques pioneered by agricultural improvers. Foremost among these were Charles (second Viscount) Townshend, who introduced turnips and clover into crop rotation on his Norfolk estates in the 1730s, thus eliminating the need for fields to lie fallow and providing cheap winter animal feeds into the bargain; Robert Bakewell, whose experiments in livestock breeding were designed to produce better quality meat and wool; and Thomas Coke (first Earl of Leicester) who demonstrated how sandy soils could be transformed using marl and manure as fertilisers, how improved strains of sheep, cattle and pigs might be bred, and whose Holkham estates became a byword for agricultural efficiency and innovation. The adoption of agricultural machinery was a nineteenth-century development rather than an eighteenth. But the seed-drill invented by Jethro Tull to replace the wasteful scattering of seed by hand dated from 1701, and Tull also devised a horse-drawn hoe to aid aeration of the soil and eliminate weeds. A machine for the threshing of corn made its appearance in the Scottish lowlands in 1758.

The agricultural revolution thus preceded the industrial, and was less well advanced by the time George III ascended the throne. Corn output increased from about 14 million quarters in 1700 to over 16 millions in 1760, most of this increase coming after 1740. During the first half of the century, particularly during the decade of the 1750s, there was a brisk export trade in wheat and wheat flour. Increases in output of meat are more difficult to quantify. Probably there was not a great rise in the number of sheep and cattle. But average weights of beasts brought to market increased substantially: cattle from 370 pounds weight in 1710 to 800 pounds in 1795, sheep from 38 pounds weight to 80 pounds over the same period.

Agriculture became a business, in which the large well-endowed units prospered and the less strong did not. Two classes in particular suffered as a result of agricultural change. The small freeholder found it harder to hold his own in a world where economies of scale were available only to those with larger farms and plenty of spare cash. The more fortunate freeholders sold their lands and became tenants on long leases. On the whole, however, the independent landowning peasantry declined both in numbers and income. Moreover, even if the change of status from freeholder to tenant might often have made financial good sense, it could also result in loss of civic influence wherever the right to vote was limited to freehold ownership. Conversely, the great landowners, who became greater still in the course of the eighteenth century, also obtained ever more pervasive political leverage as they acquired freeholds and the political privileges which went with them.

The enclosure movement had a much more immediate and devastating effect upon those who had never owned land, but who had managed to support themselves and their families through the exercise of 'rights of common' over moors, fens, commons, wastes and woodlands. These rights permitted farm labourers to supplement meagre wages by grazing cows or sheep on the common; allowed independent cultivators with few strips on the open fields to search the woodlands for animal fodder and fuel; and enabled squatters, who had never had any share in the open fields, to hunt for rabbits, burn charcoal, and actually live on the common or waste lands. For people such as these, enclosure was a personal calamity: Arthur Young explained that 'By nineteen out of twenty Enclosure Bills the poor are injured and most grossly . . . The poor in these parishes may say with truth,

"Parliament may be tender of property; all I know is, I had a cow, and an Act of Parliament has taken it from me".'

There were no significant outbreaks of rural violence in eighteenth-century England. But the fate of those evicted from the land, and unable to find more than casual or seasonal employment, was grim indeed. The Poor Law (Act of Settlement) of 1662 placed a premium upon 'settlement' in a parish; settlement was usually acquired by birth, marriage or residence and, once acquired, entitled the possessor to poor relief if destitute, sick or unable to work — but only in the parish of settlement and no other. An Act dating from the reign of William III gave protection against removal to those who, within 40 days of arriving in a parish, could produce a certificate issued by the officers of a parish where they had a 'settlement'. Nonetheless, the poor, who, as likely as not, could not produce such a certificate, were often despatched from parish to parish in a human game of 'pass the parcel' until their parish of settlement was reached; pregnant women were sent on their way with particular speed.

Yet the cost of poor relief increased by leaps and bounds during the course of the eighteenth century. In 1700 it was about £650,000; by 1776 it had reached £1.5 millions; in 1786 it stood at £2 millions; and in 1803 it was more than £4 millions. In Ireland and the Scottish Highlands holdings could be subdivided to accommodate at least some of the able-bodied poor. But even this far-from-ideal solution was not available in England and Wales. The only alternative to the poor law was to seek non-agricultural work, either industrial work in the villages or, more usually, work in nearby towns, ports or coalfields. It was in this way that the movement of population away from the agricultural countryside began well before the mid-century rise in population.

Industrial change, like agricultural innovation, was the child of the early and mid rather than the late eighteenth century. Abraham Darby established his famous works at Coalbrookdale, Shropshire, in 1709, and there pioneered the smelting of iron ore with coke so as to remove the sulphur content and facilitate the manufacture of thin castings necessary for hollow objects, such as steam cylinders. The Darby method was slow to spread. But it was at the Coalbrookdale works that the cylinders were made for the atmospheric steam engines designed by Thomas Newcomen, which were widely used for draining mines until superseded in 1765 by the superior designs of James Watt. The giant beam engines of Watt and his partner Matthew Boulton, which pumped the water and sewerage of Victorian London, began to be built at their Birmingham works in the 1770s. In 1781 the partnership produced a rotative steam engine; however, partly on account of technological difficulties and partly for economic reasons (not least, the high charges levied by Watt upon those who used his patents, which did not expire until after 1800), the potentialities of this invention were to be reserved for the nineteenth century rather than the eighteenth.

It was in the textile industry that the eighteenth-century industrial revolution was most evident, triggered by the intense jealousy between the cossetted wool trade and the newer cotton manufacturers. Cotton was first imported from India to Britain at the end of the seventeenth century. In 1701 the woollen interest secured a ban on the import of cotton calicoes printed in India; twenty years later the prohibition was extended to calicoes printed in England for home consumption. Although fustians (a mixture of cotton and linen) were exempted from 1736 onwards, the ban on the home sale of printed cotton was not finally lifted until 1774. So for much of the century the infant Lancashire cotton industry manufactured for export only, and the need to compete with the high quality Indian cottons, produced cheaply and marketed by the East India Company, added urgency to the search for efficient mechanisation. John Kay's flying shuttle (halving the number of weavers needed per loom) made its appearance in the 1730s; James Hargreaves spinning jenny dated from 1765; and Edmund Cartwright invented his power loom in 1784. But the device which had the greatest impact on the organisation of the cotton industry was Richard Arkwright's water-powered spinning frame, patented in 1769. This invention made textile spinning a factory industry and ensured that the production of cotton fabric was the first manufacturing process to be entirely mechanised. Although there were in eighteenth-century Britain numerous examples of large-scale concentration of labour (naval dockyards, shipbuilding yards, coal mines and breweries, for instance) the cotton factories that began to be established in the last quarter of the century represented a new and sinister departure: strict division of labour in a regimented atmosphere, the pace of work determined by a machine.

This was not, however, what can strictly be called a capitalist mode of production, the investment of 'anonymous' wealth in industry simply to produce a profit, or dividend, and, hence, industry whose ownership was, perhaps, far removed from industrial centres. For one thing, the banking system remained largely undeveloped for much of the century. The twenty or so banks in the City of London accepted deposits and issued notes, but dealt mainly with the aristocracy and the Treasury. A system of country banks, raising money in one locality in order to invest it in another, did not emerge until the very end of the century: in 1750 there were just twelve such banks. Capital tended to be raised privately, through friends or relatives or perhaps by persuading local merchants or brewers to risk some savings. Sometimes local attorneys or businessmen acted as brokers to arrange loans, and some of the earliest banking houses were established in this way. Coutts was founded by Thomas Coutts, a wealthy Edinburgh corn dealer who became a partner in a firm of London goldsmiths. The Gurneys were Norwich merchants and worsted manufacturers. James Barclay, a Quaker linen merchant in Cheapside, joined with some relatives in 1736 in establishing a banking business in Lombard Street, at the sign of the Spread Black Eagle.

But these were very small beginnings. For much of the eighteenth century, investment in manufacturing industry was regarded as a risky enterprise, and for that reason not to be compared with investment in land. Overseas trading ventures could, however, bring handsome rewards. The expansion of Empire into the Caribbean, America and India, the growth of the merchant marine (from about 3,300 vessels, or 260,000 tons, in 1702 to about 9,400 vessels, or 695,000 tons, in 1776), but above all the protection afforded by the Navigation Acts, which gave a monopoly of the carrying and entrepôt trade with the colonies to British or colonial vessels, in which at least three-quarters of the crews had to be British, provided the foundations upon which great fortunes could be made. Between 1700 and 1770 the total value of English exports more than doubled, from £6.5 millions to £14.3 millions. The total value of re-exports (mainly tobacco, linens, calicoes and sugar) fluctuated, but the trend was unmistakably upwards, from £2.1 millions to £4.8 millions over the same period. The value of bullion exports rarely exceeded £1 million, whereas imports of bullion rose from £6 millions to over £12 millions. Moreover, these explicit indices of wealth take no account of trade conducted by British merchants in British ships (insured in London) which did not pass through a British port:

primarily the transportation of slaves from Africa to the West Indies, and local trade in south-east Asia conducted by the East India Company. Neither do they reflect the 'repatriation' of profits to Britain by West Indian planters and East Indian nabobs. Nor, for obvious reasons, do they encompass the wealth derived from illegally traded goods, mainly the smuggling of tea, silks and French brandy.

A career in business could thus bring great rewards. But fortunes could be lost with remarkable rapidity. The chief sectors of the domestic economy were influenced by short-term fluctuations. Poor harvests in 1727, 1728, 1740, 1751 and 1756 affected not merely the farmers but, because of the resultant high corn prices, the poorer sections of society. The late 1740s and early 1750s were marked by outbreaks of cattle plague. Although wars stimulated some sections of the economy they placed new strains upon the balance of payments and interfered with foreign trade. The Seven Years' War (1756–63) certainly brought commercial and colonial gains. But in general the conflicts with France during the eighteenth century were the single most important factor in the growth of the national debt, from £36 millions in 1714 to £132 millions by 1763.

The growth of government indebtedness was a constant source of national worry, and furnished the *locus classicus* of eighteenth-century commercial stupidity, the South Sea Bubble crisis of 1720. The roots of the Bubble crisis lay in the provisions of the Treaty of Utrecht (1713), by which Great Britain acquired the *asiento de negros*, the monopoly of supplying African slaves to the Spanish-American colonies. This monopoly was not worth a great deal; but the prospect of legally breaking into the lucrative, but hitherto totally protected, trade of the Spanish Empire excited speculatory passions to an unprecedented degree. Attention focused, in particular, upon the South Sea Company, founded in 1711 by the Tory statesman Robert Harley, first Earl of Oxford, not primarily as a trading company but as an enterprise to make money by servicing part of the national debt in return for whatever trade there was with South America. The scheme also had frankly political overtones, in that it threatened the Bank of England and the Bank's Whig connections in the City of London. In February 1720 the House of Commons approved a scheme whereby the Company was to take over the whole of the national debt in return for a payment of £7 millions to the government. By June 1720

South Sea Company stock had reached the staggering level of £1,050, and the rapacious frenzy created by the scheme had led to a mushroom growth of doubtful companies dedicated to such enterprises as the purchase of bogs in Ireland, trading in hair, and other equally absurd schemes. The inevitable crash came in the autumn. By late September South Sea stock had plummetted to £190; thousands of investors had been ruined.

The Bubble crisis had two effects whose importance can hardly be overstated. The first was economic. In the middle of the crisis the government passed the 'Bubble Act', which prohibited the formation of joint-stock companies except by grant of royal charter or by private Act of Parliament; both these procedures were costly and time-consuming. General limited liablility did not appear in Britain until 1855. For over a hundred years, therefore, those who agreed to become partners in business and commercial ventures were personally liable for the debts of the companies in which they had invested. This obviously impinged upon the growth of enterprises requiring large amounts of capital. Where substantial capital needed to be raised — for docks, turnpikes, canals and railways — Acts of Parliament had to be passed so that the liability of shareholders might be limited to the amounts of their individual investments. In order for such legislation to be enacted, big business had to play the political game at Westminster. Second, the Bubble crisis brought to the fore the one experienced politician not generally touched by the scandal: Sir Robert Walpole, whose dominance of early eighteenth-century British politics rested upon, and therefore illustrates, the norms of constitutional practice as they developed in the half-century following the Glorious Revolution of 1688.

That Revolution, in many ways more permanent than the false dawn of the Civil War and Interregnum, signified the triumph of Parliament over Monarchy. The propertied classes (pre-eminently the shire gentry and the town merchants) toppled James II, who had the misfortune to be a Catholic and a believer in the exercise of rights which he undoubtedly possessed, and replaced him with his Dutch Calvinist brother-in-law William of Orange, whose one abiding passion was to use English resources to fight Louis XIV of France, and who had the good fortune to be married to James' Protestant sister, Mary. Parliament then proceeded to remodel the constitution. The Act of Rights (1689) outlawed the suspending power (the right claimed by Stuart monarchs to suspend laws without parliamentary approval) and the dispensing power (the right to veto the operation of a law in a particular case) 'as it hath beene assumed and exercised of late'. The 1689 Act also did away with the right of the monarch to maintain a standing army in peacetime without Parliament's consent; this consent was henceforth given in the form of a Mutiny Act whose duration was limited to twelve months. The necessity of ensuring the passage of the annual Mutiny Bill meant that Parliament would have to be called into session at least once a year. The Triennial Act (1694) limited the life of any one Parliament to three years, at the end of which fresh elections had to be held. In 1716 this was replaced by a Septennial Act, which extended the life of a Parliament to seven years and which remained in force until 1911.

The passage of the Septennial Act was triggered by the Jacobite rebellion of 1715 and was, in the short term, intended to postpone a general election due to be held in 1718. However, those who urged the passage of the Act also had other, longer-term aims in view. One was to reduce the burden of election expenses. Another was to increase the bargaining power of the borough-mongers (399 of the 558 members of the Commons represented borough con- stituencies) in their negotiations with the Crown, because a seat secure for seven years was worth much more than one secure for only three. The Septennial Act must not be seen as an assault on democracy. Hanoverian elections were not an appeal to public opinion to replace one administration with another. The choice of ministers remained the prerogative of the Crown, and Hanoverian monarchs made frequent changes of ministers during the lifetime of a single Parliament. Eight of the eleven Parliaments between 1716 and 1783 lasted between six and seven years. The major long-term effect of the Act was to give members of the House of Commons, once elected, a considerable degree of independence from the Crown, the ministers of the Crown, and the electorate.

The Hanoverians had, perforce, not merely to live with Parliament but to be dependent upon it. The Act of Rights had declared illegal 'levying Money for or to the use of the Crowne by pretence of Prerogative without Grant of Parlyament for longer time or in other manner then [*sic*] the same is or shall be granted'. The Act of Settlement (1701) declared that judges held their offices 'Quam diu se bene Gesserint' (during good behaviour), and not at the whim of the monarch, and stipulated that a royal pardon might not henceforth be pleaded to an impeachment by the Commons. These provisions removed the judiciary from royal control but facilitated parliamentary control of ministers, just as parliamentary control of taxation had been assured in 1689. The hereditary revenues of the Crown — £700,000 a year under William III — were hardly sufficient to allow a monarch to pursue policies and maintain the organs of government independently of the views of the Lords and Commons. From 1690 onwards, Parliament made specific appropriations to meet authorised expenditure as it arose, and by 1714 the Treasury was, as a matter of routine, preparing annual estimates for Parliamentary approval. In practice this meant the approval of the House of Commons, which during the reign of Charles II had established the principle that though the Lords might accept or reject a money Bill, such a Bill could only originate and be amended in the Commons.

Two further provisions of the Act of Settlement deserve comment. As ruler not only of England and Wales, Scotland, and Ireland, but also of the United Provinces, and with a grasp of the affairs of continental Europe few British statesmen of the period possessed, William III had endeavoured to pursue his own foreign policy, without reference to Parliament. The Act of Settlement declared that England and Englishmen were not to be obliged, without parliamentary consent, to engage in a war for the defence of territories not belonging to the English Crown. This was the first statutory limitation to be placed upon royal control of foreign policy. Taken together with parliamentary control of government expenditure, it meant that henceforth the formulation and execution of foreign policy had to be agreed between Crown and Parliament.

The Act of Settlement had also included a very sweeping provision designed to curtail royal influence in Parliament. It had provided that 'no Person who has an Office or Place of Profit under the King or recieves [sic] a Pention from the Crown shall be capable of serving as a Member of the House of Commons'. Had this provision been carried into effect it would have led inexorably to something approaching an American style of government, whereby none of the President's ministers may sit in the Congress; that is, none of the King's ministers could have become MPs, modern Cabinet government would not have been possible, and the King would have been obliged to 'lobby' in Parliament like any pressure group. As it happens, this drastic clause was never invoked. The overriding purpose of the Act of Settlement was to provide for the Protestant Hanoverian succession should the future Queen Anne die without heirs. Therefore it did not take effect until Anne's death in 1714, and this gave time to rethink the sweeping prohibition on royal 'placemen' sitting in the Commons. The Succession to the Crown Act of 1705 and the Regency Act of 1707 effected a compromise: those whose offices were in existence before 1705 were, with some exceptions, permitted to sit in the Commons, but MPs who accepted ministerial positions had to submit themselves for re-election. Hostility to royal placemen was, none the less, a recurring theme of eighteenth-century politics. Excise-men and customs-men were excluded from the Commons in 1700. A Place Act of 1742 excluded further categories of minor civil servants and in 1782, as part of the Rockingham Whigs' programme of 'economical reform', the prohibition was extended to government contractors; Crewe's Act, also of 1782, actually disfranchised the revenue officers of the Crown.

During the course of the eighteenth century, therefore, 'limited monarchy' arrived. The Crown relied upon Parliament for taxation and revenue and even in the realm of foreign relations was increasingly subject to parliamentary control. In the field of domestic legislation Parliament was supreme. William III was the last monarch to make a habit of exercising the royal veto; between 1689 and 1696 he vetoed five Bills, though in due course they all passed into law. Queen Anne's veto of the Scottish Militia Bill, in 1708, turned out to be the final occasion upon which the Crown exercised this particular power. In 1741 the philosopher and political commentator David Hume felt able to dismiss the royal veto in the following terms:

> The share of power allotted by our constitution to the House of Commons is so great, that it absolutely commands all the other parts of the government. The king's legislative power is plainly no proper check to it. For though the king has a negative [i.e. veto] in framing laws, yet this, in fact, is esteemed of so little moment, that whatever is voted by the two houses is always sure to pass into a law, and the royal assent is little better than a form. The principle weight of the crown lies in the executive power. But . . . the exercise of this power requires an immense expense, and the Commons have assumed to themselves the sole right of granting money.

How then, did eighteenth-century monarchs persuade the House of Commons to do as they wished? They could, of course, attempt to secure the return to Parliament of persons sympathetic to their aims or, better still, in their pay. The mere fact that Place Acts were passed reflects a growing hostility towards the presence in Parliament of MPs in government service. These placemen formed the nucleus of the Court and Treasury party in the Commons. Of all the English borough seats the government itself controlled perhaps 25; in alliance with wealthy local patrons, such as Lord Falmouth in Cornwall, this figure might just reach 60. Royal influence at Westminster was sustained by the Court and Treasury party, the bulk of whose members were office-holders pure and simple. The total membership fluctuated a good deal. It usually stood at around 150, or just over a quarter of the House of Commons; during the Seven Years' War it reached 220, but this was still much less than a working majority.

Nor were these placemen totally reliable. During the Excise Bill crisis of 1733, which nearly cost Walpole his majority in the Commons, Lord John Hervey confided to Queen Caroline that 'a great many in the King's service' had 'taken the quiet part of lying by [absenting themselves from Westminster] till they are ripe for a revolution in the ministry'. Walpole only avoided this 'revolution' by withdrawing the Bill. Professor J. B. Owen has calculated that of the 157 place-holders in the Commons in 1741, 33 were active members of the Opposition (some held their offices for life and were thus above royal manipulation) and another 19 voted against the government at least once during the 1741–7 Parliament. The remaining 240 or so borough seats were controlled by private patrons who returned either themselves or their relatives and who might or might not be government supporters. In the counties no single individual — not even the King — controlled the elections. Indeed, the high cost of fighting county elections (the Oxfordshire election of 1754 cost the Tories over £20,000) led to a great number of uncontested seats, a leading landowner nominating one member and the country gentry the other. Again, county MPs might or might not be numbered as government supporters.

So the Court and Treasury party by itself could never dominate the House of Commons, and the King could never acquire outright a parliamentary majority. Sustaining a majority in the Commons was an acrobatic feat of particular delicacy. It could not be undertaken by the King personally (the first two Hanoverians had little English) but had to be entrusted to a government minister — preferably himself in the Commons — who was sufficiently trusted by a majority of his fellow MPs and who enjoyed their confidence as well as that of the monarch. In attacking the government's foreign policy in the summer of 1755, the elder Pitt protested 'that the business of the House of Commons could not go on without there was a minister . . . who should go directly between the King and them'. And in trying, unsuccessfully, to persuade the Duke of Newcastle that Pitt should indeed be taken into the government to fill just such a position (effectively left vacant when Newcastle, in the Lords, had succeeded his brother Henry Pelham as First Lord of the Treasury the previous year) Lord Chancellor Hardwicke wrote of 'the *general* principle, that there must be a minister *with the King* in the House of Commons'. The following year, 1756, Pitt was, and had to be, brought into the administration, as Secretary of State for the Northern Department (virtually Foreign Secretary), paired first with the Duke of Devonshire at the Treasury and later (June 1757) with Newcastle. Pitt thereby donned the mantle worn a decade earlier by Henry Pelham and, before him, by Pelham's political tutor, Robert Walpole.

Walpole himself had always denied that he was 'a prime minister', a charge frequently levelled at him by his opponents. There had been 'first ministers' earlier in the century, such as Harley when Lord High Treasurer (the last individual to hold this office before it went into commission) between 1711 and 1714. But Harley sat in the Lords. Walpole remained in the Commons, controlled a majority there and enjoyed the confidence of two Hanoverian monarchs, a remarkable feat because it was customary for opposition politicians to court the favour of successive Princes of Wales (George II, Frederick Prince of Wales until his death in 1751, and George III) in the hope that the Prince would, once installed on the throne, dismiss his father's ministers and appoint them instead. Leicester House, the home of the Prince of Wales, thus became a shadow Court, but in 1727 Walpole circumvented it through the support of Caroline, George II's wife. Walpole also had the confidence of the City merchants and of the independent country gentry. Moreover, he turned the Treasury (of which he was First Lord) from a mere revenue-managing department into (as Hardwicke described it in 1755) 'an employment of great business' — in short, a machine to control and distribute patronage.

But the ingenuity of Robert Walpole went further than this, because he erected and maintained a particular species of Cabinet government. 'Cabinet Councils' grew out of the Privy Council, which by the late seventeenth century had become too big for either efficiency or secrecy. Queen Anne sat with the Cabinet, but George I ceased this practice in 1717 and thereafter the Cabinet deliberated upon matters referred to it by the King (and, during the reign of George III, without waiting for the King's instructions) and then drew up a minute recording the decisions taken. The evolution of Cabinet government was resisted because it prevented the House of Commons from naming or impeaching individuals suspected of having initiated particular policies. In 1738 Sir William Pulteney accused Walpole of having 'the chief direction' of the Privy Council, the Cabinet Council, and 'any more secret council', and we know from the memoirs of Lord Hervey that Walpole used the Cabinet as a way of evading personal responsibility for his policies:

> So that Sir Robert Walpole [Hervey recorded], with a dexterity equal to his power, whilst in fact he did everything alone, was responsible for nothing but in common whilst those ciphers of the Cabinet signed everything he dictated, and, without the least share of honour or power, bound themselves equally with him in case this political merchant should be bankrupt.

In the shifting sands of eighteenth-century politics, the evolution of Cabinet government and of the office of Prime Minister seemed, in some quarters, to be, or at least to be capable of becoming, instruments of royal tyranny. Had not Archbishop Laud and the Earl of Strafford ('Black Tom Tyrant') been the 'chief ministers' of Charles I, and would not a system of Cabinet government have saved these evil ministers from the scaffold?

If these arguments seem far-fetched or spurious, we must remember that only a hundred years separated the fall of Walpole from the outbreak of the Civil War and that the fear of a Stuart restoration was a fact of life, at least during the first half of the eighteenth century. The new element in the equation (though it was too novel to have yet acquired the aura of permanence and the confidence which flows therefrom) was the power of the House of Commons. With that proviso, Cabinet government and the office of Prime Minister were here to stay. In November 1778 Lord North, a true Prime Minister, told George III 'that in critical times, it is necessary that there should be one directing Minister, who should plan the whole of the operations of government'. But the following month he used the device of collective Cabinet responsibility to defend Lord George Germain, the unfortunate Colonial Secretary who was regarded as 'the principal author' of the events which were leading to the loss of some of the American colonies. As it became clear that the American war was lost, North's majority in the Commons grew smaller, and in February 1782 a motion declaring continued war in America to be impracticable was carried by 19 votes. On 18 March, faced with a vote of no confidence which he knew he could not win, North again wrote to the King:

> Your Majesty is well apprized that, in this country, the Prince on the Throne cannot, with prudence, oppose the deliberate resolution of the House of Commons . . . The Parliament have altered their sentiments, and . . . their sentiments whether just or erroneous, must ultimately prevail.

North resigned. In this way, and at the price of 13 American colonies, the House of Commons demonstrated its ultimate ascendancy over the House of Hanover.

But where did 'party' fit into this schema, and who were the Whigs and the Tories? In trying to understand the nature of eighteenth-century 'party' politics we must, of course, dismiss from our minds any notion of party deriving from later examples of mass parties, disciplined parties, parties organised from headquarters, or even parties based upon dogma. In Queen Anne's reign there did exist two broadly definable groupings, called the Whigs and the Tories, with adherents in Parliament and in the country. These parties had their origins in the politics of the 1670s and 1680s. Tories supported the principle of hereditary monarchy and, therefore, the right of James II to the English throne even though he was a Catholic; they also, somewhat paradoxically, stood for the monopolistic claims of the established Church of England. Whigs pressed for a limited monarchy, supported — and later engineered — the exclusion of James II from the throne, and favoured the imposition of political disabilities upon the Catholics but the toleration of Dissenters. The Toleration Act of 1689, which allowed English nonconformists to have their own places of worship, teachers and preachers, was a

Whig measure. The Whigs also supported the practice of 'occasional conformity', whereby nonconformists agreed to receive communion in the Anglican Church merely to qualify for civil or military office. In 1711 the Tory administration of Robert Harley and Henry St John, Viscount Bolingbroke, legislated against occasional conformity by passing an Act imposing a £40 fine and disqualification from office upon those who, after receiving the Anglican sacrament, attended nonconformist services. The Schism Act of 1714 forbade nonconformists to teach or to maintain schools. Both the Schism and the Occasional Conformity Acts were repealed by the Whigs in 1719, and annually from 1727 onwards an Indemnity Act was passed in order to allow nonconformists to hold municipal offices.

It is likely that after the Glorious Revolution all but the most implacable Tories gave up the true Stuart cause, deriving consolation from the fact that Mary, James II's eldest daughter, shared the throne with Dutch William, and that William was succeeded by Mary's younger sister, Anne. Most Tories had in any case shared with the Whigs a total opposition to James' attempts to re-Catholicise England. But the Tory politicians who had been denied office in the 1690s found a new source of grievance in England's involvement in Continental wars, which they regarded as detrimental to the national well-being and a subordination of English interests to Dutch. The claims of the Old Pretender (James Edward Stuart, James II's son) were forgotten, the Act of Settlement was supported, and the Tories concentrated their energies upon exploiting the two issues which dominated Anne's reign: increasing war-weariness and the cry of 'The Church in danger'.

In pursuing these themes the Tories found allies amongst the independent country gentlemen in Parliament, who supported the Anglican ascendancy and opposed high war taxation. A 'country party' thus came into being, juxtaposed to the Court party and with Tory politicians at its head. Harley also exploited the personal quarrel between Queen Anne and the Duchess of Marlborough. His chance of power came in 1710, when the Whig 'junta' (Lords Somers, Wharton, Halifax and Sunderland, and Robert Walpole) foolishly prosecuted Dr Henry Sacheverell for having preached against the ideals of the Glorious Revolution and for having accused the Whig ministry of hostility to the established Church. The London mobs attacked dissenting chapels and the

Bank of England, symbols of Whig dominance in the City. Harley became head of a Tory ministry; the general election of 1710 gave him a majority in the Commons.

During Anne's reign, therefore, a distinct and viable two-party system emerged, sustained by real issues of perceived and immediate importance. The Tories, as we have seen, legislated against nonconformity and brought the war to an end. The Peace of Utrecht (1713), though naturally denounced by the Whigs, prevented a union of the French and Spanish crowns, and provided for French recognition of the Hanoverian succession. England gained Nova Scotia, Newfoundland, the Hudson Bay territories, Fort James in Senegambia, Gibraltar and Minorca; English merchants acquired the right to trade with Spain on equal terms with the French, and England was granted the over-valued *asiento*.

But the succession question proved to be the undoing of the Tory party. In the summer of 1714, as Anne's life drew to a close, some of the most prominent Tory politicians, led by Bolingbroke, made contact with the Jacobite gentry (located mainly in the old Royalist north of England, and, of course, in Scotland) and gave serious consideration to a hare-brained scheme for a Jacobite administration under the Old Pretender once the Queen was dead. The total failure of the Old Pretender's invasion of Scotland (with French troops) in 1708 ought to have told them that the course they were pursuing was doomed. But the Tory leaders seem to have over-estimated their own popularity and, much more seriously, to have misjudged totally the outlook of the great mass of the Tory squirearchy, who had no intention of becoming party to an armed revolt. The fear of the Tory leadership, that the Hanoverian succession would lead to its exclusion from office, became a self-fulfilling prophecy, and the actual involvement of a few Tory politicians, including Bolingbroke (now fled to France), in the Jacobite rebellion of 1715 sealed the fate of the party.

In the first place, Tory and Jacobite became interchangeable terms, and almost synonymous with treason. George I naturally concluded that only Whig politicians could be safely entrusted with the conduct of his government; the more serious Jacobite revolt of 1745 confirmed George II in the fears and beliefs of his father. Secondly, and consequentially, those who wished to pursue political careers under the first two Hanoverians had to call themselves Whigs; political conflict in this period was, therefore, Whig against Whig.

Tories who had no serious Jacobite sympathies, but who wished to maintain their independence of the Hanoverian Court and the Whig ministers to be found there, did not attempt to resurrect the old political divisions. The Stuart cause was dead and the Hanoverians firmly established. The Church was manifestly no longer in danger. There were isolated instances of Anglican xenophobia later in the century, such as the Jew Bill riots of 1753 which forced the Pelhams to repeal the Jewish Naturalisation Act, and the anti-Catholic Gordon riots of 1780, but in both cases religious prejudice was really a cover for underlying political and economic grievances. The annual Indemnity Acts for dissenters were passed automatically; Jews were loyal and valued supporters of the Hanoverian throne; and, significantly, the Roman Catholic Relief Act of 1778 (the passage of which was the ostensible cause of the Gordon riots) was not repealed. Certainly by 1760, religion had ceased to be an issue of major political significance in England, though in Ireland, and to a lesser extent in Scotland, Roman Catholics were still politically suspect.

Other issues which might have been exploited by the Tories also became less contentious. As more of the landed gentry invested in commerce and industry, and as the merchant classes purchased or married themselves to great estates, the conflict between landed and monied interests became less important. One reason why the Excise Bill crisis of 1733 proved so dangerous to Walpole's ministry was that it witnessed an alliance between Whig merchants and Tory landed gentry, even though one object of the ill-fated measure was to facilitate a reduction of the land tax by raising excise duties. The Tories had protested against the War of the Spanish Succession because it had involved expensive military commitments on the European mainland, instead of a relatively cheap naval and colonial war which could bring financial benefits to the nation. The Wars of Jenkins' Ear (1739–48) and of the Austrian Succession (1740–48) were not quite in this mould. Yet they were aimed at the Spanish monopoly of trade with South America and at the French colonial possessions in India and North America, and were but a prelude to the more extensive Seven Years' War (1756–63), from which Britain gained extensive territories in North America and the Caribbean. Already (thanks to the exploits of Robert Clive) in control of much of India, Britain was, by 1763, the world's leading colonial power.

The one remaining issue which the Tories might have exploited was that of the royal prerogative. But far from wishing to see it strengthened, as they had done at the beginning of the century, the Tories now desired its limitation. It is easy to see why. When Walpole did finally fall from office in February 1742, driven to resignation by the loss of his Commons' majority following mismanagement of the war with Spain, he was replaced with other Whig politicians: John Carteret, then Henry Pelham and his brother the Duke of Newcastle, and, later, the elder Pitt. This use of royal power to sustain a one-party regime was not at all to the liking of Tory politicians. Little wonder, therefore, that in a formal electoral alliance between the Tories and Frederick, Prince of Wales, in June 1747, the Prince agreed to 'setting bounds to the Prerogative' and 'totally to abolish for the future all Distinction of Party'.

But Frederick did not outlive his father. In the Commons the Tories therefore reconciled themselves to forming a permanent backbench opposition of about 140 MPs, joining the 'Country' (i.e. opposition) Whig politicians with almost unfailing regularity, but neither wanting nor expecting to be taken into the government. By 1760 the Tories had more or less lost their separate identity. 'Court' and 'Country' ('ins' and 'outs') rather than 'Whig' and 'Tory' thus formed the warp and weft of eighteenth-century politics after 1715. The Court included the Whig politicians in office at any particular time, supported by the Court and Treasury party and by sympathetic independents. The Country was composed of those politicians out of favour, supported by opposition independents, of which the Tories formed but a part. 'Does any candid and intelligent man seriously believe, [Bishop John Douglas asked in 1761] that at this time of day, there subsists any party distinction amongst us, that is not merely nominal? Are not the *tories* friends of the *royal family*? Have they not long ago laid aside their aversion to the dissenters? Do they not think the toleration and establishment, both necessary parts of the constitution? And can a *whig* distinguish these from his own principles?'

But when George III came to the throne the pattern of politics thus established was about to undergo a violent upheaval. George III's break with political convention was the talk of the age. He was accused of an 'aggression' upon and of 'subverting' the constitution. This accusation was made not only at the time, by Edmund Burke ('the power of the Crown, almost dead and rotten, as Prerogative, has grown up anew', Burke wrote in *Thoughts on the Cause on the Present Discontents*, April 1770), but also by a subsequent generation of influential 'Whig' historians, such as Lord Macaulay and Thomas Erskine May. Their argument was that the new King had plotted to gain complete control of the patronage system, had thereby built up a party of 'King's Friends' and Tories and, with their assistance, had reduced Parliament to a rubber stamp for sinister policies aimed at the restoration of absolute rule, both within the kingdom (as the trials and travails of John Wilkes seemed to prove) and in the colonies (leading to the troubles in America). The American settlers rescued themselves from this situation by a just rebellion. But England — so the argument went — was in chains until, in the 1830s, Lord John Russell and Charles Grey, the political heirs of Burke and Charles James Fox, dealt the fatal blow (parliamentary reform) which put paid, once and for all, to the personal rule of the sovereign.

Like all myths this one had a kernel of truth. George III was determined to have done with the Whig families whom he believed, somewhat simplistically (for he was only 23 when he ascended the throne) to have enslaved his grandfather and, somewhat less simplistically, to be at the centre of a corrupt system of political influence. What he desired, apart from high political office for his 'dearest friend', Lord Bute, was a broad-based administration which transcended 'party' and which was genuinely popular. Had he stopped to think, he would have realised that the Pitt-Newcastle coalition (1757–61), which had successfully conducted a major war with truly national support, fulfilled all these criteria. But he did not stop to think. Newcastle was the epitome of 'those ministers of the late reign who have attempted to fetter and enslave him' (as Bute put it to the Duke of Bedford in 1763) and Pitt had damned himself, in the King's eyes, by his association with the Newcastle regime. They were dismissed and replaced by Bute (1761–3), who simply did not know how to drive the political machine. Bute gave way to Grenville (1763–5), Grenville to Rockingham (1765–6), Rockingham to Chatham (1766–8), Chatham to Grafton (1768–70) and Grafton to Lord North (1770–82). In North the King found a man of political experience and acumen on whom he could lean and who provided the stability in government that had eluded him for a decade. When the reverses in America forced North to resign, the search began again, and was concluded the following year, 1783, with the appointment of William Pitt the Younger as First Lord of the Treasury.

But George III was no tyrant. In matters of constitutional pro-
priety he was, in fact, a stickler for adhering to established con-
ventions and did not interfere with ministers once he had appointed them. Rejecting a supplication from the Duke of Bedford
to thwart the plans of the Rockingham Whigs to repeal Grenville's
Act of 1765 imposing a stamp duty upon the American colonies
(the Stamp Act, repealed in 1766), the King declared that, 'I do
not think it constitutional for the Crown personally to interfere in
measures which it has been thought proper to refer to the choice of
Parliament.' As for the contention that George III plotted with the
Tories, this argument simply does not stand up to examination. By
1760 the old Tory party was dead. Many Tories supported the
elder Pitt's foreign policy and a few, such as Sir Francis
Dashwood, accepted ministerial appointments. But the overwhelming majority of George III's ministers were Whigs: Lord
North, who had held office under Newcastle, was a Court Whig;
the younger Pitt was a Rockingham Whig who held office under
the Earl of Shelburne, 1782–3.

There was no Tory revival under George III. The King's Friends
were the old Court and Treasury party which the first two
Hanoverians had kindly placed at the disposal of the Whig
magnates; George III merely reminded them — not that many
needed reminding — where their true allegiance lay. Between
1714 and 1760 the Whig grandees had managed to grasp most of
the important levers in the machinery of politics. George III
reasserted rights which were undoubtedly his. The old Whig
families, particularly those who followed Charles Watson-
Wentworth, second Marquis of Rockingham, the leading Whig
once Newcastle had been driven from office by Bute, naturally did
not find this state of affairs at all congenial. Whig families like the
Devonshires, who could hardly remember when they had last
opposed royal goverment, found themselves proscribed at Court,
and with their support Rockingham formed a party of wealthy
malcontents.

The Rockingham Whigs made virtues out of necessities. They,
of course, opposed Bute, and so championed the idea of
economical reform and the reduction of the monarch's role in
government. Since much of this royal influence was associated, in
the 1760s and 1770s, with the policy of taxing the American
colonies, they opposed that too and, for good measure, they took
up other causes, such as those of John Wilkes, which could be

capable of interpretation as resistance to tyranny. In order to justify their organised and systematic opposition to the King and his successive administrations, the Rockinghams formulated a wholly novel concept of 'party'. In the past, organised opposition to the King's government, even if conducted in a party framework, had had treasonable overtones. Now, using the argument that the King was attempting to overthrow the constitution, Burke (the theoretician and codifier of Rockingham prejudices) legitimated the idea of party: 'a body of men united for promoting by their joint endeavours the national interest upon some particular principle in which they are all agreed.' The Rockingham Whigs thus came to have a political programme and sought power, as Burke specified, on 'manly and honourable maxims, [which] will easily be distinguished from the mean and interested struggle for place and emolument'. But the redefinition which the Rockinghams sought of the terms upon which the political game was played out went further than this. 'All Opposition', Burke instructed them, 'is absolutely crippled if it can obtain no kind of support out-of-doors.' In their attempts to force a political programme upon the King, the Rockingham Whigs took shameless advantage of all manner of extra-parliamentary agitations. And it so happened that in the 1760s and 1770s there were plenty of opportunities for campaigns of this sort.

Pre-eminently, and hanging like an albatross about the neck of the King, were the American colonies — or, more correctly (because it is too easily forgotten that only some of these colonies rebelled), the thirteen colonies on the eastern seaboard of North America, stretching from Canada (acquired from the French by stages between 1713 and 1763) to Florida (acquired from Spain in 1763). The thirteen colonies, where Roman Catholics and Puritans freely practised their religions and where there was more real democracy than anywhere on the British mainland, had long since reached the stage at which they were capable of self-government. To their west, beyond the Appalachians, lay vast territories whose natural wealth was incalculable. With the French and Spanish threats removed, the two million inhabitants of these colonies looked forward not merely to the exploitation of these resources, but to being able to trade with whom they pleased, the Navigation Acts and British colonial policy notwithstanding.

The British had other ideas. Not only had Britain spent great sums of money during the Seven Years' War to free the colonists from the Spanish and French threats, but the Treasury had reimbursed the colonial governments to the tune of £1.2 millions for expenses they had incurred. Now there were garrisons to build and maintain, for the loyalty of French settlers to their new masters could obviously not be assumed, and a watch had to be kept over the Indian tribes. It seemed very reasonable that the colonists should assume some of the financial burden hitherto borne solely by the British taxpayer. The task of finding a method by which this sharing of the burden might be accomplished fell to George Grenville, and his preferred solution was to extend to the American colonies the tax on legal documents and newspapers long imposed in England. But Grenville's Stamp Act of 1765 imposed a direct tax upon classes of persons who were not represented in the British legislature; it was taxation without representation, and the colonists were having none of it. In a welter of peaceful resolutions and violent reactions in the colonies, applauded at home by the elder Pitt and the London mob, Rockingham replaced Grenville and the Act was repealed.

So the drama of American independence began to be played out in an atmosphere of intransigence on both sides. Although the Stamp Act was removed from the statute book, a Declaratory Act was passed (1766) asserting the right of the British Parliament to legislate for the colonies. The following year Charles Townshend, Chancellor of the Exchequer under Pitt (Chatham) promoted the American Import Duties Act, which imposed duties on lead, glass, paper, paint and tea imported from Britain. Little money was got by these duties, but colonial passions were raised to new heights. Confrontations between the British army and American civilians grew more desperate; in 1770 five colonists died when troops opened fire on a crowd in Boston, Massachusetts (the so-called 'Boston massacre'). Lord North repealed most of the Townshend duties but retained that on tea and in 1773, in an attempt to ease the plight of the East India Company, he legislated to allow the Company to ship tea directly to America without its having to pass through England; it could thus be offered for sale at lower prices than hitherto. This threatened the livelihoods of legitimate colonial merchants and of the smugglers; on 16 December 1773 the colonists dumped 340 chests of tea into Boston harbour.

The Boston Tea Party was, and was meant to be, a challenge to the British Parliament; even Rockingham and Chatham were moved to condemn the event. North's government reacted swiftly.

The Boston Port Act (1774) closed Boston to all shipping until compensation had been paid to the East India Company. The Massachusetts Government Act revoked the colony's charter, giving the Governor virtually absolute authority. The Quartering Act empowered the new Governor, General Gage, to billet troops in private houses. The Administration of Justice Act provided for defendants (such as British soldiers) to stand trial in Britain, or in another colony. These four measures were quickly dubbed by the colonists 'the Intolerable Acts'; but they were largely aimed at one colony, Massachusetts. What united the colonists in a determination to take up arms was not the Intolerable Acts by themselves, but these measures taken in conjunction with the Quebec Act, passed at the same time, which granted full civil rights to Roman Catholics, extended the boundary of Quebec south to the Ohio river and west to the Mississippi, and retained French civil law, which did not provide for trial by jury. In the thirteen colonies the Quebec Act was portrayed as a new 'popish plot', a foretaste of the despotism that lay in store for the colonists unless they acted to defend themselves. In April 1775 war broke out at Lexington and Concord.

In retrospect it is easy to see that the British position, from both the political and military points of view, was hopelessly unrealistic. It was one thing to put down rebellions in Scotland or Ireland, where lines of communication were short and where the government in London could know fairly quickly how matters were progressing. But America was several weeks' sailing distance from Britain; the news of the defeat of Lord Cornwallis at Yorktown, Virginia, on 19 October 1781 did not reach Westminster until 25 November. Add to this poor generalship, a navy and an army run down by the economy drive of the previous decade, and the entry into the conflict of, first, France and Spain, and later (because of British insistence on the right to search neutral ships) of Holland, Russia, Sweden, Denmark and Prussia, and the odds against British success were heavy indeed.

In any case, what would a British victory have meant? Almost certainly a vast expenditure, for the foreseeable future, on maintaining and supplying a British army of occupation within the colonies and a British navy to patrol the coast and the waters of the Caribbean. Realistically, the British government ought to have offered some compromise, perhaps a form of internal self-rule. In fact such proposals were made, but only after the defeat of General Burgoyne at Saratoga in 1777. The proposals were too late in coming, for the colonists could already smell outright victory. Moreover their position had moved, by stages, away from demands for freedom of trade (which could have been met by the lifting of all customs duties and the modification of the Navigation Acts) and for 'no taxation without representation' (which could have been granted by the election of American MPs to Westminster). To the concept of the supremacy of Parliament the colonists responded with the notion, derived from Locke, of the existence of natural law and the right of rebellion against a tyrant, and with the demand, derived from Tom Paine (whose pamphlet *Common Sense* was published in 1775) for total independence.

No British King or Parliament in the late eighteenth century could have conceded those principles without a fight. As things turned out, and given the strength and the extent of the international forces ranged against them, the British did not emerge from the conflict totally humiliated. At the Peace of Versailles, 1783, the independence of the thirteen colonies was recognised, Florida was returned to Spain and some territorial concessions were made to France in Africa and the West Indies. But Britain retained Gibraltar, won back the Bahamas, and obtained the right to trade freely with the Spice Islands of the Dutch East Indies. French efforts to recover former possessions in the Indian subcontinent were successfully resisted.

One effect of events across the Atlantic was to give British statesmen a more realistic appreciation of the difficulties of keeping in subjection a people who wished to rule themselves. The ease with which relations between England and Scotland had been regulated at the beginning of the century had been in some respects misleading. For a time, following the failure of the scheme to establish a Scottish colony in Panama (the Darien scheme), it had appeared that England and Scotland were set on a collision course. In 1704 the Edinburgh Parliament had even passed an Act of Security, providing that on Queen Anne's death the Scottish Crown would pass to someone other than the King of England (a Stuart perhaps?); this would almost certainly have led to war. But wiser counsels had later prevailed on both sides of the border; in 1707 the Westminster and Edinburgh Parliaments had agreed to an Act of Union. The Edinburgh Parliament was abolished, Scotland was henceforth represented by 45 MPs and 16 peers at Westminster, England took over the Scottish national debt, and the Scottish share of national taxation was fixed at one-fortieth of England's. Only in the tribalised Catholic Highlands did real hostility to England persist after mid-century.

Tragically, the course of Anglo-Irish relations did not follow the Anglo-Scottish pattern. Perhaps this was because English politicians realised that the differences between the societies of England and Ireland were greater than the similarities. The great majority of Irish men and women were Catholics, against whom the Irish penal laws discriminated with deliberate ferocity. Irish Catholics could not, for instance, purchase land, inherit land from a Protestant, hold public office or sit in the Dublin Parliament. Ireland was kept under military occupation and economic thralldom; over three-quarters of the land of Ireland was held by Protestant English landlords (often absentee), and the Navigation Laws were applied to Ireland as to any other colony; Irish trade was not allowed to threaten English. The Dublin Parliament was not independent in the way that the Edinburgh Parliament had been; under Poyning's Law of 1494, statutes passed in Ireland were valid only if approved at Westminster.

The imposition upon Ireland of commercial dependence and political servility achieved a remarkable transformation in the attitude of Irish Protestants. While unwilling to grant 'power-sharing' to the Catholics, the Protestant landowning gentry, led by Henry Grattan, did wish for the guarantee of some basic liberties (such as habeas corpus) for all Irish people, and for some independent status for the Irish Parliament. All that the English would offer was an Octennial Act (1768) to ensure that the Dublin legislature was re-elected at least once every eight years; elections to that legislature remained as corrupt as ever.

The American war affected the Irish situation in two ways. First, the Irish copied the tactics of the American colonists and refused, in 1778, to import goods manufactured in England. Lord North responded by agreeing to grant the Irish access to American and African colonial markets, and the right to trade with Turkey and the Near East. Secondly companies of 'Volunteers' sprang up, with the purpose (it was said) of defending Ireland from the French and Spanish fleets, now that Irish troops had been withdrawn to fight in America. At first the Volunteers were exclusively Protestant, but later Catholics joined them. A nationalist citizen-army was thus created in Ireland, and in 1782 the Volunteers met together to demand home rule. Rockingham and

Shelburne had to grant it. Legislation passed in 1782–3 gave legislative independence to the Dublin Parliament, with the King as sovereign. Grattan and his colleagues remained answerable to London, and London still determined foreign and (in practice) commercial policy. But it was an autonomy of sorts.

The American Revolution began with fiscal and territorial disputes, but the issues to which it gave rise had deep political significance. As we have seen, the Rockingham Whigs used events in America as a justification for their assertion that the King and his 'Tory' ministers were intent upon a restoration of Stuart despotism. The experiences of John Wilkes were cited as proof positive that this policy was not being applied merely to overseas territories. Wilkes was an unlikely champion of the rights of the individual. The wealthy son of a wealthy distiller, he was an uncontrollable womaniser by night and, by day, a pornographer and a political agitator in search of a cause. Elected to Parliament in 1757, Wilkes had founded a scurrilous political weekly, the *North Briton* (the reference was to the Scotsman Lord Bute), number 45 of which (1763) carried an attack on George III's speech defending the Treaty of Paris. Arrested on a general warrant for seditious libel, Wilkes successfully claimed immunity from arrest as an MP and eventually, in 1769, obtained damages from the Secretary of State, the Earl of Halifax.

Meanwhile, Wilkes had alienated his supporters in Parliament by printing an obscene poem. The Commons declared that privilege could not protect him, he fled to France and was declared an outlaw. Then, to escape his French creditors, he returned to Britain and (in 1768) was elected MP for Middlesex. In all, Wilkes was elected and re-elected for that constituency four times; on each occasion the Commons expelled him. So he spent a not uncongenial time in prison and upon his release, in 1770, was elected an alderman for the City of London, becoming Lord Mayor in 1774. Lord North wisely took a conciliatory line. Wilkes was allowed to take his seat as MP for Middlesex, and remained in the Commons until 1790. He did not, however, forget his parliamentary enemies. In 1776, when still a City alderman and a magistrate, he refused to permit the Serjeant-at-arms to arrest a printer who had published accounts of parliamentary proceedings, which were still considered secret.

John Wilkes thus wrote himself into the history books as one who suffered in the cause of liberty — 'Wilkes and Liberty', as the popular cry put it. A Society of the Supporters of the Bill of Rights was formed to further his cause, and in the Commons a small but distinct group of 'Wilkite' MPs spoke in his defence. The wealthy Whig merchants of the City of London joined with radical elements among the lower middle and working classes of Middlesex to uphold his rights, and theirs.

Wilkes' own flirtation with radicalism appears to have ended with the Gordon Riots (June 1780) which, as a City alderman, he opposed. But the controversies surrounding his political career mirrored, at a lesser and more immediate level, those which at the very same time were raging about the policy of George III and his ministers towards the American colonies. The King and his evil counsellors (it was argued) had seized control of Parliament through bribery and corruption, and were intent upon stifling liberty. In April 1780 a Society for Promoting Constitutional Reform was founded and in the same year Major John Cartwright, whose career in the service of democratic ideals spanned half a century, launched a campaign for the abolition of the property qualification for membership of the House of Commons and for the payment of MPs. In a pamphlet, *Take Your Choice* published four years earlier, he had demanded universal manhood suffrage, annual parliaments and equal parliamentary constituencies.

Cartwright, and his friend Horne Tooke (imprisoned for wanting to collect funds for the American colonists) formed a tangible link between the Levellers of the seventeenth century and the Chartists of the nineteenth. Cartwright and Tooke were, however, on the political fringe. The Rockingham Whigs, briefly in government between 1765 and 1766, hoped to occupy office once more, and they had only to wait until events in America and unrest in England eroded parliamentary confidence in Lord North's government. No more than George III did the Rockinghams wish for political reform of the sort Cartwright was proposing. Their cry was 'economical reform', by which they meant reform of the civil service in order to lessen the cost of government and so reduce the number of placemen in the Commons and the money available to the Crown for political purposes. In Yorkshire a movement led by an Anglican clergyman, the Reverend Christopher Wyvill, was already organising petitions denouncing the high cost of government and the influence of the executive upon Parliament. When men of property in the shires joined City merchants and the London mob in demanding reform, the so-called 'King's Friends' in the Commons displayed discretion, not valour: North's parliamentary majority disappeared.

So in March 1782 the Marquis of Rockingham was given an opportunity to form a 'party' government with an agreed programme which the King had to accept: American independence; the disqualification of government contractors from sitting in the Commons; the disfranchising of revenue officers; and civil service reform along the lines proposed by Burke. The Civil Establishment Act of 1782 abolished the office of Third Secretary of State for the Colonies and did away with the Board of Trade and a large number of minor posts in the Royal Household; it also forbade government pensions to be paid except at the Exchequer (i.e. not through any 'private list'). Another Act passed at the same time obliged the Paymaster General to pay government money into an official account at the Bank of England.

Rockingham did not live long enough to see this programme carried into effect. He died in July 1782 and it fell to Shelburne to carry out the peace negotiations with America and her allies. The death of Rockingham led to the withdrawal from the government of Charles James Fox, a friend of Burke and one of the staunchest parliamentary opponents of North's colonial policies. Fox's career illustrates perfectly the extent to which political principle could become the tool of personal ambition at this time. Fox is customarily hailed as a liberal, and it is true that he espoused many radical causes. But he had originally entered Parliament, in 1768, as a Court Whig (he was the third son of Lord Holland) and only broke with North, for personal reasons, in 1774. Personal considerations led him to break with Shelburne and personal considerations drove him to an alliance with North, in February 1783, in order to bring down Shelburne's administration.

In 1782 George III had had to bow to majority opinion in the House of Commons, dispense with North and agree to the Rockingham programme. Now, the foisting upon him of the unholy and hypocritical alliance of Fox and North, even though under the nominal leadership of the Duke of Portland, represented political opportunism of the most blatant sort. The King was right to call it 'unprincipled' and at once set about undermining it. In December 1783 the House of Lords, at the King's behest, threw out proposals for the reform of the East India Company which would have given key positions to Foxite Whigs. George III dismissed the government and appointed William Pitt the Younger as

First Lord of the Treasury. Within the space of two years, therefore, the most conspicuous victory of Commons over monarchy in
eighteenth-century Britain had been followed by the most au-
dacious victory of monarch over Commons.

But this was in no sense a return to the politics of the Stuarts.
No-one seriously contemplated government without Parliament
and no-one seriously proposed the end of monarchy. We may
observe here that during the course of the eighteenth century the
mind of the nation ceased to be preoccupied with matters which
had so agitated the society of 'early modern' Britain. Religion was
no longer a major divisive force in national life, largely because
those who dissented from the doctrines of the Established Church
were no longer regarded as politically suspect; heresy was divorced
from treason. The suspension of Convocation (the assembly of the
bishops and representatives of the lower clergy) in 1717 was generally welcomed; it was not again summoned till 1855.

However, the nonconformist merchants and industrialists whose
wealth and commercial influence became ever more prominent as
the eighteenth century progressed did not suggest that the
Anglican Church be disestablished; nor did the Dissenting De-
puties, formed as a representative body in 1733, ask for an enlargement of their privileges. The Church of England did become
'latitudinarian' in doctrine, and there was certainly more than a
trace of worldliness and materialism observable within it. Yet, in
trying to achieve a balanced view of eighteenth-century
ecclesiastics, we must recall that Charles and John Wesley, the
founders of Methodism (1729), were Anglicans and that, in
bringing the Christian message to the neglected industrial workers
of Hanoverian Britain, Methodism was a powerful restatement of
the Anglican Church's national character.

In the arts, too, the preoccupation was no longer with the
metaphysical and supernatural — 'the other world' — but with
practical ethical and social questions, sometimes presented in the
form of sophisticated political satire (as evidenced in the writings
of Jonathan Swift and Alexander Pope), sometimes in popular
theatrical form (as in the earthy *Beggar's Opera* of John Gay), and
sometimes through visual presentations. The satirical engravings
of William Hogarth achieved a wide following. His *Gin Lane*,
exposing the evils of gin drinking, so aroused public opinion that
Parliament was forced to legislate in 1751 (the Gin Act) to ban
retailing of spirits by distillers and shopkeepers.

Patronage remained important in architecture, painting and music. But in the literary field the eighteenth century saw the emergence of the professional writer who could expect to earn a living from his pen without having to satisfy the whims of a wealthy benefactor. Circulating libraries were established and, more importantly, a newspaper press emerged both in London and the provinces. In 1700, 50,000 copies of provincial newspapers were sold each week; by 1760 and the figure had reached 200,000. Since newspapers were commonly passed from hand to hand (and then the contents by word of mouth), this indicates the existence of a significant reading puplic. 'Knowledge', wrote Dr Samuel Johnson, 'is diffused among our people by the news-paper.' In these ways, and notwithstanding the corruption of the age, 'public opinion' emerged as a social force in its own right.

2 THE IMPACT OF INDUSTRIALISATION

The half-century which separated George III's dismissal of the Fox-North coalition and the passage of the Great Reform Bill witnessed a transformation in British politics and society more profound and more permanent than the upheavals of the seventeenth century. In 1783 the monarch still possessed real political authority in the day-to-day affairs of the government; by 1832 that authority had largely disappeared. In 1783 Britain was still largely an agricultural society, in which landownership provided the key to social and political influence. After 1832 the landed aristocracy, though still very important, had been forced to share power with the industrialists; henceforth the British economy was to be based increasingly on industrial production, and the British Parliament was to be preoccupied with the needs of, and problems resulting from, industrialisation. In 1783 it was widely assumed that the British Empire was in decline; but by 1832 it was clear that a new Empire was in the making, and that Britain's international influence had never been greater. In 1783 Fox had been deprived of political power by royal decree; in 1832 his friend and disciple Charles Grey retained political power with royal support.

The period 1783–1832 thus displayed different varieties of change, each radical in its own way. It is therefore important to keep in mind that the period also displayed elements of stability and continuity. Between them, William Pitt and his lieutenant Robert Jenkinson, second Earl of Liverpool, held the office of Prime Minister for over thirty of these fifty years. Only once, at the very end of the period, can one speak of the possibility of violent revolutionary change; it was the monarch himself who nipped this possibility in the bud. Though some of the movements of popular protest in the period undoubtedly aimed at the overthrow of the established order, they were small in number. Most of the movements were rooted in economic grievances, not in the idea of social and constitutional upheaval. The industrial bourgeoisie did indeed wish to share political power with the landed aristocracy; but they did not wish to overthrow monarchy or to abolish the hereditary peerage. The major purpose of the 1832 Reform Act was not to introduce 'democracy', but to purify the then existing system of parliamentary representation; it was a profoundly backward-looking measure.

It is tempting to see in the long wars with revolutionary and Napoleonic France a major source of the transformations experienced by the British people at this time. The wars stimulated the domestic economy and acted as a spur to industrial production. Military spending, which had stood at about £15 millions per year of war in the mid-eighteenth century, rose to £40 millions per year of war (in current prices) between 1793 and 1815. In all, the military expenditure directly incurred by Britain in the French wars amounted to £1,000 millions. Since much of this money was spent in the purchase of arms, ships and other military equipment, manufacturing industry benefited both directly and through the stimulus given to ancilliary trades. There was, for example, a notable expansion of the business of timber merchants and naval contractors in the south of England, serving the naval ports of the Medway and English Channel as well as London.

Although government contracts accounted for no more than 10 per cent of iron production, the iron industry benefited from the war economy because the interruption of iron imports from the Baltic stimulated domestic production. Skills developed to improve the quality of military hardware were put to domestic uses; in Birmingham and Sheffield the techniques of small-arms production were applied to more general areas of precision metalwork. In other sectors of industry the stimulus from government contracts was more direct. This was particularly true of production at the cheaper end of the textile market. Moreover, just as the wars with France hastened the development of more efficient production methods, so they stimulated the search for new markets to replace those lost in Europe; the British blockade of France and her allies led directly to the finding of new trading partners in South America and the Far East.

Against these factors, however, must be set the stark realities of the depressive effects of the French wars. In the short term the blockade led to widespread dislocation in the pattern of trade with Europe, while the cotton trade with America suffered severe dislocation, more especially in the period 1810–12. Government spending had inflationary tendencies during the wars, while the sharp contraction in such spending after 1815, coupled with the operation of Sinking Funds to try and reduce the National Debt (£153.4 millions in 1779, £844.3 millions in 1819) had predictably negative effects upon economic growth. Between 1790 and 1820 the annual average public revenue rose from £21.0 millions to £70.2 millions, most of this increase being derived from customs and excise duties and property and income taxes; between them these imposts accounted for three-quarters of government revenue by the end of the wars. Military recruitment sapped the labour market by as many as half a million men at the height of the conflict. This pushed up money wages by over 60 per cent between 1790 and 1815, but the ravages of inflation meant that real wages rose by — at most — 15 per cent over the same period.

It is tempting to argue that the wartime labour shortage must have promoted the mechanisation of production methods. In fact, very few technological inventions of fundamental importance can be attributed to the demands of the conflict with France. John Wilkinson's development of an accurate method of boring cannon, which made possible the building of a true cylinder for steam engines, dated from the time of the American war, in 1774. Admiralty spending certainly extended the use of iron and copper in ship construction. But during this period the means most commonly used by employers to overcome the shortage of adult male workers was the recruitment of female and child labour.

In the mines children were used as 'trappers', working ventilation flaps, and women were employed hauling coal wagons underground. Mill owners made bargains with the heads of families to employ entire family units: children worked with their fathers and mothers in the same conditions and for the same hours — but not for the same wages. In cotton factories the proportion of employees under 14 years of age appears to have risen by 1835 to about 13 per cent of the labour force, over half of which was composed of women and girls. Their conditions of work were largely unregulated. The Health and Morals of Apprentices Act (commonly known as the Factory Act) of 1802, introduced by the radical Tory mill owner Sir Robert Peel (father of the future Prime Minister), applied only to pauper apprentices sent to work in cotton mills from parish workhouses, a fruitful source of child labour. In 1819, again owing to Peel's endeavours, the twelve-hour daily limit prescribed in the 1802 Act was extended to all children working as cotton operatives; the 1819 legislation also prohibited the employment of such children under nine years of age. Without adequate inspection and enforcement, however, the legislation was generally ignored. Child labour was cheap labour, and never in short supply.

It is wise, therefore, not to place too much emphasis upon the French wars as a factor of prime importance in the origins of the Industrial Revolution. Indeed, there was no one ultimate cause. But in listing the factors which, taken together, produced the conditions necessary for the first phase of the industrialisation of Britain, population growth must rank very high. Economies cannot expand without demand. From 1760 to 1800 the population of England and Wales grew at a rate of between 7 and 9 per cent per decade; between 1801 and 1831 the rate of increase for Great Britain never fell below 14 per cent per decade, and in the period 1801–10 reached 17 per cent. By 1831 the population of Great Britain had grown from 7.8 millions to 16.4 millions, compared with 1760; it had, therefore, more than doubled. During the remainder of the nineteenth century the rate of increase in England and Wales never fell below 11 per cent per decade, so that by 1901 the population of Great Britain stood at over 37 millions. But this dramatic increase was not uniformly felt throughout the country. It was noted in the previous chapter that during the eighteenth century population growth had been more rapid in areas of industrial concentration, such as Warwickshire and Lancashire. Between the censuses of 1801 and 1841 the population of Birmingham rose from 71,000 to 202,000, of Manchester from 75,000 to 252,000, and of Liverpool from 82,000 to 299,000; over the same period London's population grew from just over a million to over two millions.

This expanding population created demand, and offered itself as a highly accessible mass market to industries which had already experienced growth earlier in the eighteenth century, besides prompting investment in transport, housing and urban improvement. Above all, the rising population needed to be fed. Agricultural techniques did not change drastically until the advent of steam-driven machinery in the mid-nineteenth century. But agricultural output experienced a sharp upturn. Corn production increased by a half between 1760 and 1815. Wheat prices rose from 42 shillings a quarter in 1775 to over 100 shillings a quarter in 1810–14; prices as high as 126 shillings were recorded at this time. Therefore, in spite of high war taxation and the raising of wages and rents, the late-eighteenth and early-nineteenth centuries (at least down to the coming of peace in 1815) were periods of buoyant agricultural prosperity.

The enclosure movement entered a new phase of intensity. Between 1781 and 1790, 287 private Enclosure Acts were passed; in the following decade the figure reached 506, and between 1801 and 1810 no less than 906 such Acts were authorised. General Enclosure Acts in 1801, 1836 and 1845 facilitated the movement by giving powers of enclosure, by agreement, to a majority of local landowners. Enclosure affected the country unevenly. The principal areas involved were in the Midlands, eastern England and the East Riding of Yorkshire; most of northern England, the west country and Wales were already enclosed. None the less, between 1760 and 1815 over seven million acres were enclosed by Act of Parliament. Nearly a quarter of this acreage was composed of waste and common land.

The needs of the domestic market wrought another important change in the pattern of agriculture production. Prior to the outbreak of war with France, years of good harvests had produced significant surpluses of grain for export. After 1793 England ceased to be an exporter of wheat and flour. Wheat imports, hitherto necessary only in lean years, were to become an increasingly substantial component of the country's total imports. As yet, however, grain imports constituted only a fraction of total home consumption (less than 2 per cent in 1815). During the reigns of George III and George IV, English agriculture was able to feed most of the country's growing population most of the time. Agriculture accounted for a third of the national income and employed over a third of the labour force.

Between 1784 and 1832 Britain was, therefore, still predominantly an agricultural country. But agriculture, though not yet in decline itself, was becoming less important in relation to the manufacturing sector. By 1801 the British economy boasted the lowest level of agricultural occupation in Europe: 30 per cent of the labour force was engaged in manufacturing and mining, with another 11 per cent in trade and transport. Although changing methods of agricultural production resulted in real hardship, the social protests which characterised the turn of the eighteenth and nineteenth centuries did not stem predominantly from the farming sector, but from within the industrial community. It is indeed doubtful whether we would be justified in talking of an agricultural 'revolution'. But industrial changes were radical and profound; here the epithet 'revolutionary' does not seem at all out of place.

Home demand for the products of industry is easier to describe than to quantify, because reliable statistics exist only in relation to the export trade. Not even the onset of the French wars altered significantly the upward trend of exports, which grew in value from an annual average of £10 millions (England and Wales) in the decade 1760–69 to £35 millions in 1810–19. The annual average of imports rose from £10.7 millions to £31.6 millions over the same period, and of re-exports from £4.8 millions to £11.7 millions. Exports of iron, steel and coal roughly doubled; those of cotton increased by about 7,000 per cent. By the 1820s the total value of the British export trade had reached an average of £46.1 millions a year, and of imports £38.3 millions. However, although manufactured goods accounted for over 80 per cent of the export trade, only a third of the country's industrial output was destined for export. The domestic market provided the basis for industrial growth.

The first phase of Britain's industrial revolution had two outstanding features: technological advance in metal extraction and textile production; and innovations in the funding of commercial ventures. By 1800 the widespread adoption of Darby's method of producing pig-iron by smelting iron ore with coke had led to the movement of the smelting furnaces away from forest areas, such as the Weald of Sussex and the Forest of Dean, to the coalfields of the Midlands and South Wales. In 1784 the Hampshire ironmaster Henry Cort devised the 'puddling' process and the rolling mill, thus enabling bar iron and wrought iron to be manufactured with coal rather than charcoal. The entire iron industry thus became concentrated within the coalfields.

Production of pig-iron, which had stood at not more than 25,000 tons by 1750, reached *circa* 244,000 tons in 1806 and 455,000 tons in 1823. Iron widely replaced timber and stone as a major building material, while the development of more durable forms of the metal made possible the construction of more powerful stationary steam engines and, ultimately, of steam locomotives. Although the railway line between Stockton and Darlington (opened 1825) is generally regarded as the first locomotive-hauled railway, and that between Liverpool and Manchester (1830) as the first public passenger-carrying steam railway, the engineer Richard Trevithick had built the first steam-operated passenger railway as early as 1801, and produced the first railway locomotive three years later. Steam locomotives were working on a number of colliery lines before 1825, and no less than 23 railway Acts had been approved by Parliament before the Stockton and Darlington line was proposed in 1823, almost all of them in order to facilitate the carriage of coal but almost all of them horse-drawn tramways. George Stephenson's contribution was twofold: he designed boilers capable of producing sufficient quantities of steam over extended periods of time and he demonstrated that the friction of an iron-edge wheel on an iron rail was perfectly adequate for heavy haulage. The victory of Stephenson's *Rocket* in the Rainhill trials (1829) ensured not merely that his engines would operate the Liverpool and Manchester line, but that steam power would supersede horse power on the railways. None of this would have been possible without progress in iron technology.

Yet, although railways existed before 1830, the railway era should not be pre-dated. In the age of Pitt and Lord Liverpool railways were a decided novelty; raw materials and manufactured goods were commonly carried by waterways. The Bridgewater Canal, built by the self-educated engineer James Brindley to carry the Duke of Bridgewater's coals from his Worsley colliery to Manchester, was opened in 1761. A feat of civil engineering, its successful operation was proof that such a venture could be commercially viable; it was extended to Liverpool in 1776. The two major periods of canal-building were in the 1770s and 1790s. By 1830 Britain had acquired 2,000 miles of canals, a vast experience in the surveying, cutting and tunnelling of canal projects, and in the human organisation of the workforce needed for such undertakings. Canals and improved navigation of existing rivers not only facilitated the transport of bulky raw materials; they were cheaper and quicker than horse-drawn land traffic. In 1792 it was over three times as costly to send goods from Birmingham to Liverpool by land as by canal; the Bridgewater Canal cut the price of coal in Manchester by a half. Canals therefore stimulated demand for the goods whose production they made easier.

In the field of textile production, steam replaced water power. During the eighteenth century the use of water power in the wollen and cotton industries had necessitated the siting of woollen mills and cotton factories on the banks of fast-flowing streams, in the rural areas of Lancashire and the West Riding. But this had many balancing disadvantages. Production could be stopped by flood or drought; mills located in remote upland villages were badly placed from the point of view of ease of access. From the

1780s the introduction of steam power led to the gradual relocation of cotton-spinning and wollen mills within or adjacent to the coalfields, in towns such as Leeds, Halifax, Bradford, Bolton, Preston and Stockport. The number of cotton-spinning mills in Manchester grew from two, in 1790, to 66 in 1821. By 1830 Britain had 185,000 cotton-factory operatives; thirty years later the figure had more than doubled.

The mechanisation of the weaving process was, of course, related to the introduction of power spinning, but in an indirect way. At first, the increased output from the spinning mills resulted in more work for the weavers. The number of handloom weavers, far from declining in the early-nineteenth century, actually grew from 184,000 in 1806 to 240,000 in the 1830s. Thereafter, it is true, the weavers fought a desperate battle — which they inevitably lost — against factory-based machine production. Between 1830 and 1840 their numbers declined by nearly half, and by 1860 there were reputed to be only 10,000 left at work in the cotton industry. But the point is worth making, in relation to the social unrest during and immediately after the Napoleonic wars, that the advent of power-driven machinery did not, of itself, cause widespread unemployment.

The replacement of the domestic by the factory system is one of the hallmarks of the industrial revolution. Scarcely less important, however, was the revolution in the supply of finance capital. Knitting frames and spinning wheels did not require much initial outlay; but the erection of a water- or steam-driven mill might easily cost £15,000. Sums of this magnitude could rarely be provided locally, or from friends or relatives. As it happened, there was plenty of capital ready for investment, the fruits of eighteenth-century agricultural profits and commercial speculation. Much of this went into the National Debt, because the Usury Laws, which between 1714 and 1832 prohibited commercial interest rates above 5 per cent, did not apply to government stock. In fact, except in time of war, this rate was rarely exceeded or even reached, suggesting that there was a great deal of capital about, searching for investment opportunities.

Low interest rates were clearly important in facilitating industrial borrowing. The movement of capital was made possible by the spectacular growth of country banks, from a dozen (in England and Wales) in 1750 to 660 by 1824. Most country bankers had made their money in other ways, perhaps in industry or as merchants, and used the banks they created to channel their savings into profitable investments. By law, country banks were (except in Scotland) limited to six partners; they were restricted from competition with the Bank of England, and tended to lend on short-term and often high-risk business. Confining themselves to a single locality, they relied upon a growing army of bill-brokers to provide mobility of capital between different geographical areas. Much country banking was a gamble. At times of financial crisis bankruptcies were commonplace. In 1815 alone, 15 country banks were declared insolvent, and 35 more the following year. After the banking crises of 1825, steps were taken to strengthen the system. Legislation in 1826 permitted joint-stock banks to operate outside a 65-mile radius of London, and allowed banks to issue notes ('paper money') under the same condition; after 1833 note issue was allowed within this area. None the less, the nature of the risks commonly undertaken by joint-stock banks meant that the enactments of 1826 and 1833 were of only limited benefit.

Even without the French wars, therefore, the first phase of the industrial revolution would have been a time of uncertainty, of risk, even of fear. The period was one of paradox: great wealth and great poverty; fortunes easily made and lost; newer technologies creating employment but also unemployment. Nowhere are these paradoxes more noticeably in evidence than in the condition of the working classes.

For some sections of the working population real wages rose — apart from short-term fluctuations — throughout the period. As was indicated earlier, there was a growth in real wages of an average of slightly under 1 per cent per annum between 1790 and 1830. Indices of bread prices show that the cost of bread in London was about the same in 1830 and 1840 as in 1790, and that prices fell substantially in the first two decades of the nineteenth century; between 1790 and 1800 the cost of bread in London fell by over a third. Consumption of beer, spirits, tea and sugar fell, but not drastically so. The widespread use of child and female labour raised family incomes. Factory wages were not only higher than those of agricultural workers and those working at home; they were more regular.

It is right to regard cheaper food and good employment prospects as an improvement in the standard of living. Most members of the manual working classes were better clothed, better fed and better housed than their grandparents. But industrialisation brought with it a cyclical pattern of boom and slump. In years of slump — 1816, 1819, 1826–7, 1830–31, 1842–3 — there was heavy unemployment. At times of bad harvests — 1792–3, 1795–6, 1799–1800 and 1808–12 — food prices rose. Between 1790 and 1842 there was an unmistakable relationship between food prices and trade fluctuations on the one hand, and outbreaks of public disorder on the other. There were widespread food riots in 1795–6 and 1800–01. The Luddite 'revolts' of 1811–12 and 1816–17 coincided with soaring food prices, as did the Peterloo 'massacre' in Manchester in 1819, the 'Captain Swing' riots of 1830–31 in the south of England and East Anglia, and the 'Plug Plot' riots in Lancashire in 1842.

These outbreaks had immediate and less immediate causes. True Luddism (1811–17) — the breaking of machinery — was limited both as to area and occupation: the wool croppers or shearmen of the West Riding; the cotton weavers of South Lancashire; and the framework knitters of Nottinghamshire, Leicestershire and Derbyshire. The destruction of machinery was not a mindless act of reactionary thuggery. The position of the croppers illustrates this point. The status of the croppers was threatened by the gig-mill (the use of which had been outlawed by a statute dating from 1552) and by the shearing frame, a much more recent invention. The croppers were well organised, and able to enforce a closed shop. They were also aware of their constitutional rights, not only under the law already mentioned but also under the Statute of Artificers of 1563, which enforced a seven-year apprenticeship, and by reason of an Act of 1555 which limited the number of looms any one master might employ.

The croppers were not opposed to the introduction of machinery, but they wished such introduction to be gradual, so that displaced men might be found alternative employment, aided by a tax of sixpence per yard upon cloth finished by machine. The masters, however, would not hear of such a proposal. From 1803 onwards Parliament voted an annual Act suspending all the protective legislation the croppers had previously enjoyed. In 1809 every piece of protective legislation in the wool industry was repealed. 'Luddism appeared,' Professor E. P. Thompson has written, 'with an almost inevitable logic':

We will never lay down Arms [till] The House of Commons passes an Act to put down all Machinery hurtful to Com-

monality, and repeal that to hang Frame Breakers. But we. We
petition no more — that won't do — fighting must.
                    Signed by the General of the Army of Redressers
                    Redressers for ever Amen   *Ned Ludd* Clerk

The experience of the framework-knitters, or stockingers, told a
similar story. A major grievance of the Nottinghamshire
framework-knitters related to 'cut-ups' — that is, hosiery manufactured by steam-driven machinery. But the introduction of
machinery was by no means the only source of complaint. In 1787
the stockingers had negotiated wage agreements with the masters,
but from 1807 onwards wage rates fell because — so the
stockingers alleged — the Nottingham hosiers had entered into an
agreement to reduce wages and were seeking to evade restrictions
on the employment of unskilled labourers and the number of
apprentices (practices known as 'colting'). At first the stockingers
used constitutional methods to try and obtain redress. A test case
against colting was actually found proven, but the jury awarded a
mere one shilling damages. In 1811 evidence was produced to the
Nottingham magistrates of a wage-reduction agreement among the
masters; in theory such an agreement was illegal under the Combination Act of 1800. The Town Clerk declined to serve a warrant.
In 1812 the Nottingham 'United Committee of Framework-
Knitters' attempted to promote a Bill to regulate abuses in the
industry. It was emasculated beyond recognition in the Commons
and killed off in the Lords, where Viscount Sidmouth, the Home
Secretary, 'trusted in God that no such principle would be again
attempted to be introduced in any Bill brought up to that House'.
    The cotton workers were initially more fortunate. In 1800 and
1803 they had secured the passage of the Cotton Arbitration Acts,
giving magistrates powers to arbitrate in wage disputes in the
industry and to enforce minimum wages. This victory was a hollow
one, but not primarily because the magistracy was allied by rank
and sentiment to the masters, whose views on economic wage rates
they could usually be relied upon to follow. In 1812 the cotton
weavers of Glasgow brought and won a test case against manufacturers who refused to pay the minimum wages upon which the
magistrates had decided. The manufacturers ignored the ruling,
and a strike was organised. The strike leaders were thereupon
sentenced to terms of imprisonment ranging from four to eighteen
months. The manufacturers went unpunished.

We must not imagine that the men who were driven to machine-breaking did not understand why the law was being applied with such obvious bias. The Nottingham framework-knitters Committee declared:

> It is well known, that governments will not interfere with the regulation of the *quantum* of wages which shall be paid for a certain *quantum* of labour . . . It is true that Government has interfered in the regulation of wages in times long since gone by; but the writings of Dr Adam Smith have altered the opinion of the polished part of society, on this subject.

The skilled artisan classes of the early industrial revolution believed that the institution of apprenticeship, and in particular the ability to limit the recruitment of apprentices, would protect their jobs and strengthen their bargaining power. The Statute of Artificers had made a seven-year apprenticeship compulsory in 61 named trades; custom and practice had extended its operation to other employments. For example, apprenticeship was rigorously enforced by the Liverpool shipwrights' trade society, the Thames caulkers' society and the London Society of Bookbinders. Many 'trade clubs' actually employed attorneys to prosecute masters in cases of alleged infringement of the apprenticeship laws. Such clubs were craft trade unions by another name; other trade unions existed under the guise of friendly or burial societies.

In this connection, the Combination Acts of 1799 and 1800 were not as important as is sometimes supposed. The Act of 1799 declared that any agreement 'for obtaining an advance of Wages' was illegal and punishable on conviction, before one magistrate, with three months' imprisonment. This legislation was extended, with some valueless arbitration clauses, by the Act of 1800, which required that two magistrates should try such cases and that combinations of employers to determine wage levels or hours of employment would also be illegal henceforth. The shallowness of this last provision, and of the arbitration clauses, have already been indicated. But it must be remembered that combining 'in restraint of trade' had always been a criminal offence under the common law doctrine of conspiracy, and was punishable by imprisonment or transportation, and that the 1563 Statute had made it illegal for work to be left unfinished. The impact of the Combination Acts lay in the scope they gave for official meddling in all alleged combinations. A Home Office correspondent confided in 1802 that the Acts afforded 'a very convenient pretext for summoning and examining upon Oath any suspected Persons'.

The purpose of the legislation of 1799 and 1800 was therefore political rather than economic. The onus of bringing cases under the Acts was placed upon employers, who were often reluctant to use them as anything more than a threat. However, prosecutions frequently took place under the common law or for leaving work unfinished. The testimony of Gravener Henson, the leader of the framework-knitters, speaks for itself:

> Very few prosecutions have been made to effect under the Combination Acts, but hundreds have been made under this law, and the labourer can never be free unless this law is modified; the combination is nothing; it is the law with regards the finishing of work, which masters employ to harass and keep down the wages of their workpeople.

Beyond these considerations, and of far greater significance in any judgement on the condition of the working classes at this time, was the repeal of the entire corpus of protective legislation. As we have seen, the statutory protection for wool workers, suspended between 1803 and 1808, was removed in 1809. The apprenticeship clauses of the Statute of Artificers were repealed in 1813, and the following year saw the repeal of those parts of the 1563 Statute which had empowered magistrates to enforce minimum wages; significantly, the provision making it an offence to leave work unfinished was left intact. Also in 1814, the Sheffield Cutlers' Act did away with apprenticeship restrictions in the cutlery industry. Trade clubs which brought actions under legislation still on the statute book found the courts unwilling to mete out more than token punishments. We should also note that the same Parliament which removed protection from the workers approved a Corn Law (1815) banning the import of grain until the home price had reached 80 shillings a quarter. Three years earlier, machine-breaking had been made a capital offence and twelve Luddites had been hanged at York.

The trade clubs of skilled artisans survived, and were often successful in enforcing the closed shop in spite of the constraints of the law. The radical tailor Francis Place argued (in 1834) that during the Napoleonic wars the conditions of London artisans had improved partly because of the higher wages obtained through the efforts of trade clubs and industrial action. But life was more insecure than before, and conditions in the hastily built town dwellings were grim. People who migrated from the countryside into the towns in search of work often found it, but brought to their new surroundings a wholly inappropriate set of assumptions and norms. The agricultural labourer would often have a garden or smallholding to supplement money wages; farmers were accustomed to paying their workers in kind. Indeed actual money — cash — did not have the importance for those who worked on the land that it possessed for those who were employed in factories. The urban slums of the industrial revolution did not have gardens. Factory workers were dependent for all their necessities — the food they ate, the clothes they wore, the wood or coal they burnt and the roofs over their heads — upon their weekly wages. Money which agricultural labourers commonly squandered on drink needed to be saved by town-dwellers for the bare essentials of life. A stricter regime of self-discipline had to be learnt. This process took time. Other rural habits proved dis-astrous when brought into an urban environment. In rural areas sanitation was primitive; fresh water was drawn from streams or wells. In the towns this lack of provision led inexorably to disease and death.

In the countryside a certain mutual respect had existed between all who worked on and lived off the land. Work in a factory was disciplined, severe, impersonal and often destructive of family ties. These effects cannot be measured. They were none the less keenly felt. But of all the difficulties faced by the factory workers of the late-eighteenth and nineteenth centuries, the most in-tractable arose from loss of earnings due to cyclical un-employment, accident, ill health or old age. The skilled artisans evolved a set of mechanisms to help cope with these calamities. Trade clubs developed the 'tramping' system, by which accredited members of a trade could be sure of food and lodging from local branches as they tramped the country looking for work. Tramping was not a pleasant experience. In the 1820s the 'grand tour' of all the branches of the brushmakers' society comprised 1,200 miles; in the 1850s the compositors' 'grand tour' was 2,800 miles. The early socialist John Francis Bray, a printer by trade, described in later life how tramping when in his early twenties (1830–32) involved 'walks of twenty to thirty miles a day, half-fed and a shelter in some low lodging-house whose vermin prevented sleep'. This experience, he added ominously, 'was enough to set any man to thinking of the causes of these miseries'.

The trade clubs both promoted and reflected the social gospel of thrift, sobriety, hard work and self-help which Nonconformist and Evangelical doctrine championed, and which the Sunday schools and mechanics' institutes enthusiastically supported. These values found practical expression in the friendly society movement. Friendly or benefit societies evolved from the trade societies and clubs of the eighteenth century. They were given legal status and protection in 1793 and were not affected by the Combination Laws or other repressive legislation of the period. It is thought that by 1815 membership of friendly societies was about one million; this figure had doubled by 1850. In return for modest weekly subscriptions the societies provided equally modest but dependable benefits payable in case of ill health or unemployment and, perhaps, a payment to provide for a respectable non-pauper funeral and a widow's or orphan's pension. The typical friendly society was governed by a series of elaborate rules covering not merely entitlement to benefit but also the personal conduct of members. Some societies engaged in secret rituals, which made them ideal vehicles for clandestine trade-union activity. But in general friendly societies were encouraged by the authorities and often actively supported by factory owners; in 1821 a register of friendly societies was established in London, and the societies were permitted to invest in the National Debt. 'It is a great benefit of Friendly Societies,' the vicar of Harrow declared in 1817, 'that they teach a man to avert his eye from the workhouse: to look to the blessing of God on his own endeavours; to get his bread by the sweat of his brow.'

The friendly-society movement was confined to skilled artisans, small shopkeepers and other members of the lower middle classes. For the unskilled, and those unable to afford or enjoy the advantages which membership of a society conferred, a much harsher fate lay in store. Faced with the choice between reviving wage regulation and abandoning the poor to the whims of local charitable instincts, the ruling classes hesitated for a time and then chose the latter course. In a few counties — Devon, Hampshire and Suffolk — lists of minimum wages were either issued or threatened if wage levels were not raised sufficiently. Overall, however, wage protection, along with apprenticeship rules and other protective regulations, was abandoned. Gilbert's Act of 1782 authorised subsidisation of wages from parish funds. In 1785, following a poor harvest, the Cambridgeshire justices used this legislation to ensure that all wages in the county were raised to a fixed level. Similar action was taken in Dorset in 1792 and in Buckinghamshire, Oxfordshire and Berkshire in 1795. The amount of subsidy was generally calculated according to the size of family and the price of bread, and the adoption of the system (often incorrectly termed 'the Speenhamland system', from the place where the Berkshire magistrates met) was made easier in 1796, when an Act of 1722 restricting the payment of outdoor relief was repealed.

But the supplementation of wages from parish funds, originally intended as an emergency measure, became permanent in some areas (southern England, East Anglia and the East and North Ridings of Yorkshire). Elsewhere it was never adopted. Where the system was in force it tended to keep wages low, since farmers knew that whatever they paid would be supplemented. The system was held to have discouraged mobility of labour and to have encouraged larger families; payments rose with the number of children, legitimate or illegitimate. Those able, but unwilling, to work had no incentive to find employment, while those wanting to work found wage levels artificially depressed. In the major industrial and urban areas the system did not operate; instead, workhouses were established. An Act of 1795 enabled parishes to form unions for the creation of such establishments, wherein the starving might obtain sustenance and shelter, but at a terrible price in terms of dignity and freedom.

The idea that there could be such a thing as the 'deserving' poor, who might justifiably call upon the state for help, was already under attack, as part of the more general campaign against government regulation of the economy. During the last two decades of the eighteenth century the case for the abolition of the poor laws was made ever more insistently, especially by Joseph Townsend, whose *Dissertation on the Poor Laws* appeared in 1786, and by T.R. Malthus, whose *Essay on the Principle of Population as it Affects the Future Improvement of Society* was published (anonymously) in 1798. Malthus argued that increases in population would never be matched by increases in production, and that the way to deal with the population explosion was to allow natural disasters, such as famine, to take their toll and not to provide food and warmth, which only encouraged the birth-rate. Among the ruling classes these ideas became ever more popular as the burden of the poor rate increased and post-1815 social unrest intensified. In 1817 a Select Committee of the House of Commons accepted the arguments for abolition.

As a matter of fact the poor laws never were abolished; but their drastic modification in 1834 was clearly anticipated by the way in which they were administered prior to this reform. Adam Smith's brilliant invective against government interference with the economy *(The Wealth of Nations,* 1776) influenced late-eighteenth-century politicians to an extent which can scarcely be exaggerated. They did not slavishly follow through the logic of *laissez-faire,* and in the case of the 1815 Corn Law they clearly rejected it. Yet Smith provided them with an academic cloak of respectability with which to justify unbridled industrialisation. Condemning a wage-regulation Bill introduced in 1795 by the brewer Samuel Whitbread, William Pitt declared that:

> It was necessary to argue the general inexpediency of any legislative interference . . . The most celebrated writers upon political economy . . . leave ample testimony of their truth . . . trade, industry and barter would always find their own level, and be impeded by regulations which violated their natural operation.

Now both Whitbread and Pitt were Whigs. But in their clash over the desirability of minimim wage control we see them at odds over fundamental issues of principle. The industrial revolution had profound effects upon British politics; so did the French Revolution and the Napoleonic wars. These developments now require examination.

For several months after their dismissal by George III, Fox and North waged a guerrilla campaign in Parliament against Pitt's ministry. They forgot, however, that support of the Kings's government was a cardinal maxim of the majority of the independents, to be discarded only in times of the gravest emergency. On 8 March 1784 an opposition motion deploring George III's action was carried, but by only one vote. Later that month Parliament was dissolved, and there took place the most intensely fought general election of the century, from which the King and Pitt emerged with a majority of over one hundred.

It is true that royal patronage played a part in this victory. However, the sum of £31,848 disbursed from the Secret Service Fund in 1784 was less than that spent at either of the two previous general elections. John Robinson, who as Secretary to the Treasury under North was widely regarded as the leading election pundit of the age, had predicted for the government a gain of 60 seats; the gain was actually 70. Robinson thought that government victories would come in close constituencies, where bargains might be struck with borough patrons; in fact, many of the gains came in the more open constituencies, where public opinion counted for something. In Yorkshire, generally considered in the past to have been a Rockingham stronghold, the Foxites did not bother to contest a single seat.

The second Viscount Palmerston, father of the future Whig Prime Minister and at this time a friend of Fox, had already predicted that Pitt would gain a handsome majority 'from the epidemical kind of spirit that has gone about the country in favour of the King's Prerogative against the House of Commons'. If the victory belonged to anyone it belonged to George III. Pitt was just 24 years of age, the son of a famous father but largely untried and as yet without any personal following to speak of in the country or in Parliament; he was, indeed, the only member of his Cabinet not in the House of Lords. Between the summers of 1784 and 1785 he was defeated four times in the Commons: over the scrutiny of the Westminster poll (where he made a clumsy attempt to have Fox's election overturned); over proposed fortifications at Plymouth and Portsmouth (rejected, on grounds of economy, by the casting vote of the Speaker); over proposals to do away with 36 close boroughs and to widen the county franchise (defeated by 248 votes to 174); and over plans for an economic union with Ireland (sabotaged in the Commons as a result of sustained pressure by Josiah Wedgwood and his Grand Chamber of Manufacturers).

Yet Pitt learnt from his mistakes, whereas Fox did not learn from his. Fox was a likeable and generous extrovert, but almost totally undiscriminating in his attacks on government policy, obsessed with the idea that George III was intent on sabotaging his political career. Fox also adopted political postures which were frankly anti-monarchical and occasionally unpatriotic. In consequence, he was not able to exploit Pitt's early defeats or the crisis brought about by the King's supposed madness (1788–9), when, as a friend of the Prince of Wales, he was pushed into the position of advocating an unrestricted Regency, while it was Pitt who persuaded Parliament to support a Regency Bill with strict limitations, a 'constitutional' Regency. Fox seems never to have grasped the subtleties of a political system in which the wishes both of the monarch and of the parliamentary classes needed to be addressed. So, by the time of his death in 1806 he had held high office for only a few months. Pitt also died in 1806, but had been Prime Minister for nearly twenty years.

Pitt, Fox's junior by ten years, was a brilliant orator but, except within a small circle of close friends and relations, an icy, aloof figure, calculating, devious and unprincipled. He had been secretly implicated in the King's pressure upon the House of Lords in 1783. He did indeed resign over George III's opposition to Catholic Emancipation, in 1801, but in a manner which left the way open for his return to office three years later, when all talk of Catholic relief was forgotten. Following his early parliamentary defeats, his youthful flirtation with radical reform was quickly cast aside. He had a thoroughly pragmatic and non-partisan view of politics. He had served his political apprenticeship within the circle of the Rockingham Whigs, but actually presided over the most repressive and illiberal administration of the eighteenth century. Because of its elevation of the absolute authority of central government (no longer, it should be noted, the personal rule of the sovereign) at the expense of the rights of the individual, Pitt's administration came to be known as 'Tory', and after his death he came to be thought of as 'Tory' too, though he himself would certainly have denied this. Why, then, was he able to retain power for so long?

In the first place, it must be conceded at once that, though without much pretension to originality, William Pitt was an exceedingly able administrator, carefully adapting the ideas of others to the problems which faced Britain at the end of the American war. Foremost among these was the need to bridge the gap between government expenditure and revenue. The National Debt stood at about £238 millions, with annual interest charges approaching £9 millions; but government revenue was only about £15 millions per annum. Pitt responded to this situation in a variety of ways. From Walpole he borrowed (1786) the idea of a Sinking Fund to reduce the Debt. Specifically, one million pounds per annum were to be applied by a body of independent commissioners to purchase government stock, interest from which was to

be re-invested in the Fund. By 1793 the Debt had been reduced by
£11 millions. But the scheme had about it the air of a confidence
trick, because the government was paying interest to itself. After
1783 the scheme was in any case self-defeating; the high cost of the
French wars led to a situation in which the money paid into the
Fund could only be raised by borrowing at high rates of interest.

Pitt also extended the concept of the bonded warehouse and
took steps to reduce smuggling by lowering import duties on
commodities such as tea (on which the duty was reduced from 119
to 25 per cent), and by authorising the confiscation of ships built
for smuggling and outlawing the practice of 'hovering' off the coast
with contraband cargoes. More dramatically, he introduced a
plethora of novel taxes, mainly on luxury items such as wigs, hair
powder and domestic servants but, less wisely, on bricks, candles
and shopkeepers. Some of these taxes were easily evaded; others
were palpably short-sighted. Increases in excise duties on cotton
textile products (1784) were rapidly withdrawn after protests.
Taxes on printed and bleached textiles, and on coals, were
similarly abandoned. The shop tax was brought to an end in 1789.
More permanent was the income tax, first levied in 1799 at the rate
of two shillings in the pound and continued, save for a short break
between 1802 and 1803, until 1816. This tax was novel in concept,
but unpopular and disappointing in its results. Pitt had expected to
raise some £10 millions per annum through this tax, but the yield
was only about half this figure.

An alternative to raising revenue was to lower expenditure.
Here again, Pitt borrowed heavily from the ideas of others. The
abolition of nearly 1,000 sinecures was merely a particular
application of 'economical reform'. Other administrative innovations, such as the establishment of an Audit Office and the
introduction of open bidding for government contracts and of
public tender for government stocks, were based on the Reports of
the Commissioners for Examining the Public Accounts. Nor was
Pitt's introduction of the Consolidated Fund (the payment of all
revenues into a central pool, thus necessitating the employment of
fewer civil servants) entirely novel; Lord North had put forward
just such a proposal. We should also note that Pitt's unsuccessful
attempt to achieve free trade with Ireland and his 1786 trade treaty
with France were, like so many of his economic policies, heavily
influenced by the writings of Adam Smith.

Yet it would be churlish not to acknowledge Pitt's twin

achievements. He did put all these ideas into practice, whereas others had only talked about them or applied them half-heartedly. And he did restore the country's financial position. Between 1783 and 1792 the annual revenue of the government was increased by £4 millions. The burden of government indebtedness was being reduced, and showed every prospect of being liquidated. Pitt's financial policies prepared Britain for the long wars with France. But they depended for their ultimate success upon there being no increase in the level of military expenditure. The French wars thus proved to be their undoing.

As in peacetime, so in the years after 1792, Pitt did not show himself to be a particularly brilliant or original leader. He wisely declined to become involved in the attacks by Prussia and Austria upon the infant French republic, but felt that the French annexation of the Austrian Netherlands posed a threat (in terms of French control of the Channel ports) which could not be ignored. Pitt's war policy was entirely orthodox. British military commitments on the European mainland were kept to a minimum, but subsidies were paid to Prussia, Russia, Austria, Holland, Spain and Sardinia. Meanwhile, British naval power was used to make colonial gains in the West Indies, the Mediterranean and the Far East. When anti-French coalitions collapsed in 1797 and again in 1801, and Britain stood alone against France, it was naval supremacy which saved the country from invasion and which sheltered the nation from the full effects of Napoleon's continental victories.

None the less, at Amiens in March 1802 Henry Addington, Pitt's successor as Prime Minister, had to surrender almost all Britain's territorial conquests as the price of peace with France. Pitt's second ministry (May 1804-February 1806) was preoccupied with the renewal of hostilities. The naval victory at Trafalgar (1805) proved the only success against Napoleon in a catalogue of Russian and Austrian defeats. In January 1806 Pitt himself died, at the age of 46, worn out with overwork and depressed by the knowledge of French success. He can be criticised for not attacking the French on land, where alone their power might be broken, and where, in the years from 1810 to 1815, they were finally overcome, first in Russia, then in Portugal and Spain, and finally in France and Belgium. Yet it cannot be doubted that the possession of a strong navy not only proved a vital component of these final land victories, but enabled Britain to withstand

Napoleon's blockade of her ports, to maintain a successful counter-blockade, to defend and consolidate her Indian empire, and to make further territorial acquisitions, such as Ceylon, the Cape of Good Hope, Trinidad and other West Indian islands, Malta and Heligoland. Pitt had helped lay the foundations of a new British Empire.

The French Revolution, and British reaction to it, provide further clues to the reasons for Pitt's long tenure of office. Events in France had a traumatic effect on the mosaic of political groupings in Britain. The outbreak of the Revolution, in May 1789, and the fall of the Bastille on 14 July, coincided with the centenary of the Act of Rights in England and, therefore, of the triumph of parliamentary government over royal despotism. Fox and his friends were quick to emphasise the parallels between the English and French experiences; Dr Richard Price, the radical Dissenter, publicly declared that the Glorious Revolution of 1688–9, and the French imitation of it a hundred years later, were proof that the true source of lawful authority in a state lay with the people, who must always be free to overthrow and replace a bad form of government. Even Pitt was moved to express the hope that France would 'enjoy just that kind of liberty which I venerate'. There was a renaissance among older radical societies, such as the London Revolution Society (dating from 1688) and the (Wilkite) Society of the Supporters of the Bill of Rights. In 1792 Fox encouraged a group of younger Whigs, including the future Earl Grey, to form the Society of the Friends of the People; it produced a scheme of parliamentary reform which included household suffrage in the boroughs. Working-class radical movements were also rekindled. The shoemaker Thomas Hardy founded the London Corresponding Society, not merely to mobilise support for the French Revolution but to encourage discussion of domestic social questions, such as the loss of common land through enclosure, and conditions of work in the factories.

From this general euphoria Edmund Burke stood aloof. In his *Reflections on the Revolution in France*, published in November 1790, he denounced the Revolution as a threat to liberty and predicted that it would end in anarchy, atheism and military dictatorship. But Burke did not stop at this point. He argued that the Glorious Revolution of 1688 had been a conservative act, in harmony with the traditions of the English people. It had been a bloodless revolution, whereas that in France would be very different, the antithesis of 1688 rather than its imitation. This view turned out to be broadly correct. More importantly, Burke's exposition of what can only be termed a conservative political theory led to a dramatic public rift with Fox, in the House of Commons, on 6 May 1791. In answer to a whispered enquiry from Fox as to whether they might still remain friends, Burke loudly proclaimed that their friendship 'was at an end'. By 1792 the former theoretician of the Rockingham Whigs had become a supporter of Pitt's government.

But the advantages which accrued to Pitt from this rupture between two great Whig leaders went much deeper than this. As the French Revolution turned ever more bloody, and as the apprehensions of serious domestic disorder grew ever more real (there were serious riots in Birmingham in July 1791, when the house and laboratory of the Unitarian Dr Joseph Priestley were burnt down), so public opinion — by no means confined to aristocratic opinion — hardened against reform and reformers alike. The French declaration of war on Britain and Holland, on 1 February 1793, proved a momentous turning point. For most of the opposition Whig leaders it was no longer possible to support (assuming they still supported) the ideals of the French Revolution and at the same time wage war upon those who led it. Parliamentary opposition to the King's government now smacked of disloyalty. In 1794 the main body of opposition Whigs, led by the Duke of Portland, joined Pitt's administration in order to 'maintain the Constitution and save the country'. Portland himself became Home Secretary, where he instituted a series of draconian measures to counter subversion: the suspension of Habeas Corpus (1794); the Seditious Meetings and Treasonable Practices Acts (1795); the increase in stamp duty on newspapers and the registration of printing presses (1795); the Combination Acts (1799 and 1800); the prosecution of radical leaders and reform societies; the suppression of social protest, whether its basis was political or merely economic.

Parliamentary opposition to the government was left in the hands of Fox and a handful of close friends, such as Grey and the poet Sheridan. In 1797 Grey was bold enough to introduce a motion in favour of electoral reform; it was defeated by 237 votes to 91. For a time thereafter Fox and his friends refused to attend the Commons at all. It was not until 1803 that Fox himself acknowledged the necessity of waging war against Napoleon, and it was only in the very last year of his life that he seems to have come to terms with the fact of widespread popular support for the war, accepting office as Foreign Secretary in the 'Ministry of All the Talents' which followed Pitt's death.

The secession to his side of the major Whig groupings and — significantly — of the independent gentry in the Commons, thus consolidated Pitt's political leadership of the country. He trimmed his sails to take advantage of an atmosphere in which the war assumed the aspect of a crusade, and in which anti-revolutionary societies, such as the Association for Preserving Liberty and Property, outnumbered those dedicated to reform. His own popularity enabled him to maintain a tighter discipline over his Cabinet than any previous First Lord of the Treasury. In March 1803 he conveyed to Lord Melville his opinion,

> with regard to the absolute necessity there is in the conduct of the affairs of this country, that there should be an avowed and real Minister possessing the chief weight in the council, and the principal place in the confidence of the King . . . That power must rest in the person generally called the First Minister, and that Minister ought . . . to be the person at the head of the finances.

There evolved, largely through the necessities of war, a new conception of the role of a Prime Minister, and of Cabinet solidarity. In 1792 Pitt had forced George III to dismiss Lord Chancellor Thurlow, after Thurlow had attacked his financial policy. But in 1797 George Canning, the under-secretary for foreign affairs, recorded that the Cabinet had been persuaded by Lord Grenville (Foreign Secretary) to agree upon complete secrecy on the subject of peace negotiations with France, '*to tie up Pitt's tongue*'. By 1806 Viscount Castlereagh, who held office in Pitt's second ministry, could state that the members of the Cabinet had 'always been considered by the country . . . both as individually and collectively responsible for the measures of government'.

The King's ill health also played a part in this process. George III continued to take a very active interest in the affairs of government throughout and beyond Pitt's ministries. As late as March 1807 he forced the All Talents Cabinet, headed by Grenville, to withdraw a Bill which would have allowed Roman Catholics to take commissions in the armed forces. The members of the

Cabinet declined to give the King the 'positive assurance' he desired, that the question of concessions to the Catholics would never again be raised by them, and the government resigned. But, evidently, George III's recurring illness, and his advancing years (he was 63 years of age by the turn of the century; his father had died aged 44) prompted politicians to more overt opposition to the royal will, and his final breakdown, in 1810, led to the installation of a Prince Regent for whom there was little popular support or respect.

It was not only the monarchy's reputation which suffered in the years of Regency (1810–20) and of George IV's own reign (1820–30). During the Napoleonic wars the scope of government had grown to an extent where it would have been impossible for even an able, healthy monarch to have attended to all the details of the administration, as George III had done in his younger days. The administrative and economical reforms of the 1780s and 1790s, and especially the abolition of sinecures, had a profound cumulative effect upon the personal influence of the monarch. During the reign of George IV there were — at most — only 70 office-holders in the Commons, compared with about 180 when Pitt had first become Prime Minister. The number of boroughs under government control was also reduced by an important piece of parliamentary reform approved during the war years.

In 1809, following the revelation that the Duke of York's mistress, Mrs Clarke, had accepted bribes from those who wished to further their careers in the public service, the Portland government hurriedly passed an Act making it a penal offence to solicit money for procuring offices. The independent element in the Commons, already shocked, was further angered by well-substantiated accusations that both Spencer Perceval (Chancellor of the Exchequer) and Castlereagh (Secretary of War) had used public money to buy seats at Westminster for their friends. In this atmosphere the government was quite unable to prevent the passage of a Bill, introduced by a Whig country gentleman, John Christian Curwen, to prohibit the sale of seats in the Commons. 'Mr Curwen's bill,' Lord Liverpool admitted in 1812, 'has put an end to all money transactions between Government and the supposed proprietors of boroughs.'

As Treasury influence over elections diminished, so the Court and Treasury party withered away. But the pattern of eighteenth-century politics was not immediately replaced by another. Party ties remained loose and party-political labels were still vague. The five years following the resignation of the All Talents administration were characterised, so far as Westminster politics were concerned, by uneasy alliances of mostly second-rate politicians, united only by a desire to prosecute the war to a successful conclusion, and by a feeling that the Protestant Church was in danger from those who wished — mainly on account of the Irish situation — to further the cause of Catholic Emancipation. Portland, though himself too old and too ill to be able to attend more than a few Cabinet meetings, held a ministry together between March 1807 and October 1809. He was succeeded by the unfortunate Perceval, shot dead by the bankrupt John Bellingham in the lobby of the Commons on 11 May 1812. Thus began the premiership of Lord Liverpool (1812–27), under whom a stable government of remarkable longevity was united as much by common fears as by common ambitions.

Portland and Perceval would not have accepted the description 'Tory'; they and their followers thought of themselves as the 'Friends of Mr Pitt'. But the repressive policies they pursued were commonly referred to as Tory policies and Canning, who held office under Portland but not under Perceval nor, until 1816, under Liverpool, was happy to call himself a 'Tory' politician. Immediately following Perceval's death, members of Liverpool's administration denied that they were anything but a 'Whig Government'; this was a piece of wishful nostalgia and a pretence which was not maintained for very long. The second-generation Pittites who formed the backbone of Liverpool's ministry — Liverpool himself, Castlereagh, Canning, Viscount Sidmouth (Addington) and Lord Harrowby — possessed a common ideology: the defence of property and the Protestant Church, and the abhorrence of political reform and religious toleration. By 1826 Liverpool could safely write that he was 'no Whig'.

The true heirs of a reforming Whig tradition, jealous for the liberties of the subject, were the Foxites. Fox's 1792 Libel Act, which gave juries the power to decide whether written words actually were libellous, and the abolition of the slave trade by the All Talents ministry in 1807, as well as the very survival of the Foxite group after Fox's death, demonstrated that this tradition was still strong. At the general election of 1807 the terms 'Whig' and 'Tory' were commonly used, in relation to support for or opposition to the King's government, and in relation to the

Catholic question, which was increasingly becoming a testing ground of political attitudes. Pitt had at least resigned over the Emancipation issue; those who professed to be his 'friends' would have none of it, while the rump of the old Foxite Whigs, now led by Grey, wrote it into their national party propaganda.

From 1812, therefore, so long as we remember that we are observing two sets of politicians who, despite their differences, agreed on a wide variety of basic assumptions — for instance that there must never be 'democracy' in Britain, and that power must remain in the hands of a reasonably small group of privileged and wealthy people — and so long as we recall that those who played the political game were wealthy and independent themselves (to a degree which makes nonsense of any assumption of party 'discipline' at this time), we are none the less justified in agreeing with the opinion of J. W. Croker, the Secretary of the Admiralty, who told the future King William IV in January 1828 that 'there were two marked and distinct parties in the country, which might for brevity be fairly called Whig and Tory'. The questions posed by the French Revolution and the Napoleonic wars had thus resulted in the disintegration of the norms of eighteenth-century politics. The political and social problems which beset the nation in the early nineteenth century caused a major realignment.

For the first time, the Irish question affected domestic British politics. The concessions of the late 1770s and early 1780s had satisfied, in some measure, the ambitions of the Protestant Ascendancy in Ireland, who now enjoyed legislative independence and (following the failure of Pitt's proposed commercial treaty) a form of tariff protection to assist the development of Irish industry. The lot of the Catholic majority also improved. By the 1780s most of the penal code against Catholics had been repealed, thus allowing, for example, the establishment of Catholic schools and making it possible for Catholics to buy and inherit land. In 1793 a Catholic Relief Act had even extended voting rights to Catholics who held freehold land to the value of 40 shillings per annum (thus bringing the Irish franchise into line with that of the English counties); Catholics were additionally permitted to serve on juries, hold minor offices and bear arms.

Yet Roman Catholics — in Ireland or England — were still unable to hold major offices or be elected to Parliament. These disabilities formed the basis of the struggle for Catholic Emancipation, which, strictly speaking, was not an Irish issue at all. The fierce debate over Catholic Emancipation can only be understood within the context of a wider dispute over the extent to which the British constitution was or ought to have been a 'Protestant' or even an 'Anglican' constitution. It was a dispute which rumbled on, with varying degrees of ferocity, from the arguments over Occasional Conformity in the early-eighteenth century to the campaign for Jewish emancipation (achieved between 1858 and 1860) and the attempt — ultimately unsuccessful — to prevent the atheist Charles Bradlaugh taking his seat at Westminster in the early 1880s. The Bradlaugh case was, indeed, the theatre of the absurd. But George III's utter conviction that to consent to Catholic Emancipation would be a violation of his coronation oath to defend the Anglican Church, was neither absurd nor to be explained away as the stubbornness of an old man with a diseased mind. His denunciation of Pitt's proposal as 'the most Jacobinical thing I ever heard of' was widely applauded by MPs and constituents alike. Even the Prince Regent — who, after all, shared his bed with a Catholic lady — would not risk further public ignominy by publicly consenting to such a proposition. Catholics, like Jews and Unitarians, might be individually charming people; but the Westminster Parliament was a Protestant Parliament and the British constitution was a Protestant constitution, in the direction of which non-Protestants were to play — at most — a subordinate role.

The significance of the issue of Catholic Emancipation therefore extended well beyond the boundaries of Ireland. But it was the impact of Catholic disabilities within Ireland that gave the issue a unique and dramatic quality because, in an Ireland which now had legislative independence, these disabilities prevented the majority of the population from taking part in the work of the legislature. To make matters worse, the Irish peasantry were obliged to pay tithes to an Anglican established church, which owned a great deal of land but was regarded, even by the Presbyterians of Ulster, as alien. The land question itself became much more acute as the population of Ireland grew from two millions in 1700 to four millions in 1800, and then doubled again by 1840. Pressure of population growth led to the rapid subdivision of tenants' holdings, so that by 1841 half of these holdings were under five acres. Except in Ulster, tenants were not usually compensated for improvements made to the land they farmed. Evictions and agrarian violence, commonplace in the mid-nineteenth century, were not unknown even in the late eighteenth.

Under Pitt, however, the Irish question was a severely political one. We have already noted that the main protagonists for legislative independence were Protestants. In 1791, and in emulation of events in France, radical Protestants, led by the barrister Wolfe Tone, founded the Society of United Irishmen. They intended, with French assistance, to establish an ' independent Irish Republic. After the outbreak of war between Britain and France, Pitt had to take seriously the possibility that the French would use Ireland as a springboard for an invasion of England; there was, indeed, a miniscule landing of Frenchmen in Wales in 1797 and an abortive revolt by the United Irishmen the following year. To deal with this situation Pitt evolved a policy which had two major elements. He calculated, correctly, that he would have the support of the Ascendancy for the abolition of the Dublin Parliament, Ireland being represented henceforth by 28 lay peers, four bishops and 100 MPs at Westminster. As part of the United Kingdom of Great Britain and Ireland, the Irish economy was thus brought within the British mercantilist structure, enjoying free trade with the mainland.

The Act of Union was passed in both countries in 1800 and came into effect on 1 January 1801. It afforded the Presbyterian Ulstermen the best possible guarantee against the prospect of subservience to a Catholic majority, and it therefore dealt a heavy blow at Irish Protestant nationalism. The economic and social position of the Ascendancy remained intact. But the Union was only one part of Pitt's overall strategy. The other was to legislate for Catholic Emancipation, and to offer further substantial olive branches to the Catholics of Ireland by exempting them from the tithe and instituting state payment of the Catholic priesthood. These over-ambitious plans were thwarted by George III. Yet they remained part of Pitt's legacy to his Tory heirs, especially Canning, who in 1812 persuaded the Commons to approve a motion calling for consideration of the Emancipation question.

Canning's political influence in the 1820s gave the Emancipationist renewed hope. Moreover, the quiet repeal of the Test and Corporation Acts by the Duke of Wellington's government in 1828 seemed to indicate that, even in a Parliament dominated by ultra-Tories, a degree of religious indifference would ensure their ultimate victory. In fact, the repeal of the Test and Corporation Acts, so permitting Dissenters to hold municipal and government office, was not a matter of great principle, since the Dissenting community had for the past century enjoyed the advantages of an annual Indemnity Act. What forced the issue of Emancipation was the ferment caused by Daniel O'Connell's election for County Claire in June 1828.

O'Connell, a brilliant Catholic lawyer in Dublin, saw in the Emancipation question a way of furthering his eventual aim of dismantling the Union, and in 1823 he had founded the Catholic Association as a pressure group to mobilise Irish Catholic voters. His candidature at Clare was deliberate — he stood against Vesey Fitzgerald, a Protestant Emancipationist landlord but also a Tory minister — and his victory made Emancipation inevitable. The Emancipation Act was carried by Wellington's government the following year, but with a bad grace. Peel, the Home Secretary, supported the measure in order to preserve the Union; Wellington feared civil war in Ireland if it were not approved. In a fit of spite he secured, in a quite separate Act, the disfranchisement of most Irish Roman Catholics to whom Pitt had given the vote in 1793, by the simple expedient of raising the Irish county franchise from 40 shillings to £10.

The enactment of Catholic Emancipation, following so soon upon the repeal of the Test and Corporation Acts, was both a landmark and a signpost. At one level it signalled, if not quite the end then certainly the beginning of the end of the political privileges of Anglicanism. Those who dissented from the doctrines of the Church of England continued to suffer discrimination: they were still obliged to pay rates to the Anglican church; there were difficulties over marriage and burial; there was exclusion from Oxford and Cambridge universities; the one university non-Anglicans could enter — London — was unable to grant degrees. Removal of these remaining disabilities became part of the Whig creed, and was to be the foundation-stone of the alliance between Whiggery and Nonconformity upon which the mid-nineteenth-century Liberal party was based. At another level, Catholic Emancipation brought the spectre of Irish nationalism quite literally into the Palace of Westminster, in the persons of the Irish Catholic MPs — initially numbering about 30 — who took their seats in the Commons. Though inclined by temperament to follow the Whigs, these members kept their own counsel as a third force of increasing importance in the political life of both countries. At a third level, the enactment of Emancipation was a public acknowledgement of a deep split within the Tory ranks, between those who were ready to fight in their last ditch in defence of the old order, and those who were prepared to give ground in the hope that the best of the old might be preserved in the new.

This important difference of outlook, which was to lead ultimately to the break-up of the early-nineteenth-century Tory party, came into public view in the 1820s, but its origins reached back into the condition of England following Wellington's victory at Waterloo. The run-down of a war economy can always, if not carefully controlled, bring great social distress and profound economic uncertainty. As we have seen, in the years immediately preceding Waterloo the legislative regulation of wage levels had been largely removed or rendered ineffective. The repeal, in 1824, of the Spitalfields Act of 1773 (which had provided for agreed rates of remuneration in the silk industry) inaugurated a period, lasting until 1909, when wage rates were determined solely by the free play of market forces. However, while workers were left to the mercy of the open market, farmers were not.

The Corn Law of 1815 protected farmers from the possibility that cheap foreign grain would force down prices. Two years later Parliament increased the duty payable on imported wool. These measures were passed at a time when, following the cessation of government contracts, industry was experiencing a sharp re-cession. The demobilisation of about 200,000 ex-servicemen flooded the labour market and thus aggravated an unemployment problem which would have been severe in any case; between 1815 and 1818 the amount of ratepayers' money (not including charitable contributions) spent in poor relief increased from £5.5 millions to £7.9 millions annually. In 1816, to satisfy the organised opposition of commercial and business interests, Pitt's income tax was abolished; since it had provided the Treasury with (by 1815) about one-fifth of its income, its demise obliged the government to rely much more on indirect taxation, which annoyed the rich but hurt the poor.

Scarcely less damaging to working-class interests was the restor-ation of the gold standard in 1821. Payments of gold in exchange for Bank of England notes had been suspended in 1797. The resumption of cash payments, so strongly advocated by *laissez-faire* economists such as David Ricardo (an MP from 1819 to his death in 1823), was beneficial to Britain's overseas trade but had an inevitable deflationary effect at home, restricting the supply of paper money and so pushing up prices. The return to gold was supported by the agricultural interest, which saw it as a piece of economic realism, but was condemned by industrialists, who correctly foresaw its depressive effect on the domestic economy. The Birmingham banker Thomas Attwood subsequently observed that it had created 'more misery, more poverty, more discord . . . than Attila caused in the Roman Empire'.

Misery, poverty and discord were certainly the most distinctive features of British society at this time. A catalogue of uprisings, agitations and plots filled the post-Waterloo years. The Luddites were active from 1811 to 1817. On 2 December 1816 there was a riot at Spa Fields, London, following public meetings addressed by Henry Hunt, a popular radical interested in parliamentary reform, and Thomas Spence, who advocated land nationalisation and the abolition of all taxes save that on incomes. Some extremists, led by Arthur Thistlewood, determined to seize the Tower of London and set up a Committee of Public Safety, but were easily overcome; one person was wounded. Early in the new year the Prince Regent's coach was attacked, some said with bullets but perhaps only with stones. In the spring hundreds of unemployed Lancashire weavers set off to walk from Manchester to London to petition the Regent for relief; their courage deserted them at Macclesfield, where the 'March of the Blanketeers' petered out. The following June there took place at Pentrich, in Derbyshire, the only true uprising of the period. Again, unemployed textile workers were involved, this time in a real plot hatched by one Jeremiah Brandreth to overthrow the government. Troops suppressed the conspiracy near Nottingham; 23 of the conspirators were found guilty of high treason and four of them, including Brandreth, were hanged.

There was a revival of trade in 1817, and a good harvest. A recession in 1818 prompted a series of strikes (not revolts), but a bad harvest was the prelude to the bloodiest encounter of the period, on 16 August 1819, when the military killed 11 people gathered at St Peter's Fields, Manchester, to hear 'Orator' Hunt speak on parliamentary reform; several hundred more were injured. 'Peterloo' marked a high point of post-war civil discontent. Arthur Thistlewood's plot of February 1820, to murder members of the Cabinet and proclaim a republic, was nothing but pathetic melodrama. The plotters were betrayed by government agents (who may well have instigated the business) and five of the ringleaders were executed.

What proper interpretation should be placed upon the unrest of the years 1815–20? The government was convinced, or at least claimed to be convinced, that Luddism, Spa Fields, the Blanketeers, Pentrich, Peterloo and Cato Street were but the tip of an iceberg, and that the state itself was in mortal danger from well-organised revolutionaries. This was their justification for a series of measures more repressive than any that had been introduced by a peacetime administration since the seventeenth century: the suspension of Habeas Corpus and the Gagging Acts of 1817, providing for the licensing of meetings and increasing the penalties for expressing treasonable thoughts; the Six Acts of 1819, which gave magistrates sweeping powers to seize allegedly subversive literature, suppress drilling and confiscate weapons, prevent 'seditious meetings' and make 'certain publications' liable to newspaper stamp duty; the employment of spies and *agents provocateurs*; and the deployment and use of troops to maintain law and order.

But though there undoubtedly were some 'physical force' revolutionaries at large, an examination of the causes of the unrest does not support the view of Lord Liverpool and his colleagues as to the ultimate intentions of the majority of the disaffected. It is true that the main thrust of the Six Acts was aimed at remedying defects in existing legislation, and that the two that interfered most seriously with the liberty of the individual — the prohibition of unauthorised meetings and the powers given to magistrates to search for arms — were only temporary. The Liverpool administration had, however, misdirected itself as to the ultimate causes of the widespread popular discontent. The thousands of people who witnessed the horrors of Peterloo had no intention of overthrowing the government. Their concern was with the undeniable fact that Manchester, a town of some 135,000 inhabitants and now of considerable importance in the economic life of the country, had not a single MP at Westminster; they hoped to follow the example of the citizenry of Birmingham (also unrepresented in the Commons), who had chosen their own 'legislatorial attorney' (Sir Charles Wolseley, later jailed on a charge of sedition) to fill this gap. If to demand representation in the Westminster Parliament, rather than its overthrow, was revolutionary, then there were far more revolutionaries to be found among the middle classes, the *nouveaux riches* of the industrial revolution, than among the agricultural labourers or the textile workers, whose wants would have been entirely satisfied by modest employment and one hot meal a day. Orator Hunt did not desire to abolish the House of Commons but to be elected to it, an ambition he realised in 1830.

As with Catholic Emancipation, the Tories were deeply split on the issue of parliamentary reform, but less so on the desirability of change in other directions. From 1820 the economy recovered and unemployment fell. In 1822 the replacement of Sidmouth by Peel brought to the headship of the Home Office a champion of penal reform, much influenced by the ideas of Sir Samuel Romilly, Elizabeth Fry, John Howard and other prison reformers. Peel reduced the list of capital offences by about a hundred, and introduced regular inspection of prisons. In 1829, believing (correctly) that deterrence is better than punishment, he created in London a body of 3,000 paid constables — the Metropolitan Police — controlled by a Commissioner responsible to the Home Secretary. The idea of a professional, but non-military, corps of law-enforcement officers, accountable to elected representatives of the people, quickly spread to the provinces; there were to be no more Peterloos.

If there was some suspicion within Tory ranks over the policies of Robert Peel, there was none over the implementation of freer trade. Two men, Frederick Robinson (who in 1823 moved from the resurrected Board of Trade to the Exchequer) and William Huskisson (who succeeded him at the Board of Trade), were responsible for implementing a policy of economic *laissez-faire*. In 1821 tariffs were reduced on imported timber. The following year the Navigation Laws were modified, thus making it easier, in particular, for European nations to trade with Britain in goods originating outside Europe, and permitting colonies to trade more freely with Europe and Africa. In 1824, overcoming the opposition of farmers and manufacturers, the duties on imported wool and silk were removed; import duties generally were lowered, from 50 to 20 per cent on manufactured goods and from 20 to 10 per cent on raw materials. A series of reciprocal trade treaties was negotiated with European states.

This policy of freer trade caught the upswing in industrial production at the right moment; between 1821 and 1827 revenues from customs duties increased by 64 per cent. It also had an unexpected political repercussion. Radicals in Parliament argued that, since British workers were now less protected from foreign competition, and completely unprotected from the effects of the trade cycle, there was no point in continuing to prohibit 'combinations'. In 1824 Pitt's Combination Acts were repealed, with hardly any parliamentary debate or public concern. An immediate outbreak of strikes and contract-breaking led to their partial re-enactment the following year. None the less, though still subject to the common law of conspiracy, trade unions could henceforth legally exist, organise and bargain on behalf of their members.

These reforms were carried through from a variety of motives: paternalistic humanitarianism; economic ideology; political opportunism. There was also an element of enlightened fear. A majority of the Tories agreed with the Whigs that, whatever its origins, post-war radicalism had benefited from a mixture of economic distress, affecting the lower orders, and political ambition, affecting the middle classes. The prevailing climate of *laissez-faire* meant that only the symptoms of economic distress could be attacked; a little-noticed effect of the legislation of 1824 was to remove the former prohibition on the emigration of artisans. But the ever more insistent demands of the bourgeoisie for a share in government could not be brushed aside so lightly. The years following Waterloo witnessed a growing agitation for parliamentary reform, popularised by Major John Cartwright's Hampden Clubs and at the meetings addressed by Hunt and other radical demagogues. To make matters worse, in 1816 William Cobbett discovered he could avoid stamp duty on his weekly *Political Register* by publishing it as a pamphlet instead of a newspaper; the price was, in consequence, slashed from a shilling to twopence, with an inevitable increase in circulation. T. J. Wooler, who produced the radical newspaper *Black Dwarf* in a similar way, brought out a cheap edition of Bentham's *Plan of Parliamentary Reform*.

Ideas which had not been heard of since the Puritan Revolution, such as universal suffrage and annual parliaments, became popular talking points. During the 1820s the issue of parliamentary reform was overshadowed by that of Catholic Emancipation, and appeared in any case to have become less urgent with the improvement in the state of the economy. None the less, Cobbett kept the subject alive in his lecture tours and in January 1830 Attwood founded the Birmingham Political Union to campaign for reform. As the possibility of serious social disorder faded, the industrial bourgeoisie became more interested in reform along two well-defined avenues: first, overhaul of the borough franchise in order to sweep away a miscellany of ancient voting qualifications and to institute instead a standard £10 householder qualification; second, a general redistribution of seats (this had not occurred since Tudor times) in order to allow the new centres of industry to be represented in Parliament.

The justice of these moderate middle-class demands might appear too obvious to have required much discussion. Cornwall returned 44 MPs to Parliament, mostly from decayed or uninhabited borough constituencies. Birmingham, Manchester, Leeds, Sheffield, Wolverhampton, Huddersfield and Gateshead were unrepresented; even London only had eight MPs. The old system was unfair in another way, in that there was an imbalance in favour of the agricultural south of England; of the 203 English borough constituencies only 74 were located in the 23 northern counties. The borough franchise, replete with 'burgage', 'scot and lot' and 'potwalloper' privileges, was almost totally corrupt. The electorates of British boroughs averaged only 300, and only 55 boroughs had electorates of over 500. Even where the borough franchise was reasonably open, as at Preston, aristocratic influence could be very strong. Only in the counties, the electorates of which (averaging 4,000 voters) were too big to bribe on a large scale, was there to be found anything approaching free and fair elections; in the counties there was a great deal of deference to the views of local landowners but relatively little corruption.

The necessity of some reform was not a matter of fundamental dispute between Whigs and Tories; many 'ultra' Tories supported the principle of reform as a way of purifying the existing electoral system. The eighteenth century had been littered with attempts to root out corruption. In addition to the Place Acts, legislation in 1729 and 1770 had attempted to take disputes over the franchise and election returns out of parliamentary politics. Pitt himself favoured parliamentary reform. Curwen's Act had curbed government influence in the electoral process. The notorious 'nomination' borough of Grampound had been disfranchised in 1821 and its two seats given to Yorkshire. In February 1830, when Wellington was still in office, the Whig leader Lord John Russell had attempted to introduce a modest parliamentary reform Bill; so had the ultra-Tory Marquess of Blandford. Following their successful enactment of Catholic Emancipation, it was widely expected that Wellington and Peel would press ahead with parliamentary reform proposals of their own.

Yet although there was a wide measure of agreement on the necessity for some reform of the electoral system, there was no such agreement as to the scope of the reform, or its purpose. The Tories argued that the basis of the old system had been that the direction of the nation's affairs was given over to the landowning classes. They were anxious, therefore, to extend the vote to an assortment of leaseholders, particularly the £50 per annum tenants-at-will whose enfranchisement was proposed by the Tory Marquess of Chandos and who, because of their susceptibility to landlord influence, could be counted upon to support Toryism. The Whigs believed that the basis of the system was the enfranchisement of property and that reform was necessary because new forms of property — industrial property — had arisen which were not encompassed within the old constitution. They therefore proposed, and ultimately carried, the abolition of all customary voting rights in the boroughs and their replacement by a standard £10 householder qualification. They also insisted on the disfranchisement of 56 rotten boroughs (representing 111 seats) and on a reduction of the representation of 31 other boroughs, releasing a further 32 seats. Of the seats thus made available for redistribution, 65 were given to industrial towns, 65 to the counties, eight to Scotland and five to Ireland

The Reform Acts of 1832 (separate legislation covered England and Wales, Scotland, and Ireland) which implemented these proposals, are generally accorded an importance out of all proportion to their effects upon the political system. The aim of the legislation was to purify and refine the existing system, not to replace it by any other. In introducing the English Bill, in March 1831, Lord John Russell stressed that the effects of the £10 householder vote would be to extend the franchise to 'about half a million of persons, and all these connected with the property of the country, having a valuable stake amongst us, and deeply interested in our institutions'. The legislation preserved and extended the eighteenth-century idea that the House of Commons should be representative of interests, not people. Frome was enfranchised because it had a woollen industry, and would 'represent' the south-west of England. Totnes, with 179 voters, returned two MPs, but so did Liverpool, whose electors numbered over 8,000. County MPs now totalled 253, as against 188 in the unreformed House of Commons; borough representation dropped from 465 to 399.

What the Whigs had done was to preserve the eighteenth-century constitution by bringing within its pale the industrialists and men of business who might otherwise have provided leadership and backing for dangerous democratic movements. There was certainly nothing remotely democratic about the Acts of 1832. Although their effect was to increase the British electorate by about 38 per cent, less than three-quarters of a million persons were entitled to vote as a result of their implementation: about one in five of the adult male population in England and Wales, and about one in eight in Scotland. In a large number of towns the working-class vote was actually reduced: in the small boroughs about one-quarter of adult males were enfranchised, but in the large manufacturing towns the proportion was only about one in forty-five.

Whigs and Tories agreed in ruling out any idea of the secret ballot. Wellington was later relieved to find that 'the gentry . . . influence as many voters as ever they did'. Nor was there any drastic or far-reaching change in the social composition of the House of Commons. The diarist Charles Greville (Clerk of the Privy Council) noted in 1833 that the first session of the reformed Parliament 'turns out to be very much like every other Parliament . . . the hopes and fears of mankind have been equally disappointed'. The radical *Black Book* of 1834 was a good deal blunter when it proclaimed that 'the aristocratic interests still have a numerical preponderance'. Indeed, Grey's government, which passed the reform legislation, was itself so thoroughly aristocratic that of the 14 members of the Cabinet only four sat in the Commons; it was hardly to be expected that a government such as this would have dealt harshly with the landowning interests in which it was rooted.

The terms of the legislation were, therefore, noteworthy but not of fundamental significance; they constituted a backward-looking measure, the passage of which (so the Whigs hoped) would put an end to agitation for further reform. In one sense the Whigs were right. Later Reform Acts had nothing in common with those of 1832, and it is quite erroneous to see in the 1832 legislation the ancestor of democratic government in Britain. Yet, modest and conservative though they undoubtedly were, the Whig proposals aroused more public interest than any subsequent reform of the electoral system. They were rejected once by the Commons (March 1831) and twice by the Lords (October 1831 and May

1832); Grey had to extract a promise from William IV to create enough Whig peers, if necessary, to pass the measure (June 1832); there were riots in Derby, Nottingham and Bristol; the smell of revolution was unmistakable, and more authentic than at any time since Waterloo.

How is this remarkable public concern and agitation to be explained? The answer seems to be, not that the Whig proposals constituted the first reform of Parliament by itself (clearly they did not), but that their passage into law was desired by a very substantial body of national opinion. The election of 1831 was dominated by the proposed reforms and many candidates pledged themselves to support Lord John Russell's Bill. Those who were successful could indeed claim that they had been 'mandated' by their electors. The Burkean concept of parliamentary government, that MPs were elected to represent the national interest as they conceived it, rather than the particular wishes of their constituents, was thus under attack. The electorate may have been very small, but it existed none the less, and had to be deferred to. The monarch had, in consequence, forced the Lords to give way to the Commons. The voter-registration provisions of the 1832 reform stimulated the growth of party organisation, and the strength of party organisation was ultimately to lead not only to the disappearance of royal influence in Parliament but also to the diminution of aristocratic influence. The more professionally organised political clubs which came into existence — the Tory Carlton (1832) and the Whig Reform (1836) — came to have some say in the choice of candidates and in the disbursement of election expenses.

Although, therefore, the Whigs were quite justified in pointing to the fact that the Continental Revolutions of 1848 did not take root in Britain, and in pointing to their 1832 reform as a major reason for this, and for the general domestic tranquillity in the country in the mid-nineteenth century, the Tories were also justified in regarding the fact that the Acts were passed at all as a watershed. Extra-parliamentary public opinion secured the passage of the Reform Acts in 1832. Therein lay their importance and their message.

3 AN AGE OF PROSPERITY

The development of British society during the middle years of the nineteenth century possesses a superficial symmetry. The period was ushered in with the calling of the first reformed Parliament, and was brought to a close with the passage of the second Reform Act. Historians have professed to see a natural relationship between the Acts of 1867 and 1832, and it is sometimes argued that both were part of an even grander project: the creation of a democracy. On a social level, the process of unfettered mechanisation and factory organisation which had characterised the previous half-century was now followed by a stocktaking, in the course of which steps were taken to correct, or at least to modify, some of the worst features of the industrialised society. But were these steps really taken solely on humanitarian grounds? Its world economic supremacy as yet unchallenged, the United Kingdom was able to extend its influence to virtually every part of the globe by a combination of commercial penetration and military persistence, symbolised by the hegemony of Lord Palmerston at the Foreign Office and fortified by the conviction that free trade was (as *The Times* put it in 1859) 'not so much a prevalent opinion as an article of faith'. How, then, are we to explain that at precisely the time at which free trade triumphed as an economic doctrine, administrative *laissez-faire* was abandoned?

These middle years certainly seem to have exuded unashamed self-confidence. The Great Exhibition of 1851 was, after all, a celebration not merely of British achievement but of the belief in the efficacy of British institutions and of the British approach to social and industrial organisation. The bourgeoisie assumed an ever greater prominence in the direction of the nation's affairs, secure — for the time being — in the knowledge that the relative prosperity of the period made the possibility of class conflict remote indeed. One of the best-selling books of the period was *Self-Help*, a slim volume published in 1859 and written by the Scottish doctor and journalist Samuel Smiles. Smiles had made detailed studies of the lives of the leading engineers of the age, all of whom were self-made men. In *Self-Help* he extolled the virtues of thrift and hard work. 'The spirit of self-help,' he explained, 'is the root of all genuine growth in the individual; and exhibited in the lives of the many, it constitutes the true source of national vigour and strength.'

This opinion was shared by many of the middle and working classes alike. Socialism remained a utopian curiosity. Robert Owen's New Lanark experiment at the beginning of the century was not repeated. The Grand National Consolidated Trades Union (GNCTU), of which Owen became President, collapsed in 1834, the year of its foundation. A band of self-styled Christian Socialists, led by Charles Kingsley, the Anglican minister and novelist, Thomas Hughes, the author of *Tom Brown's Schooldays*, and J.M. Ludlow, later to become Registrar of Friendly Societies, attempted to revive working-class interest in Christianity by encouraging co-operative workshops; by the mid-1850s this movement, too, was in ruins.

The only successful co-operative venture of the period was the foundation of a consumers' co-operative by some of Owen's disciples in Rochdale in 1844. Customers of the Rochdale shop, and of the many others founded on the same principle, provided the capital with which they were established, and shared in their profits. Thus, although goods were sold at the market price, they could in effect be purchased more cheaply than elsewhere. Moreover, the food products so supplied were unadulterated, an important consideration at a time when adulteration of foodstuffs (such as the mixing of brown sugar with sand) was commonplace. So popular and effective was this form of economic organisation that by the 1880s a string of co-operative factories and wholesale facilities had been established to service the retail outlets. Co-operative societies of this type acquired friendly-society status in 1852 and were allowed to become limited liability companies in 1862. Yet, despite the idealism of the Rochdale pioneers, and their plans 'to arrange the powers of production, distribution, education, and government', the movement developed along lines far removed from socialism. It became merely a form of profit-sharing in which customers were shareholders in an essentially capitalist enterprise. There is, indeed, no better testimony to the popularity of capitalism among the working classes of mid-Victorian England than the high street 'co-ops' which flourished in the poorer districts of the industrial conurbations.

The trade-union movement, too, was a paradigm of moderation. Early attempts, following the partial repeal of the Combination Acts, to form national unions catering for more than one trade all foundered — as they were bound to — on the rock of sectionalism and craft rivalry. The Grand General Union of Operative Spinners of Great Britain and Ireland, formed by John Doherty in Manchester in 1829, disintegrated in 1832, and his National Association for the Protection of Labour also broke up. The GNCTU belied its name; it was formed in London and its paid-up membership, which did not exceed about 16,000, was composed largely of tailors, shoemakers and silk weavers. Its collapse was due not merely to the hostility of employers and the authorities, but also to the fact that it appealed mainly to economically weak groups of workers, and to poor organisation and financial ineptitude, its end being hastened by the disappearance of its treasurer, who made off with the funds.

The attempt by a group of agricultural labourers in Dorset to form a branch of the GNCTU, and their subsequent trial and transportation to Australia, made the union's activities appear much more sinister than they actually were. The Tolpuddle Martyrs (as they became known) were not punished for belonging to or forming a union; they fell foul of the Act of 1797 against administering unlawful oaths. The Home Secretary, Lord Melbourne, chose to make an example of them because he feared a recurrence of the agricultural riots which had taken place in Kent in 1830 (the Captain Swing riots). But the maximum sentence of seven years' transportation led to a public outcry, and by 1838 all six 'martyrs' had been returned to Britain. Melbourne really need not have worried about the intentions of the Dorset labourers. One of their rules had stated:

> That the objects of this society can never be promoted by any act or acts of violence, but on the contrary, all such proceedings must tend to injure the cause and destroy the society itself. This order therefore will not counternance [sic] any violation of the laws.

The development of trade unionism in the late 1830s and 1840s must be distinguished from Chartism, which was, in some respects, a movement with revolutionary potential. The trade unions of the 1840s were craft unions, the members of which comprised the 'aristocracy of labour': skilled literate working men. Though strike

action was not unknown it was frowned upon, and generally unsuccessful. Employers countered industrial militancy by a combination of ruthless intimidation of troublemakers and generous
paternalism; the railway companies, for example, provided
dwellings, schools, hospitals and various other forms of welfare
provision. The typical unions of the mid-century, such as the
Typographers, Boilermakers and Engineers, saw their prime task
as the strengthening of the apprenticeship system in order to
maintain wage levels; beyond that, they were little more than
friendly societies, providing pension, sickness and death benefits.
It certainly never occurred to them to use industrial muscle in
order to bring about political change or to acquire parliamentary
representation.

The merger, in 1851, of the Journeymen Steam Engine Makers
(established in Manchester in 1826) with a number of other engineering societies to form the Amalgamated Society of Engineers
is generally regarded as having inaugurated a new era in the
history of the trade-union movement. There was nothing new in
national unions, of course, and the combination of high subscriptions and membership restricted to skilled artisans was commonplace in the eighteenth century; the membership fee of the
Engineers was one shilling a week, at a time when unskilled
workers in industry could expect to earn no more than about
twenty shillings a week at most. None the less, after 1850 the
organisation of skilled workers on a national basis became the rule
rather than the exception; the example of the Engineers was
followed by the Builders and the Flint Glass Makers (1851), the
Spinners (1852) and the Weavers (1858). These 'New Model'
unions were capable of militancy, but in the main their leaderships
were cautious and conservative, pursuing a policy of low profile
while building up membership and financial resources. The system
of tramping was phased out. Unions encouraged temperance and
literary pursuits; their journals preached the virtues of poetry, not
politics. The middle classes were impressed. By the mid-1860s
trade unions had become an accepted and respectable facet of
industrial society. The passage of the Master and Servant Act, in
1867, restricting imprisonment for breach of contract to extreme
or aggravated breaches, was an acknowledgement of this fact.

Later generations of trade unionists saw the relationship between employers and unions in the mid-nineteenth century as
altogether too cosy. Both sides held to the same moral values and

political beliefs, both worshipped at the altar of free trade, and both regarded unemployment as a natural phenomenon, like a bad harvest: one could protect oneself against its effects, but one could not prevent it happening. There is little evidence of the existence of a unitary working-class consciousness in Britain at this time. The Victorians — even Karl Marx's collaborator Friedrich Engels — spoke of 'the working classes' rather than of the 'working class'. The class divisions of the age were between different types of Labour and different types of Capital. The evidence of poll books shows that shopkeepers and craftsmen were more likely to vote Liberal than Conservative, and that labourers, where they had the vote, were more likely to vote Conservative than Liberal.

The Victorian 'upper classes' were persons of the highest rank. They belonged to a social rather than to an economic group; they were the titled, hereditary aristocracy. The term 'middle classes' came into general usage in the early-nineteenth century, and originally denoted those next in the social hierarchy below the upper classes. But in the reaction against the power and privileges of the landed aristocracy the term acquired an economic dimension: the 'industrious classes', those, that is, who used their capital in a productive manner. John Stuart Mill talked about the 'three classes' of 'landlords, capitalists and labourers', and Marx, who lived in London as a refugee from 1848 to his death in 1883, spoke in much the same terms about the three 'great social classes . . . wage labourers, capitalists and landlords'.

The term 'middle classes', which was thus originally social in its purport, became an economic term, and one, moreover, which implied not merely a certain kind of wealth but also an economic relationship (that of employer) with those — 'the working classes' — whose only wealth lay in the labour they sold to their employers in return for wages. We must add, however, that the Victorians thought of the working classes as belonging pre-eminently to the industrial sector. There was a basic truth in the famous assertion of Engels, in *The Condition of the Working Class in England* (1845) that 'The history of the English working classes begins in the last half of the eighteenth century, with the invention of the steam engine and the machines for manufacturing cotton'. Marx and Engels located the working classes in the factories, the mines, the railway companies, the textile mills, and the ironworks, and labelled them as the proletariat, 'the class of modern wage labourers', Engels explained in the 1888 edition of the *Communist Manifesto* (first published 40 years previously) 'who, having no means of production of their own, are reduced to selling their labour in order to live'.

But even Marx did not go so far as to claim that British society was composed of only two classes. Industry was severely hierarchical. In 1866 the ironmaster and MP W.O. Foster explained why it had proved difficult to organise working men's clubs:

> Some receive considerable wages, some little. The high grade of iron workers associate with second and third class tradesmen and do not want to meet in a club the faces they have seen all day.

Analysis of census returns for 1841 and 1851 suggests that in urban communities as far apart as South Shields, Northampton and Oldham about 46 per cent of working men were semi-skilled, 18 per cent were engaged in crafts and a similar proportion were skilled masters, clerical workers and shopkeepers, 14 per cent were paupers and labourers, and only 4 per cent were well-to-do, industrialists, professional people and the like. Quite clearly, the major divide was that between the artisan and the unskilled labourer.

Trade-union membership was a privilege only a small minority of working men and women enjoyed. In 1851 Henry Mayhew, the meticulous chronicler of London life, recorded that only 10 per cent of the craft workers of the metropolis were organised in trade unions. In evidence to the Royal Commission on Trade Unions, in 1867, the secretary of a builders' association in the Midlands declared that only 10 per cent of carpenters were unionised, 19 per cent of bricklayers and less than 10 per cent of plumbers. Organised workers such as these comprised the labour aristocracy, earning wages perhaps twice as high as the unskilled, and enjoying better conditions of work and, within limits, greater security of employment. Between the skilled artisan and the unskilled labourer a gulf existed as wide as any social division to be found in Britain at the time. Unionised workers, both from the older crafts, such as watchmakers and carpenters, and from the new industries, such as the cotton operatives and the locomotive drivers, aspired to a lower middle-class lifestyle. But the railway navvies, the general labourers, the dockers, sailors and agricultural workers, as well as the great mass of female workers, enjoyed no such advantages. Mayhew recorded that,

> The transition from the artisan to the labourer is curious in many ways. In passing from the skilled operative of the west-end to the unskilled workman of the eastern quarter of London, the moral and intellectual change is so great, that it seems as if we were in a new land, and among another race.

A working-class writer explained in 1873 that 'The artisan creed with regard to the labourer is, that they are an inferior class, and that they should be made to know, and kept in their place'.

We are certainly justified in speaking of working-class consciousness at this time — that is, of an increasingly deep awareness by manual workers of their role in the economy and of their place in the social hierarchy. But we must take care not to assume that an awareness of class also meant an awareness of, let alone a predilection for, class struggle. We must guard against formulating a general argument derived from a few dramatic episodes, and, in particular, against interpreting desperately fought wage disputes as evidence of opposition to the entire capitalist system. In 1834 there was a well-organised strike of Oldham cotton operatives, who wished to force the masters to accept a maximum working day of eight hours. The strike lasted a week and had been precipitated by a police raid on a trade-union lodge and the arrest of some of its members. The attempt to gain by industrial action what Parliament was unwilling to grant by statute could be interpreted as opposition to the state as well as to employers; but such a conclusion would not be justified. In 1835, after the collapse of the strike, the spinners' delegates declared that 'we would despoil no man of his rightful property; we dream not of any absolute equality of condition'.

What the operatives of Oldham desired was not the overthrow of all capital, but a bigger say in its distribution. The same kind of verdict must be passed on other industrial disputes of the period, such as the 'Plug Plot' of 1842, a movement, again in the north of England, in which workers demonstrated their dislike of wage cuts by removing boiler plugs to prevent further production at their factories or workplaces. However, the Plug Plot, and its attendant riots, are generally regarded as a bizarre episode within a wider agitation, Chartism, which was, by any standards, the most significant political manifestation of the early Victorian working classes. Is it, perhaps, in Chartism that a genuine revolutionary proletariat is to be found?

The Chartist movement had its origins in the artisan and middle-class radicalism that flourished in London and Birmingham after the disappointments of the 1832 Reform Acts. In 1836 a group of London radicals, led by William Lovett, a cabinet-maker, established the London Working Men's Association. In collaboration with the master tailor Francis Place (who had played a central role in the partial repeal of the Combination Acts), and with the assistance of a number of radical MPs, Lovett drew up a 'People's Charter', which made its famous 'Six Points': universal suffrage (not universal male suffrage); the abolition of the property qualification necessary for election to Parliament; annual parliaments; equal-sized parliamentary constituencies; the payment of MPs; and voting by secret ballot. None of these demands was new; some, indeed, such as the abolition of the property qulification, dated back to the seventeenth century. But the London Working Men's Association hoped to give their enactment a greater sense of urgency by winning over the support of moderate working men who had felt betrayed in 1832. Contact was made with Attwood's Birmingham Political Union, which accepted the Charter at a mass meeting in August 1838; other meetings in support of the Charter were held in Manchester, Leeds and Glasgow. In May 1839, and again in May 1842, petitions said to contain, respectively, 1.3 million and 3.3 million signatures, were presented to Parliament. They were supported by less than 50 MPs.

Between 1842 and 1847 the movement was dormant, perhaps because the revival of trade took the wind out of its sails; many supporters of Chartism turned to other causes, such as the Anti-Corn Law League and the campaign for a maximum working day of ten hours in factories. But the onset of recession, in 1846–7, gave the movement a final lease of life. A new petition, alleged to contain two million signatures (many of which were certainly forged) was presented to Parliament, to the accompaniment of a great deal of silly talk of violence if it should be rejected. In the event the much publicised Kennington Common rally, on 10 April 1848, attracted a crowd estimated by *The Times* at about 20,000, which no less than 150,000 special constables had been recruited to hold in check. The petition was rejected. There was no insurrection. Chartism collapsed.

The demands of the Chartists were, of course, far too radical for a Parliament dominated by the middle and upper classes. There was much division within Chartist ranks over tactics to be pursued. Those who had drawn up the Charter were essentially moderates, not violent revolutionaries. But it was the fate of Chartism to have become a focus for discontent arising from a variety of deep-seated social and economic grievances which really had little in common with the Six Points. In Lancashire and Yorkshire, adult factory workers, who had not been protected by Lord Althorp's 1833 Factory Act, supported Chartism as a means of furthering not merely the Ten Hours movement but the state regulation of factory work generally. The Ten Hours movement dissipated Chartist energies in the 1840s, and was not triumphant until 1853. The main protagonists of factory reform — men like Michael Sadler, Richard Oastler, Anthony Ashley (Lord Shaftesbury) and the ex-Methodist minister John Raynor Stephens — were all Tories. The Chartists were not. Francis Place had declared that 'All legislative interference must be pernicious. Men must be left to make their own bargains'. The Charter stood for basic political freedoms, which were of little immediate benefit or comfort to exploited workers. Nor was Chartism especially disposed to favour the advance of the trade-union movement. Significantly, the Six Points said nothing about any enlargement of trade-union rights. Although a great many individual trade unionists joined the movement, the unions kept (for the most part) a safe distance from it. Some groups of workers who rallied to the Chartist flag — such as handloom weavers and stockingers — were clearly in depressed trades; but others — such as tailors and carpenters — were well paid, even prosperous. Chartism was not a revolt against technological change.

The Chartist movement thus gathered unto itself groups of malcontents who did not have much sympathy with or even understanding of its objectives, but who supported its efforts out of frustration at their inability to further their own. Disenchanted factory reformers, thwarted trade unionists and agitators against the 1834 Poor Law all lauded the principles of the Charter in the hope that their own causes would benefit thereby. The resultant and inevitable fragmentation of the movement was far more important as a cause of its demise than the fact (upon which too much stress is conventionally laid) that Chartism had six aims, whereas, say, the Anti-Corn Law League had only one. The Six Points of the Charter represented a coherent if as yet unattainable political package. But the horses coupled to the Chartist wagon pulled it in different directions.

It was no help that the movement fell into the hands of de-magogues, pre-eminent among whom was Feargus O'Connor, an Irish landowner and ex-MP whose newspaper, *The Northern Star*, achieved a circulation of 50,000 copies a week. In 1840 O'Connor established the National Charter Association, which soon eclipsed other Chartist organisations and which gave its blessing to acts of politically motivated violence. Chartism had its 'physical' moments: the 1839 Newport (South Wales) rising, when 14 Chartists were killed by the military and the ex-mayor, John Frost, was among those sentenced to death; the Plug Plot riots of 1842; and a few other isolated incidents. But we should also note that Chartists regularly used colourful and intimidatory language. Even Lovett, at the Chartist Convention of 1839, supported a motion advising the populace to take up arms. When we consider the number and size of Chartist meetings between 1838 and 1848, what is remarkable is that the violence was so limited.

It is also clear that the times of greatest mass support for the Chartist movement coincided with periods of severe economic depression: 1839, 1842 and 1848. J.R. Stephens had no doubt of the implication:

> The question of universal suffrage is a knife and fork question . . . a bread and cheese question . . . and if any man asks me what I mean by universal suffrage, I would answer: that every man in the land has a right to have a good coat on his back, a comfortable abode in which to shelter himself and his family, a good dinner upon his table, and no more work than is necessary for keeping him in good health and as much wages for that work as would keep him in plenty.

It is evident that the experience of Chartism embedded itself deeply into the minds of working-class people. Its social man-ifestations (such as the promotion of Chartist churches and schools) were no less important than its political campaigns. O'Connor's National Co-operative Land Company had been wound up by 1851, and he himself died in a Chiswick lunatic asylum four years later. What was left of the movement fell into the hands of socialists such as Julian Harney and Ernest Jones. By

1860 the National Charter Association was no more. Yet the effects of Chartism outlived its various formal organisations. The movement promoted and encouraged political activity among working people in Britain, and exposed them to continental movements: the *Communist Manifesto* was first published in English in Harney's newspaper, the *Red Republican*, in 1851. The Irish Chartist James Bronterre O'Brien, writing in *The Northern Star*, evolved a theory of political action based upon working-class needs. Indeed, in the 1840s and 1850s Chartism kept alive the idea and the memory of political reform, which thus remained a legitimate working-class aspiration during the more prosperous decades of the mid-century. The movement was, quite clearly, dealt a fatal blow by the fiasco of 1848. But within the next two generations all of its demands, save that for annual parliaments, had been enacted.

Chartism not only stimulated working-class consciousness. It aroused wide interest in and directed the attention of the nation towards areas of potential social reform virtually neglected hitherto, such as public health, education and factory conditions. Unfortunately, the Whigs, who reaped an immediate and predictable benefit from having enacted parliamentary reform in 1832, were not inclined to radical social policies. The Whig governments which ruled almost without interruption from 1833 to 1841 were coalitions, sustained in the Commons by the Radicals, but also by Canningites and moderate Tories. These groups, united only in their support of the Acts of 1832, were known collectively as 'Reformers', and numbered about 480 MPs. Across the floor of the House there sat 175 'anti-Reformers', a hard core of Tories led by Sir Robert Peel. Apart from the issue of parliamentary reform, Whigs and Tories were more often than not in agreement on the general lines of national policy; in the 1833 parliamentary session Peel voted against Grey, the Prime Minister, on only three occasions, and went into the government lobby to support the tax on malt proposed in the budget.

The following year witnessed a constitutional landmark. Believing Lord Melbourne, Grey's successor as Prime Minister to be an unreliable defender of the Church of England, William IV dismissed him (November 1834) and installed a Tory government led, initially, by the Duke of Wellington. Peel, who was abroad at the time, did not take over as First Lord of the Treasury until the following month; his parliamentary position was, of course, un-

tenable, and he asked for and obtained from the King a dissolution. At the general election of January 1835 the Whigs saw
their representation in the Commons decrease, to 385. But an
alliance with the Irish MPs (the Lichfield House 'compact') in
February paved the way for Melbourne's return to power, and in
April Peel resigned. Since these events no monarch has dared
dismiss an administration, and a Prime Minister's request for a
dissolution has always been granted. Although Queen Victoria's
influence on public affairs was sometimes strong, William IV's
conscious but clumsy emulation of his father, George III, has
never been repeated: he was obliged to acknowledge the
parliamentary basis of British government.

The events of 1834–5 were also important in a party sense. The
Lichfield House agreement was the first of a series of alliances
between Whigs and Radicals on the one hand, and Irish
parliamentarians on the other. The immediate advantages to each
side were obvious. Melbourne's government was sustained in
office; O'Connell dropped his campaign for the repeal of the
Union; and two pieces of useful reform legislation relating to
Ireland were passed, the Tithe Commutation Act (1838), converting tithes into a fixed rent charge, and the Irish Municipal
Corporations Act (1840) which abolished over 50 corrupt corporations and corrected a number of more general abuses in Irish
local government. But the marriage of convenience with the Irish,
and particularly with the unscrupulous and loud-mouthed leader
of the Irish parliamentary party, damaged the reputation of the
Whigs in the constituencies. In 1836 Sir Harry Verney, the Whig
MP for Buckingham, declared that 'at the present moment the
fault found with government is that they are too much influenced
by O'Connell'.

Moderate reformers grew uneasy, and by 1837 no less than 40 of
them had crossed the floor of the Commons to join the Tory
opposition, which was increasingly being regarded as the true
patriotic party of the nation. After the general election that year
the Whig/Liberal majority over the Tories fell to just 32 seats. As
Melbourne's dependence upon Irish votes grew deeper, so the
popularity of the Whigs fell. Preoccupation with Irish questions in
Parliament pushed moderates towards the Tories. Thus was established a pattern of events to become even more pronounced later
in the century, and which was to contribute not a little to the
weakness of Liberal administrations.

Peel took full advantage of the opportunities these events pre-sented for a revival of Tory fortunes. In the eyes of the party he led, Peel's besetting weakness was that he allowed himself to be ruled by his head rather than his heart. In the eyes of posterity that is precisely where his true greatness lay. Peel did not permit himself to be governed by narrow dogma. He came from bourgeois stock (his father had been a wealthy Lancashire cotton manufacturer, his grandfather a humble mill worker) and, like many of his class, he was a devoted fan of the landed aristocracy, whose continual dominance of public life he believed 'essential to the purposes of good government'. But Peel was not so blind in his devotion as to fail to recognise that the old Tory policy of total resistance to change — the policy of the 'Ultras' — was not only doomed, but dangerous into the bargain. It was for this reason that he took the opportunity provided by the 1835 election to issue to his Tamworth constituents (December 1834) a 'Manifesto' which accepted the irreversibility of the 1832 Reform Acts and which, by implication at least, repudiated Ultra-Toryism:

> I consider the Reform Bill an irrevocable settlement of a great Constitutional question . . . if the spirit of the Reform Bill implies merely a careful review of institutions, civil and ecclesiastical, undertaken in a friendly temper, combining, with a firm maintenance of established rights the correction of proved abuses and the redress of real grievances, — in that case, I can for myself and colleagues, undertake to act in such a spirit and with such intentions.

Peel recognised, and to a certain degree identified with, the policies of a newer group of radical tories, many of whom, like himself, were from commercial and industrial backgrounds, who claimed that the duty of the party was to rebuild one nation out of two and, in consequence, to side with the workers against the 'millocracy'. The logic of this approach was to demand more government intervention in the economic and social affairs of the country — more factory legislation, more social reform, less *laissez-faire*. Peel was prepared to travel some way down this road. His penal reforms of the 1820s were generally applauded. His government of 1841–6 accepted, even if it did not initiate, Ashley's Mines Act of 1842 (which prohibited all female labour under-ground, and the labour of boys under 10 years of age), and itself passed the 1844 Factory Act. This measure was, in common with all the early Factory Acts, limited to the textile industry; but it embodied the first legislative restriction upon the working hours of adult women (their hours were limited to twelve per day, as were those of young persons under 18 years of age), and it prohibited the factory employment of all children under 8 years of age; employers were obliged henceforth to fence in some types of dangerous machinery, and the powers of the factory inspectorate were increased. Peel's government also passed a remarkable Railways Act (also in 1844) which compelled every railway company to provide one covered-carriage train per day, in each direction, at a third-class fare not exceeding one penny per mile. This legislation also prescribed the terms under which all railways authorised in and after the 1844 parliamentary session might, after 21 years, be purchased by the state — the first ever nationalisation Act!

Where Peel and the bulk of the Tories parted company was in their differing attitudes towards prevailing economic orthodoxies, and in relation to the degree of protection to be afforded to the Anglican Church. On this latter issue Peel was already highly suspect, on account of his having consented to Catholic Emancipation. In the Tamworth Manifesto he expressed his support for the abortive proposal of Lord Althorp, the Whig Chancellor of the Exchequer, that the compulsory church rate (to which Dissenters were bitterly opposed) be replaced by an annual grant of £250,000 from the land tax, to be applied to the building and repair of churches. Nonconformist fury at this plan to make them (as they saw it) continue to pay church rates, but as taxpayers rather than as ratepayers, was such that the idea was dropped; compulsory church rates were not abolished until 1868. Peel also opposed the admission of Dissenters to Oxford and Cambridge universities.

It cannot therefore be argued that Peel saw no special place in the constitution for the Established Church. But he did believe that other denominations were worthy of some consideration and some civil equality. He supported Lord John Russell's proposal to licence dissenting chapels for marriages (enacted in the 1836 Marriage Act, which also brought civil marriage into existence). More seriously, he declared himself in favour of the replacement of tithes by cash payments related to corn prices (the 1836 Tithe Commutation Act; these cash payments were not abolished until 1936). Most serious of all, in 1845 Peel increased to £26,000 a year the government grant (instituted as long ago as 1803) to Maynooth

College, a seminary for the training of Irish priests and, in the same year, he consented to legislation promoted by Lord Chancellor Lyndhurst to permit Jews to hold municipal office.

Support for moderate reforms such as these was enough to damn Peel in the eyes of Tory diehards and would, by itself, be sufficient to justify the contention that he transformed the old Tory party into a Conservative party, defending what seemed worthwhile in the established order, but rooting out abuses and reforming as necessary; the party Peel led was, by 1835, generally referred to as 'Conservative'. But what marked him out as a truly great statesman was his refusal to believe that (as he wrote to a correspondent on 3 August 1846) 'gentlemen who call themselves conservatives' should be content 'with nothing but that their own passions and sordid interests should be the rule of a Minister's conduct'. 'Sir Robert Peel [Lord Robert Cecil wrote in 1865] never seems rightly to have understood the obligations which the exertions of a party impose upon a party chief.' In short, Peel was not a good party man. At the level of organisation, the main architect of the 1841 election victory was F.R. Bonham, who acted as the Conservative party's national agent in the 1830s and 1840s, building up local Conservative Associations and finding suitable candidates to fight the seats newly created in 1832. At the level of ideology, Peel did not merely refuse to challenge prevailing notions of political economy; he positively embraced them, and was accused of sacrificing his party in the process.

In the first half of the nineteenth century the principles of Utilitarianism became generally accepted among a small but highly influential group of politicians and civil servants. The leading exponents of this philosophy were Jeremy Bentham and James Mill. In his twenties, in 1776, Bentham had published his *Fragment on Government*, ridiculing the idealisation of the English legal system in the works of Sir William Blackstone and other eighteenth-century common lawyers. To every law and to every institution Bentham applied a simple test: 'What is the use of it?' Believing that man naturally pursues pleasure and eschews pain, Bentham argued (*Introduction to the Principles of Morals and Legislation*, 1789) that the duty of the legal system, and of those who frame the laws, was to achieve the greatest happiness of the greatest number. 'Actions', as James Mill's son, John Stuart Mill, put it, 'are right in proportion as they tend to promote happiness, wrong as they tend to produce the reverse of happiness.' In practical terms this meant that the state must place as few restraints as possible upon the freedom of the individual.

In 1818 Bentham announced his conversion to the view that none of this could take place until Parliament had been reformed. He died in 1832, but had already gathered around himself a number of disciples, including James Mill, at whose Political Economy Club politicians of the Whig persuasion were exposed to utilitarian ideas; Lords Althorp, Brougham and John Russell were early converts. Brougham, Lord Chancellor from 1830 to 1833, provided an especially important link between the theories of the Philosophical Radicals (as the Benthamites were known) and the practical application of utilitarian ideas. From the end of the Napoleonic Wars he had contributed articles on social reform to the Whig *Edinburgh Review*, which he had helped found in 1802. But there was another powerful influence at work. The ideas of Adam Smith had influenced a whole generation of *laissez-faire* economists, such as Ricardo, Nassau Senior and J.R. McCulloch, whose *Principles of Political Economy* appeared in 1825. In time, this new economic orthodoxy filtered down to the lower orders, having been popularised in works such as Harriet Martineau's *Illustrations of Political Economy*, which was published in serial form between 1832 and 1834. Exponents of *laissez-faire* were preoccupied with a free market in labour, the advantages of un-fettered competition in the supply of goods and services, and with exposing the evils of protectionism. These views dovetailed neatly with the insistence of the Benthamites that any law which res-tricted individual freedom must be carefully examined and, unless found to be absolutely indispensable, discarded.

But, in noting this coincidence of interest, we must also note that it was not without limit: Benthamite utilitarianism was not the same as *laissez-faire* economics. The complete triumph of free trade took place at precisely the same time as the emergence of a professional civil service, the growth of public administration and the extension of state supervision of industry. The Benthamites were not opposed root-and-branch to government intervention; they were quite prepared to be convinced that the attainment of the greatest happiness of the greatest number might require, in certain instances, more state intervention rather than less. Even McCulloch and Senior supported the right of the state to interfere with the hours and conditions of work of children. They were not prepared, however, to condone such intervention where adult workers were concerned. While free-trade economists busied themselves with the abolition of tariffs and economy in government, the typical utilitarian asked for committees and commissions of inquiry, and inspectors paid for out of the public purse.

The Whig governments of 1830–41 were heavily influenced by utilitarian ideas. They had assumed office in the midst of a great social and economic crisis, which parliamentary reform did little, by itself, to alleviate, and they were expected to give a great deal of attention to the question of 'the condition of England'. The reforms which they carried through can be subsumed under two broad headings: liberal reforms, such as the abolition of slavery (1833) and the Municipal Corporations Reform Act (1835), which were necessarily concerned with the abuse of privilege and the rights of the individual; and social reforms, touching particularly the poor law, working conditions, and education.

We have seen in the previous chapter that the old Poor Law was coming under attack at the end of the eighteenth century, as an obstacle in the way of the development of a free market in labour and as an inducement to over-population. A further worry, which emerged ever more insistently after 1815, was the cost to the ratepayer. In 1818–19 the cost of the Poor Law reached £8.9 millions, and though this proved to be a peak, expenditure on poor relief remained obstinately high; by 1831 it was again above £7 millions. Not only was the old Poor Law expensive. It did not appear to be acting as an incentive for the poor to support themselves and was alleged to be demoralising agricultural workers, especially in the south of England. To the Malthusian argument that it encouraged large families and promoted idleness, Ricardo added another objection: that the greater the proportion of the national wealth spent on poor relief, the smaller would be the proportion available for wages.

The major target of all these critics was the able-bodied poor. By introducing a deterrent workhouse at Southwell, Nottinghamshire, in the 1820s, in which 'every tenderness' was shown towards 'the infirm, the aged and the guiltless', but 'wholesome restraint' was imposed upon 'the idle, the profligate and the refractory', the Rev J.T. Becher claimed that expenditure upon the poor in that area had been reduced from £2,000, in 1821, to £551 seven years later. Incarceration of the able-bodied poor in workhouses had already been advocated by Bentham. Now the idea was taken up by McCulloch (in the 1830 edition of his *Principles*), by Senior and by Edwin Chadwick, Bentham's secretary and protégé. Chadwick proposed that the mosaic of local discretionary customs administered by amateurs be swept away and replaced by a centrally controlled and professionally run system.

In 1832 Chadwick was appointed to a Royal Commission to inquire into the Poor Law and to recommend changes; other members of the Commission included Senior, the Benthamite lawyer Walter Coulson, and the Canningite MP W.S. Bourne, who had chaired the Select Committee of 1817 which had recommended the Poor Law's abolition. The Royal Commission did not hear oral evidence. Instead it despatched assistant commissioners to report on the operation of the Poor Law in different parts of the country, and supplemented their reports by questionnaires. If this *modus operandi* appears highly sophisticated, and 'modern', it must be remembered that there was a purpose behind it. The assistant commissioners provided the evidence to support a political decision that had, in effect, already been taken; Chadwick and Senior had drafted the main body of the Report before all the data had been collected. The mass of evidence, carefully selected, simply provided a cloak of respectability for their recommendations.

The Report was published in 1834; the Poor Law Amendment Act, based upon its findings, passed easily the same year. The Report had been a thoroughgoing condemnation of the old system, in particular of the allowance system — 'most mischievous and ruinous, and till it is abandoned the spirit of industry can never be revived'. The Commission argued that this system, whereby 'the most worthless were sure of something', be replaced by one in which the person obtaining poor relief would never be in a more comfortable position than the lowest-paid labourer in work. To that end the Commission recommended the establishment of separate workhouses for the aged and sick, for children, and for able-bodied males and able-bodied females, each workhouse to serve a group, or Union, of parishes. Furthermore, 'all relief whatever to able-bodied persons or to their families, otherwise than in well-regulated workhouses . . . shall be declared unlawful and shall cease'. Finally, this new system was to be supervised by a central board of three Poor Law Commissioners (with Chadwick, as it turned out, as Secretary), under whom a body of Assistant Commissioners would work out the detailed implementation of the scheme.

In the realisation of its immediate aims the Poor Law Amendment Act must be counted a success. The level of the poor rate fell, especially in southern England, where the legislation was enforced without much difficulty, aided by a succession of good harvests and the demands which railway construction made upon the surplus labour force. In 1834 the cost of poor relief was about nine shillings per person; by 1854 the cost had fallen to six shillings. By 1840 national expenditure on the relief of poverty had fallen to £4.6 millions, and between then and 1865 it averaged from £5 millions to £6 millions, even though the total population of the United Kingdom rose from 21 to about 29 millions (that is, by over a third) during the same period. But in the northern counties there was a different story. In Lancashire the old Poor Law had worked well, with workhouses efficiently run by salaried officials. In south Lancashire and the West Riding there was mass opposition to the new Law; riots occurred in Bradford, Leeds, Huddersfield, Dewsbury and Todmorden.

The building of workhouses was not obligatory, and proceeded in fits and starts. Norwich had no workhouse until 1859, and even by 1870 about a fifth of the 647 Poor Law Unions were without new buildings. The depression of the early 1840s forced the Poor Law Commissioners to accept the fact that they could not prohibit all outdoor relief; there were simply not enough workhouses to accommodate every applicant and, in any case, out-relief was invariably cheaper than the erection and maintenance of workhouses. Some areas continued to make up wages. Indeed, in 1845 about 85 per cent of all paupers were still on outdoor relief; this figure included most (about 78 per cent) of the able-bodied. But for those in the workhouses, subject to a harsh discipline enforced by local Boards of Guardians and workhouse masters of whose activities the Commissioners could only be imperfectly aware, the experience was shocking. The French historian Hippolyte Taine, who toured England in the 1860s, remarked that even in Manchester, where the workhouses were 'spacious, perfectly clean, well-kept', nine out of ten unemployed men declined to take the workhouse Test. 'The workhouse,' Taine noted, 'is regarded as a prison; the poor consider it a point of honour not to go there.' Less well-regulated workhouses were hives of degradation, even sadism. At Andover, in 1845, a riot took place when the starving workhouse inmates fought over scraps of meat adhering to the bones brought in for crushing into manure. This scandal brought about a reorganisation of the hitherto unfettered jurisdiction of the Poor Law Commissioners. In 1847 the Commission was turned into a Board, of which some government ministers were *ex officio* members, and whose President usually sat in the Cabinet.

The essential and undeniable inhumanity of the Poor Law Amendment Act contrasts so sharply with other Whig reforms that we must remember that its justification was utility, not kindliness. Utilitarian influences were also strongly felt in the movement for factory reform, though the impact was much less harsh. This was partly because the Benthamites were opposed by a phalanx of able Tory paternalists, led by Sadler, Oastler, and the evangelicals Lord Ashley and the Rev George Bull. The Royal Commission which was established early in 1833 to enquire into factory conditions was packed with friends and disciples of Bentham, notably Thomas Tooke, Thomas Southwood Smith and the ubiquitous Chadwick. But though the Commissioners were openly sceptical of much of the horrific evidence that factory reformers had made public, and tended to agree with the manufacturers that the ultimate object of the reform agitation was to persuade Parliament to reduce the length of the adult working day, the brutal conditions under which children worked were neither denied nor minimised. These children were not 'free agents', and it was on this ground, and no other, that the Commissioners recommended state intervention. Indeed, in some important respects the 1833 Factory Act, which followed the Commission's Report, went beyond what the reformers had until then been demanding. The Act imposed a total prohibition upon work by children under nine years of age in most textile mills, and restricted the working hours of young persons under 18 to twelve per day or 69 per week; it contained admittedly modest provisions for compulsory schooling; and it provided for an inspectorate to oversee the implementation of its provisions.

By offering and agreeing to much more protection of the interests of children, the Benthamites forestalled the demand of the 'Short Time' committees in Yorkshire, Lancashire, Glasgow and elsewhere, that the adult working day should be restricted to ten hours. The inspectorate was, to begin with, an inadequate and inadequately supported institution. Four inspectors were appointed for the whole of the British Isles. Until 1844 they had no central office or travelling expenses. Later, sub-inspectors and superintendents were added to the factory service, but all these posts were filled by personal patronage; not a few of the incumbents showed themselves to be idle, ineffective and even corrupt. Factory owners were treated with excessive deference; the age regulations relating to child employment were widely (and often with parental connivance) ignored; magistrates imposed upon the owners fines that were minimal and derisory.

In time, however, the factory inspectorate adopted a much more professional approach. One of the earliest inspectors, the businessman and geologist Leonard Horner, though sceptical at the outset, became a stern advocate of the ten-hour day. Horner's ideas influenced the drafting of the 1844 Factory Act (introduced by Peel's Home Secretary, Sir James Graham), which provided for half-day working for children under 13, and placed a total prohibition upon the employment of children under 9. When it became clear that factory owners were ignoring the spirit of this legislation, by working children in relays, with two-hour gaps, Horner conducted his own campaign, within the Home Office, to persuade Sir George Grey, Home Secretary under Lord John Russell (1846–52), to withdraw instructions against prosecuting for relay working. However, the so-called 'Ten Hours' Act of 1847, which was not a government measure, did not suppress this abuse. Horner and Lord Ashley joined forces to have amending legislation passed, in 1850, forbidding the relay system in return for an extension of the working day to ten and a half hours. In 1853 Horner prepared a further and more far-reaching statute, introduced by Palmerston, then Home Secretary in the Aberdeen coalition. The Act of 1853 restricted the normal working hours of all factory workers to the period 6 a.m. to 6 p.m. But because the hours of women and young people had already been restricted to ten and a half, the practical effect of this latest measure was to establish a norm for the working hours of adult men of ten and a half also.

Historians have debated fiercely the relative importance of Benthamism and of pragmatism in the extension of state control in the mid-nineteenth century. In tracing the history of factory legislation we see how both influences were at work simultaneously. A small but very articulate and forceful group of utilitarians clearly exerted a major influence in pointing to abuses and in suggesting conceptual and methodological frameworks within which reforms might be attempted. Their concern was with effective rather than with humane government. But the factory reformers, too, were motivated by wider social purposes. One of the objects of factory reform was to give children some time during the day to acquire an education, of however rudimentary a form. In this way they would become better citizens or (in Oastler's words) 'useful members of society'.

The first state grant for general educational purposes was made, with this object very much in mind, in 1833, when £20,000 of Treasury money was shared between the two major voluntary education societies, the (Nonconformist) British and Foreign Society and the (Anglican) National Society. The total amount was, by the standards of the day, a very modest sum; in the same year the government donated £50,000 for the embellishment of the royal stables. None the less, a precedent had been established. In 1839 the education grant was increased to £30,000 and, significantly, a school inspectorate was inaugurated; in 1847 the scope of the grant was extended to include Wesleyans and Catholics. The churches monopolised the spending of the money, as they were meant to. The Whigs had, in 1839, floated the idea of non-sectarian state schools for teacher training, but backed down in the face of Anglican outrage. Under the terms of the grant of 1833, money was given only to religious societies which could themselves raise half the sums necessary for school-building purposes. The National Society was adept at persuading the landed gentry to give generous donations, pointing out that the teaching of Christian humility to the lower orders was the best way to counter seditious and upstart tendencies; Nonconformist industrialists, perhaps because they could perceive no immediate functional relationship between educational enlightenment and the requirements of machine operation, were slower to make such donations.

By 1858 the education grant had reached £900,000. But it was most unevenly spread, much of it going to wealthy areas, where the matching sums needed to qualify for state aid were more easily raised. It is probable that as late as 1840 about one-third of all children had no regular schooling. Most working-class children did not receive more than three and a half years' schooling; many received less than two. The content of the instruction they received was, typically, of the most modest kind. Sir James Kay-Shuttleworth, the first secretary of the Committee of the Privy Council on Education (established in 1839 to administer the state grant) gave it as his opinion in 1840 that 'no plan of education ought to be encouraged in which intellectual instruction is not subordinate to the regulation of the thoughts and habits of the children by the doctrine and precepts of revealed religion'. So, for the foreseeable future, the provision of state-funded education was to be the monopoly of the voluntary societies. Anglicans and Nonconformists agreed upon this, even if they disagreed about the proportions in which the public provision should be shared out. Curiously, they were able to muster some radical support for the view that the establishment of non-sectarian state schools would, on grounds both moral and political, be thoroughly retrograde:

A general state education [J.S. Mill wrote in 1859] is merely a contrivance for moulding people to be exactly like each other, and as the mould in which it casts them is that which pleases the predominant power in the government, it establishes a despotism over the mind, leading by natural tendency to one over the body.

Accordingly, the Minute appointing the first government inspectors of schools — the Rev. John Allen and Hugh Seymour Tremenheere — made it abundantly clear that they were not to 'interfere with the religious instruction, or discipline, or management of the school, it being their object to collect facts and information and report the results of their inspection to the Committee of [the Privy] Council'.

As a result of a 'Concordat' of 1840, control of appointments to the inspectorate covering Anglican schools was given over to the Church of England; this meant that in practice most of the early inspectors were clergymen. Yet they were not afraid to report the truth of what they saw, however unpalatable. 'In one school,' declared the Rev. F. Watkins, 'the Mistress (a good worker) was unable to write or to detect the most gross errors in spelling, and a large portion of the children were sitting wholly unoccupied.' In 1846 Kay-Shuttleworth persuaded the Committee of Council to institute a pupil-teacher scheme, whereby children of 13 years or more were, at the expense of the state, apprenticed to a master for five years, and entered for national examinations set by the inspectors and the Principals of the denominational training colleges. This scheme, important in itself as being the first organised system of teacher training, also provided a novel, non-manual occupation for able working-class children, leading to a salaried position and (probably) a rent-free house. Kay-Shuttleworth did not delude himself into thinking that the career of schoolmaster or mistress would appeal to the middle classes. But he ventured the opinion that the scheme would 'render the profession of schoolmaster popular among the poor, and . . . offer to their children the most powerful incentives to learning'.

In relation to both factory and education reform, the institution of inspectorates widened the activities of the state and deepened its involvement in the lives of ordinary men and women. An Inspector of Mines (Tremenheere, again) was appointed under the 1842 Mines Act. More significant, because of the even wider breach it represented with the philosophy of *laissez-faire*, was the establishment of the Railway Department of the Board of Trade. Although some areas of state involvement already examined clearly had their roots in Benthamite precepts, the gradual incursion of the power of central government into the running of the private railway companies demonstrates the potency of other, entirely practical considerations.

In the earliest phase of railway construction, in the 1830s, when Parliament authorised the building of just over 2,000 miles of track, the model used was that of the turnpike and canal companies. It was fondly imagined that a company could be empowered to build and maintain a 'rail road', and recoup the cost, plus a profit, by charging tolls to those who wished to run their own wagons and locomotives upon it, just as private citizens paid statutory tolls to sail their own barges upon the canals, or to run their own coaches upon the turnpikes. But the sheer technical complexity of railway operation and the speed at which trains could be run soon made a nonsense of this simplistic scenario. The private railway companies became, in practice, the sole carriers of goods and (in general) of people upon their lines. They were monopolies, for there could never be, on the railways, the same degree of competition that existed between road or canal carriers. In 1839 the House of Commons' Select Committee on Railways recognised that, in relation to the new form of travel, the policy of *laissez-faire* had no place:

> The intention of Parliament cannot be carried into effect . . .
> The safety of the public . . . required that upon every railway there should be one system of management under one superintending authority. On this account it is necessary that the company should possess a complete control over their line of road although they should thereby acquire an entire monopoly.

But, because this monopoly had been sanctioned by the state, politicians on all sides of the House agreed that the state was entitled to interfere with the management of the railways in order to protect the public interest. And so, in 1840, the Railway Department was established, with an inspectorate charged with the task of examining the works of all new railways before they were opened to traffic. In 1842, under pressure from the railway inspectors, Parliament gave them the power to refuse permission for any new line to be opened where they felt it would be unsafe to do so. An Act of 1846 (Lord Campbell's Act) obliged the railway companies to pay compensation if passengers (though not railway employees) were killed or injured in railway accidents.

The powers given to the early railway inspectors were, admittedly, very limited. Once a line had been opened, the Railway Department had no authority to inspect it further, or even to conduct formal inquiries following accidents. To the extent that the companies did permit the inspectors to make such inquiries, this was done purely out of courtesy. The railways were well represented in Parliament and the railway-director MPs (of whom no less than 80 were returned in 1847; by 1857 there were over 150) saw to it that their investments were shielded from too much government interference. But we should also remember that the technology of the railway system was entirely novel. No-one knew as much about running railways as the companies themselves. The early railway inspectors, prohibited by law from having close connections with the companies, had to be drawn from the ranks of the Royal Engineers; compared with the railway managers they were enlightened amateurs.

Parliament's cautious approach to railway regulation was, therefore, deliberate. With hindsight it is easy to criticise the politicians of the 1840s and 1850s for having failed to bring order into the chaos of railway construction. During the railway 'mania' of the 1840s, over 10,000 miles of line were sanctioned. Peel's government attempted to inject an element of rational planning into this commercial free-for-all by establishing (1845) a Railway Board, under Lord Dalhousie, to examine all railway bills with a view to the public interest and to preventing (in Dalhousie's words) 'the mobilisation of several capitals when the business could have been equally well or even better performed by one'. Parliament, however, refused to yield up its powers entirely to this independent Board, whose recommendations were frequently ignored; in 1848 it was dissolved.

Once the mania had ended, in the 1850s, the major railway companies inevitably began to look to the advantages of amalgamation or less formal (and less public) traffic-sharing arrangements, in order to cut costs and avoid ruinous competition between routes served by more than one line. An Act of 1854 forbade railway companies from making or giving 'any undue or unreasonable preference' in their carrying policies, but only in 1873 was special permanent machinery (the Railway Commission) established to enforce this injunction. By then, roughly 80 per cent of the 15,500 miles of track open to the public was in the hands of just 28 private companies. More seriously, the cost of obtaining private legislation to authorise railway construction, and the opportunities this system gave to landowners and solicitors to extract wholly exorbitant sums from the companies, resulted in a railway network which was extravagantly priced. In 1887 the railway economist J.S. Jeans estimated the average cost per mile of railway line in Britain at £42,486, compared with £21,236 in Germany and £11,000 in the United States of America. As a result, freight rates were higher in Britain than elsewhere. This was to have important consequences for the British economy in and after the 1870s, once America had recovered from its Civil War and after German unification.

As we have seen, public ownership of the railways was considered in 1844 but in a manner which deferred its implementation for 21 years and, except in relation to the impoverished Irish companies, was never again to be seriously contemplated during the nineteenth century. This was partly because of a widely held prejudice against state ownership, or rather in favour of the private control of capital. But it was also rooted in a deep suspicion of the involvement of the organs of central government in the conduct of economic and social affairs, and in a belief that there was no reason why the state should be any better at running great enterprises than private corporations.

Clearly there were some duties that only the state could perform, such as the taking of the national census and the uniform registration of births, deaths and marriages. The Act of 1836 establishing the office of Registrar-General of Births, Deaths and Marriages also specified (on Chadwick's initiative) that the cause of death was to appear on every death certificate. In due course this vital data enabled informed comparisons to be made between causes of death and place of domicile. It soon became apparent that there was a relationship between the incidence of disease and the level of the poor rate, and that squalor and disease were closely related to environmental factors. In 1838 William Farr, statistician to the Registrar-General, estimated that in the rural counties of Hereford, Lincoln and the North Riding, deaths from fevers, consumption, smallpox and pneumonia stood at eight or nine per thousand, whereas in the heavily populated counties of Lancashire and Middlesex the rate was, respectively, 18 and 29. Chadwick, through his experience in administering the new Poor Law, was an early convert to the view that these types of illness and mortality were preventible through state intervention. In his *Report on the Sanitary Condition of the Labouring Population* (1842) he acknowledged, publicly, that ill health, rather than laziness, was the major cause of poverty, and he argued, in typically utilitarian fashion, that it was cheaper to spend money improving living conditions than to pay out ever-increasing sums in poor relief, because where there was 'drainage, proper cleansing, better ventilation, and other means of diminishing atmospheric impurity, the frequency and intensity of . . . disease is abated'.

Chadwick's views were echoed in the Reports of the Royal Commission on the Health of Towns, appointed by Peel in 1843; the Commission recommended improved local administrations to supervise schemes of sewerage, drainage, water supply and paving. In 1844 the Health of Towns Association was established by Southwood Smith, to campaign for the implementation of these reforms through a network of local branches. Yet, in spite of overwhelming evidence of urban decay, and in spite of the formidable coalition of utilitarian and humanitarian efforts, little in the way of amelioration was immediately achieved. In 1832, following the first of the four great cholera epidemics in nineteenth-century Britain, an Act was passed giving local boards of health powers to finance (out of the poor rate) measures to combat this disease. The Vaccination Act of 1840 provided for free vaccination against smallpox, which had killed 41,000 people since 1837; in 1853 vaccination for infants was made compulsory.

The most important and potentially far-reaching public-health reform of the period was the Public Health Act of 1848. Inspired by Chadwick, the Act, which was permissive, set up a General Board of Health, responsible to Parliament, consisting of three members: Ashley, Chadwick, and Viscount Morpeth, the First Commissioner of Woods and Forests. The purpose of the Board was to supervise the establishment and operation of local boards of health, but only where 10 per cent of ratepayers petitioned for one, or if the local death-rate exceeded 23 per 1,000; the national average was then 21 per 1,000. When a local board was set up, it could be empowered to enforce drainage, provide and maintain sewers, pave and clean the streets, provide or control water supplies, close burial grounds, regulate common lodging houses, and provide public parks. These schemes were to be financed both by levying a rate and by borrowing.

The General Board of Health was immensely unpopular. One reason lay in the cost of the projects commenced under its auspices. Middle-class ratepayers, living in relatively healthy areas, were reluctant to pay for new sanitary schemes in run-down city centres. In 1835 the Whigs had reformed the municipal corporations, allowing some of the largest towns, such as Manchester and Birmingham, to become incorporated for the first time, and prescribing a uniform type of borough council, elected by all male ratepayers for a term of three years. The post-1835 municipal corporations were empowered to take over public utilities, and they naturally resented the encroachment of the General Board of Health operating from London. The corporations of Leeds and Manchester, for instance, had sponsored their own Improvement Acts in the 1840s, the 1846 Liverpool Sanitary Act made the local town council of Liverpool responsible for drainage, paving, sewerage and cleansing within its boundaries, and the Metropolitan (i.e. London) Commission of Sewers was established the following year. So the principle of central control, enshrined in the Act of 1848, was bound to come under heavy attack. The Leeds *Mercury* complained that, although all towns should have a supply of pure water and a good sewerage system, 'we could not consent to purchase these blessings by a permanent infringement of the rights of municipal bodies, and through them of the people at large'.

By the end of 1853 only 182 local boards of health had been established under the 1848 Act, and only 13 of these had completed sewerage and water works. The death of the General Board was an occasion for national rejoicing. In 1858 it was wound up, and its compulsory powers lapsed. This turn of events marked a watershed in the centralisation of public administration in nineteenth-century Britain. The 1866 Sanitary Act placed squarely upon local authorities the responsibility for removing 'nuisances' to public health, and empowered them to improve or demolish slum dwellings. In his study of *Representative Government* (1861) John Stuart Mill had already given expression to the widely held view of correct central-local relations:

> It is but a small proportion of the public business of a country, which can be well done, or safely attempted, by the central authorities; and even in our own government, the least centralized in Europe, the legislative portion at least of the governing body busies itself far too much with local affairs.

Central government had a part to play, especially where local bodies were ill fitted for particular roles (as with railway in spection) or in relation to those (such as children) who could not fend for themselves. But the overriding duty of central government was to remove restrictions to the exercise of individual and corporate endeavour.

This belief, widely held among the Whigs, also had its champions in the Conservative party. In his great reforming budgets of 1842 and 1845 Peel extended the principles of free trade set out by the Liberal Tories of the 1820s. He had come into office during a severe economic crisis (1837–42) in which, as we have seen, Chartism flourished and there were incidents of disorder. In the financial year 1841–2 there was an expected deficit of over £2.3 millions; in 1842 the cumulative deficit amounted to £7.5 millions. Peel was concerned to reduce this deficit, but not in ways which would damage the social fabric of the nation. His solution was to stimulate trade and consumption by lowering tariffs. In 1842 he cut by almost a half the 1828 levels of duty on imported wheat, reduced drastically the tariffs on 700 imported articles, and imposed an upper limit of 5 per cent on raw materials and of 20 per cent on fully manufactured goods. To compensate for the expected short-term fall in customs revenue, Peel persuaded Parliament to agree to the re-introduction of an income tax, levied at the rate of 3 per cent on incomes of over £150 p.a. from all sources.

These measures were a spectacular success. By 1844 the deficit had been transformed into a surplus of £1.2 millions. In 1845 almost all duties on imported raw materials were abolished, all export duties were removed, and the duties on about 430 imported articles were also swept away. The re-introduced income tax, which Peel had said was only a temporary measure, was now made permanent. Meanwhile, he had taken steps to reform and strengthen the monetary system. In passing the 1844 Bank Charter Act Peel aimed to remove two potent sources of monetary instability, by restricting (with a view to eventually abolishing) the right of private banks to issue paper money, and by reforming the internal organisation of the Bank of England and stipulating that all banknotes issued by it in excess of £14 millions must be supported by actual reserves of gold held in its vaults.

The Bank Charter Act was a victory for the rigid monetarism of the Currency, or Bullionist, school, with which Peel had been identified ever since his enthusiastic support for the return of the gold standard in 1819. It was a policy of which his party heartily approved. But the free trade budgets caused unease. The protection of landed property, and of the produce of the land, was a cornerstone of Tory thinking. Peel's budgets did not accord with this philosophy and, to add insult to injury, he had eased the tax burdens on the industrial bourgeoisie, the members of which most Tories still treated with contempt. Although the Conservative party of the 1840s contained some noted men of business, such as the 'Railway King' George Hudson, it was still primarily the party of the Land and the Church. In 1844 there was a revolt on the government backbenches, when 95 Tories voted for a statutory ten-hour day during the debate on Graham's Factory Bill. The following year 149 Tories voted against the Maynooth grant, which obtained parliamentary approval only with Whig support; Gladstone resigned from the government.

Peel noted the growing unrest among his supporters but was unconcerned. He had already come to the conclusion that the Corn Laws must be repealed, a policy which was, indeed, the logical sequel to his earlier budgetary measures. He believed that the removal of the protection afforded to home-grown wheat was in the national interest, being (he told the Commons) necessary to secure 'the greatest object which we or any other government can contemplate . . . to elevate the social condition of that class of the people with whom we are brought into no direct relationship by the exercise of the elective franchise' — that is, the unenfranchised lower orders of society. In 1846 Peel pushed through the repeal of the Corn Laws, but of the 367 Conservative MPs in the Commons, only 112 supported him in the division lobbies.

The events of 1846 caused a critical realignment in British politics, because the split between Peelites and Protectionists proved irreparable. Peel could not seriously plead that the demise of the Corn Laws was necessary to secure tranquillity in Ireland, as he had done over Catholic Emancipation in 1829. The Irish potato blight of 1845 was a lame excuse, for the starving Irish peasantry could not possibly have afforded to buy bread, even when baked with cheap foreign grain; the famine in Ireland was barely affected by the repeal.

Nor could Peel claim that there was a threat of grave social unrest on the mainland, as there had been at the time of the first Reform Act. The impact of the Anti-Corn Law League must not be overstated. Founded in 1839 by a group of Manchester radicals led by Richard Cobden, the League benefited from the disarray in the Chartist leadership after 1842, and became, in consequence, a major outlet for radical energies in the 1840s. It was a professionally organised and most efficient propaganda machine, with its own newspaper, *The League*, and a penchant for mass meetings conducted with almost religious fervour. But it was also an industrialists' club; Cobden was a Manchester businessman and John Bright, its most brilliant orator, was a manufacturer from Rochdale. The League's arguments in favour of repeal were not, therefore, disinterested. Repeal, it was said, would boost British exports by encouraging other countries to take in manufactured goods in return for corn. But it was also true that repeal, by reducing the price of bread, would enable employers to pay less wages.

The League played little part in obtaining the budgets of 1842 and 1845, which were passed on Peel's own initiative, following the Report of the Select Committee on Import Duties, in 1840, which, in its turn, had merely reflected the general climate of economic opinion at the time. There can be no doubt that, through its meetings, its publicity and its electoral pressure, the League encouraged this climate. But the abolition of the Corn Laws was not, ultimately, the responsibility of the League. Cobden himself believed that the major factors influencing the repeal had been the Irish famine 'and the circumstances that we had a minister who thought more of the lives of the people than his own continuance in power'. Yet it is clear that Peel had determined to do away with the Corn Laws some time before the failure of the Irish potato crop. Already intellectually converted to free trade, Peel's inherent honesty impelled him to confront the problem of the Corn Laws, no matter what the political repercussions.

The Protectionist opposition to Peel was led by Lord George Bentinck, the high-minded son of the Duke of Portland, and Benjamin Disraeli, a shrewd and unscrupulous MP whose Jewish origins might, in other circumstances, have made him *persona non grata* within his party. Disraeli's intense ambition led him to use Peel's unpopularity in order to advance his own position in the Conservative hierarchy, and his brilliant invective against Sir Robert delighted the Protectionist camp. But, unprincipled though he was, Disraeli was none the less a realist. 'Protection,' he told a friend in 1850, 'is not only dead, but damned', and he was never to attempt to resurrect it, not even in the 1870s, when imports of cheap American grain caused British farmers real hardship and when, as head of a government with a comfortable majority, he could have done so.

Why, then, given the almost universal acceptance of free trade in Britain by the mid-nineteenth century, did the Peelites and the Protectionists not patch up their differences, and reunite? To answer this question it is necessary to understand that the split was not fundamentally about protection, or the Corn Laws, but had taken place because the direction in which Peel appeared to be taking his party was more liberal than most of his colleagues were, at that time, prepared to countenance. Peel's own death, in 1850, removed an obstacle to rapprochement, but the deep personal bitterness which the Protectionists felt towards him and his followers could not be overcome. In Disraeli and the Earl of Derby, by contrast, the Conservatives felt confident that they now possessed a leadership under whom the Land and the Church would not be further compromised, and by whom the demands of the industrialists would be kept in check. Unfortunately, a party based upon such principles had little chance of forming governments in an increasingly industrial society represented through the post–1832 electoral system. The Conservative administrations of 1852, 1858 and 1866–8 were all, therefore, without parliamentary majorities.

The Peelites at first inhabited a political wilderness. Disunited on a wide variety of domestic issues, such as factory reform and Jewish political emancipation, they supported Russell's government of 1846–52 only out of fear that, otherwise, protection might have found its way back onto the statute book. After the election of 1847 their parliamentary numbers fell to 91, and during the 1850s they decreased still further, from 45, in 1852, to 23 in

1859. The major strength of the Peelites lay in their collective knowledge of government and their undoubted administrative abilities, for they included statesmen of the calibre of Sidney Herbert, Sir James Graham, Lord Cardwell, and W. E. Gladstone. In the Earl of Aberdeen's coalition of 1852–5 Peelites occupied half the Cabinet posts.

This experience of sharing office with the Whigs became a habit. Gladstone, as Chancellor of the Exchequer under Aberdeen and, from 1859 to 1865, under Palmerston, practically completed the task of removing protective tariffs: after 1860 only 48 articles remained subject to duty. Gladstone was also responsible for the imposition of succession duties upon land and houses (1853) and for the repeal of the newspaper duty (1861). During the 1850s he could not make up his mind whether to throw in his lot with the Whigs or return to the Conservative fold, where his strong Anglican sentiments would have found much sympathy; in 1858 he was invited to join the minority Conservative administration and, though he refused, he gave Derby and Disraeli his general support. Other factors weighed heavily in Gladstone's mind. The long struggle between Russell and Palmerston for the Whig leadership had ended in Palmerston's triumph. Absolved by public opinion from any responsibility for the setbacks in the Crimean War, Palmerston continued to pursue the sort of aggressive and arrogant foreign policy that had already made him a folk hero. In general, Gladstone found Palmerston obnoxious: Palmerston's excessive military estimates offended Gladstone's sense of economy, while his personal morals offended Gladstone's Christian principles.

But, as Disraeli had already discovered, politicians cannot live by ethics alone. In 1857 radical opinion had been outraged by Palmerston's having ordered a naval bombardment of Canton, in retaliation for the arrest of the Chinese crew of the British ship *Arrow*, which had been trading there illegally. Cobden moved a censure motion in the Commons and, when it was carried, Palmerston lost no time in calling a general election. He won handsomely. The Whig/Liberal majority over the Conservatives increased from 11 to 93, and there was a bonus prize in the defeat of Cobden by a Palmerstonian Liberal at Huddersfield. While he lived, Palmerston, it seemed, was unstoppable. And was he, from the Christian point of view, any more off-putting than Disraeli, who was now clearly the heir apparent to the Conservative leadership, and whose personal habits and mode of rhetoric Gladstone found equally uncongenial? Moreover, there was one aspect of foreign policy in respect of which Gladstone and Palmerston were in complete agreement: they supported Italian nationalism, and shared a determination to see Italy rid of its Austrian overlords. During the 1850s Palmerston and Gladstone both acquired considerable domestic popularity through their Italian policies and when, at the election of May 1859, Derby and Disraeli failed to gain a parliamentary majority, Gladstone agreed to serve under Palmerston in a government that was to last until Palmerston's death six years later.

Palmerston's government of 1859–65 was not a coalition, as Aberdeen's had been, but a fusion of Whigs, Liberals and Peelites sealed at the famous meeting at Willis's Rooms in June 1859, after which the Peelites disappeared as a separate political force. However, the Liberal party (as we must now call it) was much more than a collection of mainly aristocratic politicians centred upon Westminster. Outside Parliament a cheap press (made possible by the repeal of the newspaper duty), militant Nonconformity and the New Model trade unions all came together to form a body of popular Liberalism with a programme of reform aimed at the removal of privilege and the building of a somewhat less unequal society, within a framework of free trade and free bargaining, but without any significant extension of the powers of the state, and certainly without capitulation to democratic principles, at least in the foreseeable future.

Between 1851 and 1865 Liberal efforts had met with only sporadic success. In 1856 the establishment of county police forces had been made obligatory, and in 1865 the administration of prisons was removed from the jurisdiction of local authorities and given to the Home Office. In 1857 civil divorce courts were established. Dissenters were admitted to first degrees at Oxford (1854) and Cambridge (1856). There was also some reform of the home civil service. In 1853 Sir Charles Trevelyan, Assistant Secretary at the Treasury, and Sir Stafford Northcote, a Conservative MP, were commissioned by Gladstone to investigate the structure of and methods of recruitment into the civil service. The patronage system had been under increasing attack since the 1830s. The Northcote-Trevelyan Report, produced in 1854, recommended that both recruitment and promotion should depend upon open competition, and that there should be a single civil service supervised by a Civil Service Commission. 'Admission into the Civil Service', the Report announced, 'is indeed eagerly sought after, but it is for the unambitious, and the indolent or incapable, that it is chiefly desired'. The Report caused a sensation. The Peelites, led by Gladstone, welcomed it, but the Whig aristocracy, led by Palmerston, agreed with Queen Victoria that the destruction of the patronage system and its replacement by open competition would swamp the civil service with the sons of the middle classes. A Civil Service Commission was set up in 1855, but only to superintend junior posts. Gladstone's wider scheme of reform had to await Palmerston's death.

While Palmerston lived, reform of a very different and more fundamental kind was also blocked. During the 1850s Lord John Russell, forgetting that he had once spoken of the 'finality' of the 1832 Reform Acts, had introduced Bills to lower the £10 borough franchise to £6, coupled with the creation of various 'fancy franchises', such as the possession of savings-bank deposits or of a university degree. In 1859 Disraeli also attempted to pass a Reform Bill along these lines, and the following year Russell tried, again unsuccessfully, to interest Parliament in his plans. None of these proposals for parliamentary reform were the result of popular pressure. The trade unions were naturally interested in an extension of the franchise to the working-class aristocracy, but among the unenfranchised generally there was little enthusiasm for what was being offered. Russell genuinely believed that the more prosperous working-class householders and lodgers might be safely brought within the pale of the constitution. Disraeli was mainly interested in the return of a majority Conservative government, which he thought a careful widening of the franchise might bring about.

Palmerston's death removed the single greatest obstacle to reform. But the Liberals were robbed of the glory of passing a Second Reform Act by revolts from within their own ranks, which sabotaged a Bill introduced by Russell when Prime Minister in 1866. The defeat of this measure did give rise to a popular agitation, orchestrated by a Reform League in which John Bright, John Stuart Mill and the aged Chartist Ernest Jones played prominent parts. In June 1866, following Russell's resignation, Derby and Disraeli agreed to form yet another minority Conservative government. Disraeli was determined to enact some measure of franchise reform, fogetting (or perhaps simply not caring about) the fact that such a Bill, once introduced, would not be his to control.

The Bill which Disraeli introduced, in March 1867, proposed to give the vote in the boroughs to all householders who had been resident for two years and who paid their rates personally; in the counties the franchise was set at £12. There was the usual array of 'fancy franchises', and those who qualified for such franchises, and who also had a property qualification, were to be allowed two votes. During the summer of 1867 one radical amendment after another was accepted, perforce, by the government. The entire character of the proposals was changed thereby. Most of the fancy franchises were withdrawn. The residence qualification was lowered to one year. A £10 lodger franchise was introduced. Most important of all, at the behest of the Newark solicitor Grosvenor Hodgkinson, occupiers instead of owners of property were made responsible for the payment of rates, so that the restrictions inherent in the stipulation as to personal payment were largely removed; the way was now open for the enfranchisement of all urban heads of households. When the Bill became law, the only feature of it that can be said to have belonged to Disraeli was the absence of female suffrage, for which the over-optimistic J. S. Mill failed to obtain Conservative approval.

Far from being a necessary or natural sequel to the Act of 1832, that of 1867 (together with measures relating to Scotland and Ireland, which were passed the following year) represented a completely new departure. The 1832 reform had sought to preserve as much as possible of the old system. Those of 1867 and 1868 brought an entirely new system into being, not, it is true, in the counties, but certainly in the boroughs, where the enfranchisement of male heads of households brought working-class majorities onto the electoral registers. In the counties, which (thanks partly to the strength of anti-Peelite feeling) were now largely Conservative strongholds, electorates were increased by some 45 per cent. But in the boroughs the increase was of the order of 135 per cent, and in some areas the percentage increase was much greater. In Newcastle-upon-Tyne, for example, the number of voters was raised from 6,630 (1866) to 21,407 (1872), and in Leeds from 7,217 (1866) to 35,510 (1868). We should also note that the Acts provided for a modest but significant redistribution of seats, transferring 33 seats from small boroughs to large towns such as London, Manchester, Birmingham, Leeds and

Liverpool. Overall, the electorate of the United Kingdom was practically doubled; the Acts added 1.1 million voters to the existing 1.4 millions.

Clearly, the Reform Act of 1867 did not bring about democracy, or even universal manhood suffrage. In England and Wales the proportion of adults now entitled to vote was less than 17 per cent, and of adult males about 36 per cent. There was still no secret ballot. Yet old-guard Conservatives were furious when they surveyed all that Disraeli had permitted. Lord Cranbourne (the future Conservative Prime Minister Lord Salisbury) launched against Disraeli a series of attacks as bitter as anything Disraeli had hurled at Peel 21 years before; accusing him of betraying Conservatism and of borrowing his Conservative principles 'from the ethics of the political adventurer'. Even right-wing Liberals, such as Robert Lowe, fulminated against the triumph of 'the principle of numbers as against wealth and intellect'. The differences between the borough and county franchises were now so disproportionate and so glaring that further reform was inevitable; there was no finality about the Act of 1867.

It is sometimes claimed that Disraeli had wanted to bring about 'Tory democracy', by winning over the urban working-classes to a Conservative allegiance. The questions whether and to what extent such an outcome was in fact achieved must be reserved for the next chapter. Here it is necessary to make two observations. The first is that there is no evidence that Disraeli himself entertained such an ambition in 1867. He behaved as he was: an aging politician (then 63 years old) in a desperate hurry to become Prime Minister with a parliamentary majority. The second is that the urban working-class heads of households were not enfranchised by Disraeli, but by a House of Commons dominated by politicians who felt they could now trust the aristocracy of labour.

The economic fluctuations of the 1830s, and the run of bad harvests and the consequent high agricultural prices and unemployment of the 'Hungry Forties', had given way to a period of prosperity, unparalleled hitherto, that was to last until the early 1870s. In the decade of the 1850s the total value of British exports stood at an annual average of over £100 millions, an increase of 80 per cent compared with the annual average during the previous decade; in the 1860s the annual average exceeded £218 millions. In particular, exports of cotton goods approximately doubled between 1851 and 1871, as did exports of woollen goods and of iron and steel (the manufacture of which was considerably cheapened by the invention of the Bessemer process in 1856).

Within the general increase of population in the United Kingdom from 27.4 millions in 1851 to 31.6 millions in 1871, the growth of the ports was dramatic. In 1861 the inhabitants of Bristol numbered over 154,000, of Glasgow over 440,000, and of Liverpool over 470,000. London had burgeoned into a metropolis with a population in excess of three millions. As we have seen, it was during this period that the nation was provided with a railway system, which by 1870 comprised over 13,500 miles of track and represented an investment (in terms of capital and loans) of some £500 millions. The total of shipping tonnage registered in the United Kingdom increased from an annual average of 3.2 million tons in the 1840s to 5.4 millions in the 1860s; significantly, this latter figure included 700,000 tons of steam shipping, which now began to absorb ever greater quantities of home-produced coal. The annual average coal output of the nation, which had stood at 49.4 million tons in 1850, increased by over 120 per cent over the next two decades.

The expansion of the industrial economy had a further and most important social consequence. In 1851 over 1.8 million men and women were employed in the farming sector in Britain, but 475,000 worked in the heavy industrial occupations (mineral extraction, iron and steel manufacture, the railways, shipbuilding and engineering) and another 527,000, men and women, worked as cotton operatives and in ancillary trades. The 1851 census also revealed that 442,000 men were employed in the building trades, and 367,000 worked as non-agricultural labourers. By mid-century, therefore, the manufacturing industries provided virtually as much employment as agriculture. This decline of the agricultural labour force as a proportion of the total was to become even more pronounced in the second half of the century. By the end of the century agriculture accounted for a mere 8 per cent of the workforce of the country, whereas the manufacturing and mining industries comprised 46 per cent.

Certainly, at the time of the Second Reform Act the gamble of free trade appeared to have been justified. Unemployment, particularly cyclical unemployment, was always present; even among unionised workers in the engineering, metal-manufacturing and shipbuilding sectors, unemployment averaged 5 per cent between 1851 and 1873. Real wages did not increase unchecked. During the

1850s there was a great deal of real-wage fluctuation, though after 1862 the trend was unmistakably upwards, so that in 1870 (according to data presented to the Royal Statistical Society in 1909) real wages stood at 19 per cent above their 1861 level.

The mid-Victorian period was thus one of growth, but not of uniform growth, a complication which has led economic historians to question the reality of a 'Mid-Victorian Boom'. Even so, the period between the repeal of the Corn Laws and the passage of the Second Reform Act was undeniably an age of improvement, of magnificent townhalls, solid mechanics' institutes, municipal parks and pleasure-gardens, even of free public libraries (which could be built, at the ratepayers' expense, and if they so desired, under an Act of 1850). The Saturday half-holiday was becoming more widely observed, and if working men and women with pennies to spend spent them in the pubs and the music-halls, only temperance reformers and latter-day Puritans complained. The earlier nineteenth-century fear of social chaos in ungovernable urban concentrations simply did not materialise.

'A country of respectable poor,' the journalist Walter Bagehot observed in 1867 (*The English Constitution*), 'though far less happy than where there are no poor to be respectful, is nevertheless far more fitted for the best government'. The Jeremiahs of 1867 were proved wrong. Disraeli's impetuosity had indeed given the 'respectful poor' a share in the government of the country. It could not have been in safer hands.

4 THE POLITICS OF AN URBAN SOCIETY

The feelings which people have about the past, whether or not justifiable in historical terms, can often be a most useful guide to the importance they attach to their own experiences, and to the tensions of their own time. In the closing decades of the nineteenth century the British reading public developed an appetite for material which had as its subject matter the invocation of rural society and the celebration of rustic values. The immense popularity of Thomas Hardy's 'Wessex' novels rested primarily on their description of the history and folklore of a fast-disappearing closed community of landowners, farmers and peasants, practically untouched by industrialisation and able to do without many of the trappings of modernity as it was then known. 'Wessex' societies sprang up, to organise tours of the Dorset countryside Hardy had made famous, and there was a brisk trade in guidebooks to the area.

Other authors of the period based the popularity of their work upon a similar insistence on the sacredness of the nation's rural traditions. Rudyard Kipling, nowadays chiefly remembered as one who wrote on imperial and Anglo-Indian themes, achieved some of his most popular literary successes through his descriptions of the Sussex countryside in which he lived after the end of the century. Moreover, whereas Hardy's novels were clearly adult reading, Kipling's *Puck of Pook's Hill* (1906) and *Rewards and Fairies* (1910) were collections of short stories meant for young readers and, as such, were certainly more widely read. In these tales Kipling, the populariser of the Raj, was telling the children of Edwardian Britain that the roots of their identity and character lay, not in any Imperial mission, but in the rural past.

This past inevitably became mythologised. In 1904, following the shock of the South African War (1899–1902), in which the might of the British Empire had been held at bay for over two years by a relatively small army of Boer guerrillas, a group of young writers and politicians published a symposium entitled *England: A Nation*. One of the contributors, the historian R. C. K. Ensor, declared that 'our arch-achievement as a nation, the source and condition of our other greatnesses' was, quite simply 'the human wealth of a populous countryside in which all classes lived, and could live, at peace, for centuries'. The writings of Charles Dickens had already spread their message of the evils of industrialisation and of the industrial conflict to which it gave rise. Now the countryside was invoked as the complete antithesis and antidote. The artist and poet William Morris, founder of the Socialist League (1884) became a Marxist only because he wished to sweep away the factory and railway, and replace them with a medieval craft-based social order, in which there would be (he explained in *News from Nowhere*, 1891) an absence of the 'hurried and discontented humanity' he found in late-Victorian Britain. In Morris's utopian world there were to be no cities.

The realities of country life were, of course, very different from the romantic imaginings of late nineteenth-century social commentators. The most violent manifestations of political and economic protest in nineteenth-century Britain took place in rural areas, where the affinity between employers and magistrates was often far closer than in the towns, and where the system of tied cottages (that is, homes that went with the job) underpinned habits of deference which were themselves clearly wearing thin. The Reform Act of 1867 had not extended to agricutural workers, for whom, therefore, the introduction in 1872 of the secret ballot was an irrelevance. Tenant farmers, however, who were enfranchised, found the 1872 Act of little immediate benefit. Prior to the introduction of secret voting, 'political evictions' (or the threat of them) in country constituencies were a formidable weapon in the hands of landowning families. This was particularly true of the 'Celtic fringe', not merely in Ireland, where such evictions were commonplace, but in Scotland too and, more especially, in Wales, where a substantial number of such evictions had taken place in Carmarthenshire and Cardiganshire at the elections of 1859, 1865 and 1868.

In close-knit rural communities the abandonment of open voting did little, by itself, to protect the confidentiality of political beliefs, while the Corrupt and Illegal Practices Prevention Act, of 1883, was primarily aimed at curbing excessive election expenditure in the smaller boroughs (numbering around 60) where corruption was more or less a way of life. Some of these, such as Macclesfield, were disfranchised in 1885; 25 others lost their representation in the general boundary revision that year, and the remainder had their representation cut from two MPs to one. None the less, corruption continued to be a feature of borough electorates into the twentieth century (for example at Worcester in the general election of 1906) until public opinion finally brought it to an end. In the counties, however, public opinion was slower to react and it was, in any case, a very different sort of public opinion. The political influence of the landlord rested upon legal foundations. Writing in 1887, in the second edition of his treatise on *The Land Laws*, Sir Frederick Pollock explained that landlords were not bound in bad seasons to remit a percentage of the rents they normally charged, but that it was customary for them to do so:

> The landlord in return expects a certain amount of deference and compliance in various matters from his tenant . . . In the case of holdings from year to year it may be not unfairly said that being of the landlord's political party is often a tacit condition of the tenancy.

The relationship between farmers and agricultural labourers, heavily laden though it was with squirearchical paternalism, was must less genteel. Although, as we have seen, there was a continuous migration from the country to the towns, and from the fields to the factories, farm labour was still plentiful enough for wages rates to remain low. In the early 1870s a National Agricultural Labourers' Union existed in the south-east of England, the Midlands, East Anglia and the East Riding, and in 1872, consequent upon a temporary labour shortage, it was able to secure wage increases of up to 20 per cent for its members (alleged to have numbered 150,000 out of a total workforce of about 650,000). Organised by a remarkable self-employed Warwickshire craftsman and Primitive Methodist lay preacher, Joseph Arch, the Union attracted sympathy both from radical politicians, such as Joseph Chamberlain in Birmingham, and religious leaders, such as Archbishop (later Cardinal) Manning and the renowned Baptist preacher C. H. Spurgeon. But this support did not impress the landed fraternity. The farmers' response to Joseph Arch was to deprive troublemakers of the right to work by locking them out. In this way the Union was broken, with the result that by 1889 its membership had dwindled to 4,000. Arch turned to the well-tried remedy of encouraging emigration, especially to Canada, Australia and New Zealand.

But the activities of Arch's Union were a warning that the authority of the farmer and the squire was visibly weakening, and that farm labourers were as capable of disciplined and collective action as factory workers. In 1884 the Third Reform Act put the franchise in county constituencies on practically the same basis as that which had operated in the boroughs since 1867, so adding about two million voters to the electoral register and bringing the proportion of adult males enfranchised in the United Kingdom to roughly 60 per cent. The Act of 1884 did not only affect agricultural labourers; most miners lived in rural areas and they, too, benefited from the measure.

The blow which the 1884 legislation dealt to the political power of the landed aristocracy need not, by itself, have proved decisive. But it was followed almost at once by the Redistribution Act of 1885, which not only reduced the representation of the smaller towns (where the influence of the great landed families was still strong), but also accepted, in principle, the old Chartist demand for equal electoral districts. In order to achieve this result, most of the counties and the larger boroughs were divided up into single-member constituencies. For the purposes of parliamentary representation, therefore, the old historic counties were dis-membered, and the prestige which had formerly been attached to 'county' representation vanished. This had a number of important consequences. It marked a new stage in the political decline of the Whig landed families. Under the old system it had often been the case that two-member constituencies had returned a Whig and a Tory, or a Whig and a Radical; this pleasant arrangement was now no longer possible. Second, the sense of county 'community' suffered inevitable damage. Members of the country gentry, and the sons of peers, continued to sit in the House of Commons, of course, but as representatives of their ever more numerous constituents rather than as spokesmen for the landed interest, and with obligations to party organisations rather than to extended families.

Third, the reforms of 1884–5 hastened the acceptance of the principle of elected as opposed to hereditary county government. It was, significantly, a Conservative ministry which carried this new principle into law. In 1888 Charles Thomson Ritchie, President of the Local Government Board in Lord Salisbury's second administration (1886–92), promoted a Local Government Act which transferred to 61 county councils, elected by male and female household suffrage, most of the administrative tasks previously discharged by the magistrates. These duties included the maintenance of drains, roads and bridges, and the general management of county affairs; in 1890 a Local Taxation Act gave the proceeds of a new tax, on beer and spirits ('whisky money') to the county councils in order to finance schemes of technical education.

The establishment of the county councils in England and Wales and, in 1889, in Scotland, wrought a profound change in the government of the shires. To begin with, county boroughs of over 50,000 inhabitants were removed from county control and given their own form of municipal government (borough councils). London was given county status, and endowed with a County Council whose jurisdiction extended into the surrounding counties of Kent, Surrey, Middlesex and Essex, though not into the City of London. Within the county authorities some safeguards were erected against the prospect of democratic extremism. A quarter of the membership of the new councils was reserved for aldermen who were co-opted, not elected. The county councils were deliberately excluded from responsibility for poor law administration. The administration of justice remained in the hands of the magistrates, appointed by the Crown on the nomination of the Lords Lieutenant, and control of the county police forces was vested in joint committees of councillors and magistrates; in London the County Council had no say in control of the police, which remained (and remains) the responsibility of the Home Office.

Yet even when these restrictions and delimitations are taken into account, it is clear that by the end of the nineteenth century aristocratic influence in the shires had been severely eroded. Justices of the Peace, drawn from the ranks of the country gentlemen and resting their authority upon that of the Crown, had administered the counties since the fifteenth century. In an examination of the *Social Transformation of the Victorian Age*, published in 1897, T. H. Escott likened a visit to a pre–1888 county town, on a day when the magistrates were sitting at the Quarter Sessions, to 'making an excursion into feudalism'; but, following the establishment of elected county councils, 'as an object of fetish worship the County has in most districts disappeared'.

The diminished political influence of the landed aristocracy, hastened by the reform of county government, had been preceded by and, in a sense, had resulted from, a decline in its economic status. The legislation of 1888 would have been inconceivable a half-century earlier, when farming had still dominated the British economy. But in the last quarter of the nineteenth century this state of affairs was drastically altered. Prior to 1873 wheat imports had been growing steadily, but this had not resulted in a fall in prices. During the mid-Victorian boom wheat prices had sometimes reached 61 shillings a quarter; in 1875 the price fell below 50 shillings, and, after 1893, dropped below 30 shillings. In 1867 wheat and other grains accounted for about a third of the total crop acreage in Great Britain; by 1913 this proportion had fallen to about a fifth, and wheat acreage itself had fallen by a half. In former times it had been usual for rents to rise as leases were taken up or renegotiated; now, rather than allow farms to remain vacant, landlords had to accept rents which were, on average, lower by one quarter than in the years of boom. From evidence given to official inquiries, it would appear that between 1873 and 1913 farm incomes fell by 40 per cent.

The overriding cause of the agricultural depression may be deduced from the bald fact that whereas, in the 1870s, imported wheat accounted for 50 per cent of total British consumption, by the 1890s it accounted for almost 80 per cent. Encouraged by the growth of railways and the development of more efficient grain-carrying ships, wheat imports from Russia, Germany, the United States of America and Canada helped feed the United Kingdom's growing population (which by 1901 had reached 41.5 millions), while at the same time reducing costs to the consumer. The price of a 4lb loaf of bread in London actually fell from over eightpence in the 1860s to under sixpence on the eve of the Great War. Arable farmers complained long and loudly and, knowing that protection or government subsidy was out of the question, their wrath was turned upon the shipping lines and the railway companies, which were accused of offering to foreign importers deliberately pre-ferential terms. This campaign found enthusiastic allies within the manufacturing sector and was responsible for an astonishing piece of state intervention, all the more remarkable because it was carried into law by a Liberal administration. The Railway and Canal Traffic Act, passed by Lord Rosebery's administration in 1894, effectively froze at their levels on 31 December 1892 the charges which the railway companies could make for the carriage of goods and agricultural produce.

The policy of economic *laissez-faire* was thus effectively brought to an end, but the implications of the 1894 legislation went far beyond the confines of the railway companies and the canals (most of which, by this date, the railways controlled). With little hope of being able to pass on to the public even a proportion of higher operating costs, the railway companies stood firm against demands from their employees for increases in wages or shorter working hours and, in general, refused even to recognise the railway trade unions. When these unions threatened a national railway strike (1907) and actually brought one about (1911), the government of the day was inevitably drawn into the conflict, not merely because of the economic and social repercussions of such action, but because Parliament alone could release the railway companies from the straitjacket forced upon them in 1894. In this way, Rosebery's enactment paved the way for the intervention of Whitehall in industrial disputes.

Arable farmers most certainly had cause in the 1870s and 1880s to lament their fate, but it was not one shared in common throughout the farming community, some sections of which benefited substantially from railway development. For instance, the spread of the railway network stimulated the growth of an urban mass market for fresh milk. In 1870 milk had accounted for less than 14 per cent of total farm output; by 1910 this proportion was almost 25 per cent. The decades which saw the contraction of grain production also saw the rise of dairy companies, particularly in the west of England. In 1873 the first modern milk-processing factory was erected by the Anglo-Swiss Condensed Milk Company (subsequently Nestles) at Chippenham; others quickly followed, as more land in Wiltshire and Somerset was converted from mixed to dairy farming.

Market-gardening was another branch of farming to prosper in the wake of railway expansion. The last quarter of the nineteenth century saw the development of a commercial jam industry, and of canning and other food-processing enterprises in localities as far apart as Dundee, the Vale of Evesham and the Lea Valley, north of London. Rising standards of living led to the displacement of bread as a fundamental component of the family diet; instead, housewives shopped for a variety of home-grown vegetables, poultry, and meat (large quantities of which were beginning to be imported from Australia, New Zealand and Argentina in refrigerated ships). Although the extent of land dedicated to arable farming contracted by two million acres between 1866 and 1911, the amount given over to pasturage increased by six million acres over the same period. By 1911 roughly three times as much land (16 million acres) in England and Wales was being used for the rearing of cattle, sheep and pigs as was being devoted to corn production.

The vicissitudes of British agriculture at this time were thus very far from being a catastrophe. Even the term 'Great Depression' needs qualification. During the 1870s and 1880s the shift from arable farming to pasture, a process which had been in train throughout the century, was greatly accelerated. Agricultural labourers left the land and the villages to seek work in the towns, the colonies and the New World. Agriculture had not merely ceased to be the most important economic activity in Britain; it had also lost its centrality in the social system. According to the 1901 census, over three-quarters of the population of England, Scotland and Wales (that is, about 25 million persons) lived in urban areas. If some sections of the landed aristocracy and the country gentry continued to exercise political power, this was beause they sat in the House of Lords or because they had had the foresight to invest in business enterprises or to marry into the ranks of the industrialists.

Yet for industry, too, the last quarter of the nineteenth century witnessed a sharp check to the almost uninterrupted growth to which people had been accustomed hitherto. We must beware of reading too much into the complaints of contemporary economists if we wish to understand the true nature and extent of the changes that were taking place. Compared with the depression of the 1930s, the 'great depression in trade and industry', alleged to have been experienced in Britain between 1873 and 1896 was, quite simply, a myth. Population and — therefore — consumption continued to expand. In Great Britain (but not Ireland) the population increased at a decennial rate of over 10 per cent until 1911, though (significantly) the rate exhibited a slow decline after 1881: creeping affluence was leading people to limit family size. More importantly, the national income rose, throughout this period, at a rate faster than that of the population, and faster than it had done in the first half of the nineteenth century. Net national income per head of the population (at current prices) stood at £29.9 in 1870, £36.9 in 1890, and £44.2 in 1910. Real wages continued to grow, as they had been doing more or less continuously since 1850, though much of this growth was derived from falling prices, and only a little from increasing money wages. We should also bear in mind that there was a noticeable increase in unemployment. From 1855 to 1875 the national rate of unemployment had been of the order of 4.6 per cent; between 1875 and 1895 this figure rose to 5.4 per cent, though it fell to just 4.0 per cent between 1896 and 1914. This rise in unemployment in roughly the last quarter of the nineteenth century was to have some effect upon the character of trade unionism at this time.

None the less, indices of output of any of the major industrial products show that the period 1873–96 was one of buoyancy and growth. Total United Kingdom output of coal, which had barely reached 100 million tons per annum in the 1860s, reached 200 millions in the 1890s and 256 millions in 1910, by which time the coal industry employed , for the first time, over one million men. Iron ore production, it is true, fell from an annual average of over 17.4 million tons in the early 1880s to 13.4 million by 1900; but exports of iron and steel, which had not reached two million tons at any time before 1865, never fell below three million tons in any year between 1880 and 1905, and stood at 4.5 million tons on the eve of the First World War. The closing decades of the nineteenth century also witnessed record levels of production in the cotton and woollen manufacturing sectors, in shipbuilding and in house construction. In the late 1870s, for the first time ever, over 100,000 houses were built in Great Britain annually.

Upon what, therefore, did contemporaries base their strongly held conviction that they were living through a 'depression', and why did the government feel this 'depression' keenly enough to appoint a Royal Commission upon the subject, in 1886? To begin with, the plight of arable farming and the fall in landed rents could not be denied; the landed interest was still strongly represented in Parliament, and its pessimism inevitably infected the entire political establishment. Second, a fall in prices and profits was certainly in evidence. Appearing before the Royal Commission, the eminent Cambridge economist Alfred Marshall, though denying the existence of a general depression in the economy, recognised that there was 'a depression of prices, a depression of interest, a depression of profits'. Indeed, by the late 1890s the average price of industrial products stood at only 75 per cent of its 1875 value.

Now, a fall in prices need not, of itself, have given grounds for alarm. The fall might have been due to more efficient methods of production, or to a greater volume of business. In this instance, however, it is clear that such explanations can only have been marginal. The late Victorians were preoccupied with the spectre of foreign competition, and with good reason, as the following table shows:

Table 4.1: UK Exports and Imports, 1860–1909 (annual averages per decade)

	Exports (£millions)	% Increase[a]	Imports (£millions)	% Increase[a]
1860–69	159.7		260.9	
1870–79	218.1	36.6	360.6	38.2
1880–89	230.3	5.6	393.6	9.2
1890–99	237.1	3.0	435.8	10.7
1900–09	333.3	40.6	570.4	30.9

Note: a. over previous decade.
Source: B.R. Mitchell and P. Deane, *Abstract of British Historical Statistics*(1962).

In the 1870s, the proportionate increases in exports and imports over the 1860s were within a few percentage points of each other. But in the 1880s the value of imports grew at almost twice the rate of exports, and in the 1890s the gap became wider still. What is more, the imports were no longer simply of food and raw materials, but consisted also of manufactured goods, the average value of which rose from negligible amounts in mid-century (less than £3 millions annually) to over £30 millions by 1900. But it was not so much the absolute level or value of imported manufactured goods that worried the Victorians, as the trend that was represented thereby. Britain was no longer the workshop of the world.

By exporting machinery, capital and labour, Britain had helped other nations industrialise to the point where, protected by tariff barriers, they could provide sufficiently for their own domestic consumption and still possess spare capacity for the purposes of export. The rigid class-based compartmentalisation of the British education system, and its comparative lack of emphasis on technical education, had begun to tell. In 1895 a Royal Commission on Secondary Education pointed to the fact that the educational opportunities open to most youngsters were 'still far behind the requirements of our time', and declared that some, at least, of the setbacks experienced by British industry and commerce in world markets were due to the 'superior preparation' of Britain's Continental competitors. Those British students seeking the best instruction in science and technology went to German universities. In 1872 there were only twelve persons reading natural sciences at Cambridge; most of these were training to become medical practitioners. Germany already boasted no less than 20 multi-faculty universities and eleven special 'technical' universities. Observing (to a gathering of the Social Science Association, four years later) that only a fraction of young men in England and Wales who could benefit from a university education actually received one, the Rector of Lincoln College, Oxford, Mark Pattison, declared that the situation was 'nothing less than a state of national destitution'.

At the great public schools science and technology had virtually no place in the curriculum; the instruction given was heavily biased towards the classics, and to the training of the sons of the industrial middle classes for 'white collar' professions — the law, medicine, the civil service. This is not to say that there was no technical education to be had in the British Isles. The self-financing mechanics' institutes, which by the mid-nineteenth century boasted over 50,000 members, trained artisans in technical skills. In 1880 the City and Guilds of London Institute was founded, to conduct examinations in practical subjects. As the century drew to its close, a number of civic 'university colleges' were established, in Manchester, Liverpool, Leeds, Birmingham, Nottingham and Newcastle-upon-Tyne, where technical education and scientific research were given a high status, and where close links were deliberately fostered with local industries. Elsewhere, technical colleges were built, as at Sheffield (Firth College) and Edinburgh (Heriot Watt). But government involvement in these schemes was minimal. In 1889 the Treasury began making very modest grants to the university colleges and the following year, as we have seen, 'whisky money' was used to finance technical education. In 1871 Gladstone's first administration (1868–74) had abolished religious tests for all undergraduates (except those reading divinity) at Oxford and Cambridge, and there followed important reforms in the ancient universities, one result of which was to make money available for the construction of scientific laboratories — the Clarendon at Oxford and the Cavendish at Cambridge.

Yet, laudable though they were, these innovations and reforms were exceedingly modest by comparison with the size of the problem facing the British economy at the time. Belgium produced steam engines as efficient as those made in Britain, and at a cheaper price. Once it had recovered from the Civil War (1861–5), industrial production in the USA soon outstripped that of the United Kingdom. British steel output grew, but by 1896 it had been overtaken by both the USA and Germany. Exporting to these countries became much more difficult; profit margins had, in consequence, to be cut, and these countries competed much more keenly in export markets (such as South America and the Ottoman Empire) that British manufacturers had once had all to themselves.

During the 'Great Depression', therefore, the British economy continued to grow, but it declined relative to the economies of Germany and the USA. It was this which contemporary observers found most dispiriting. To it, however, must be added a psychological element. Mid-Victorians had been accustomed to unfettered growth and expansion in the home market. By the 1870s the process of primary industrialisation had been concluded. The railway system was practically complete. Innovations on the scale of the Bessemer converter (1856), the Siemen's 'open hearth' process (1866) and the Thomas-Gilchrist process (1879), all of which had considerably reduced the cost of steel production, were not to be seen again in the metallurgical and engineering sectors until after the First World War. The domestic economy had, in many respects, become saturated; for the time being, only lower prices could stimulate demand. Yet it is also clear that the productivity of British industry declined during this period. The rate of growth of output per man-year fell from 1.3 per cent per annum in the period 1856–73 to 0.9 per cent between 1873 and 1913: the decline, that is, was of the order of one-third. In coal-mining this decline in productivity was absolute, and not merely a fall in the rate of growth; between 1873 and 1913 productivity in the mines fell by 0.1 per cent.

Much of this deterioration in productivity is to be explained by failure to invest in new plant and machinery. Labour was cheap and plentiful, and in times of economic expansion the temptation to employ even more cheap labour, rather than invest in expensive but more efficient machinery, proved too great. Investors with spare capital took it abroad, into the Empire (especially India), and the interest thus earned masked only too efficiently the growing gap between exports and imports. It has been calculated that, as a percentage of the national income, gross domestic capital formation in the United Kingdom was less than half that to be found in Germany and the USA at this time.

Some sections of the British economy, such as heavy engineering and armaments (Armstrongs and Vickers), shipbuilding (Harland and Woolf, John Brown) and pharmaceutical retailing (Boots) proved highly innovative. There was something of a revolution in the marketing and retailing of consumer goods. Marks and Spencer set up their first 'Penny Bazaar' in Manchester in 1897. Multiple grocery outlets were already in existence. Thomas Lipton had established his first grocery shop in 1872; by the turn of the century there were 242 branches throughout the country, and rival chains run by J.J. Sainsbury, Home and Colonial and, of course, the Co-op. There was also a grasp of the potentialities of advertising. The soap manufacturer W.H. Lever deliberately employed advertising executives, who formed part of a growing public relations profession whose imagination and creativity may be sampled in the pages of the newspapers and magazines of the Victorian and Edwardian periods.

But other sectors of British industry showed every sign of retardation, even of senility. In the USA, Switzerland and Germany the older techniques (such as mule-spinning) for the production of cotton textiles were being abandoned in favour of ring-spinning and automatic looms. The necessary machinery was being made and exported by Lancashire-based firms such as Platts of Oldham, but was not being adopted in British factories, because labour skilled in the older techniques was relatively cheaper in Britain than in America and elsewhere. There was investment in cotton mills in Lancashire in the late-nineteenth century, but only in the sense that new buildings were erected to house outmoded technology — hardly a recipe for industrial growth in an ever more competitive international market. Machinery used in the dairy industry came increasingly from the Netherlands, Denmark, Sweden and France. Innovations in farm machinery were imported from the United States, which also manufactured the sewing machines used in the clothing sweatshops of London, Leeds and Manchester, and the typewriters used in the City offices.

The glass-making firm of Pilkingtons successfully fought off foreign competition, but only by adopting techniques pioneered in Belgium and Germany. In the technologies of metal extraction and manufacture, in electrical engineering and in the chemical industry, Germany led the world by 1900; German chemical industrialists, such as Ludwig Mond, invested in Britain only because the labour was so cheap. Britain did develop a motor-car industry, consisting (by 1914) of about 200 small firms producing individually-built vehicles for the very wealthy. The idea of mass-producing cheaper cars, as Henry Ford was doing in the USA, appears not to have occurred to British entrepreneurs at this time. In 1914 one-third of the motor vehicles running on British roads were imported, most of them from America. The Morris 'Oxford', the first car to be mass-produced in Britain, did not emerge from the Cowley works of William Morris (later Lord Nuffield) until 1913. Much of the technology of British automobile production also came from abroad. When Asquith's government declared war on the Kaiser, it was horrified to discover that the magnetos (forerunners of the modern high-voltage coils) in use in British internal combustion engines all came from Germany!

Throughout the 'Great Depression', therefore, the United Kingdom remained very prosperous, but became progressively less confident that this prosperity could last; at the same time, the national capacity for invention and innovation waned. Effective remedial action, such as the modernisation of plant and machinery and the reform of the educational system, was not undertaken in a sufficiently comprehensive or far-reaching manner. Economic planning to take account of the changing circumstances was practically non-existent. Just as old machinery, trusted and tried, remained in service even though more efficient equipment was available, so the much venerated doctrine of free trade was viewed as a sacred object, the destruction of which was not to be contemplated.

The coincidence of the mid-Victorian 'boom' with the triumph of free trade suggested to most contemporaries that prosperity and free trade went hand-in-hand, and the conclusion of a commercial treaty with France, in 1860, inspired hopes that other countries would follow down the free-trade road. This was not to be. Bismarck's Germany adopted protectionist measures in 1879, Tsarist Russia, Hapsburg Austria-Hungary, Switzerland and the Third French Republic in the early 1880s. In 1883, 1890 and 1897 the USA imposed deliberately harsh duties on foreign imports. All these moves were aimed at British manufacturers; the American McKinley tariff of 1890, for example, dealt a heavy blow at the exporting capacity of the South Wales tinplate industry. Even the self-governing British colonies resorted to tariffs as a means of nurturing their own industries. Canada erected high tariff walls in 1879, as did the Australian State of Victoria; when the Australian Commonwealth Act was passed, in 1900, the whole of Australia effectively became protectionist.

But the British government did not retaliate. The principles of free trade did come under close scrutiny. In 1881 the Fair Trade League was formed, to campaign on behalf of home producers for protection from foreign competition. During the 1890s meetings of the Trades Union Congress passed resolutions calling for restrictions upon the entry of foreign labour into the country. Among Conservative politicians hopes were re-kindled that the fiscal policies of Peel and Gladstone might soon be overthrown. Indeed, in 1902 Sir Michael Hicks Beach, Chancellor of the Exchequer in Lord Salisbury's third administration (1895–1902), used the excuse of the Boer War to re-impose what was termed a 'registration' duty of threepence per hundredweight on imported corn, and fivepence on flour; three years later the government of Salisbury's nephew, A.J. Balfour, passed an Aliens Immigration Act, designed (not very effectively) to control the hitherto almost unrestricted right of entry of foreigners into Britain. However, the Aliens Act was really aimed at Jewish refugees from Tsarist persecution, and the campaign to have it placed on the statute book had been heavily racialist; for these reasons it incurred the displeasure of Liberal politicians and, though the Liberal government which took office in December 1905 did not repeal what had clearly been a popular measure, they saw to it that the Act remained largely a dead letter. The Hicks Beach registration duty, and the possibility that it might be extended, had already stirred up a hornet's nest within Conservative circles; accordingly, it had been repealed in April 1903.

The following month, in a speech at Birmingham, Joseph Chamberlain, the Colonial Secretary, stunned his newfound Conservative colleagues, and his former Liberal colleagues, by announcing his abandonment of free trade and his belief in imperial preference and fiscal retaliation against foreign tariffs. The idea of using protectionist duties to force down foreign tariff barriers appealed to Balfour, but split the Cabinet. Chamberlain resigned from the government, in order to be free to undertake a national campaign for 'Tariff Reform'. Ostensibly his aim was to unify the

Empire by giving preferential treatment to colonial imports. But the colonies, heavily protectionist themselves, were not over-enthusiastic about this plan, and most of Chamberlain's support — and money — came from British manufacturers and farmers anxious to protect their own prices and profits. Tariff Reform caused the gradual collapse of Balfour's government and brought the Liberals into office and then, in January 1906, into power with a large parliamentary majority. Later that year Chamberlain suffered a serious stroke, and though he lived till July 1914, the Tariff Reform movement was effectively deprived of its most eloquent advocate. Free trade survived until 1932.

There is a parallel of sorts between the failure of British industrialists to adapt quickly enough to changing circumstances in the last 30 years of the nineteenth century, and the failure of the Liberal and Conservative parties to address themselves wholeheartedly enough to changing national needs. Under Gladstone the Liberal party proved conspicuously unable to unify itself. Until the 1880s it remained an uneasy coalition of Whig aristocrats, professional and industrial interests (some of whom could be described as radical) and adherents drawn from the more affluent, enfranchised sections of the working-classes. Some Liberal constituency associations did adopt working-men as party candidates, and a few (generally trade-union officials) were successfully returned as 'Lib-Lab' MPs. The first two working-class MPs, Alexander McDonald and Thomas Burt, were, in this way, elected to Parliament in 1874; in 1886 Gladstone appointed a former stonemason, Henry Broadhurst (elected 1880) to a junior post in the Home Office.

But as long as Gladstone led the Liberal party, the extent to which it might become thoroughly radical remained in doubt. By nature an elitist, Gladstone distrusted career radicals, such as Chamberlain and Charles Dilke. They were included in his Cabinets of 1880–5 as a gesture, and were swamped by a clutch of peers of the realm. At that time the majority of Liberal MPs shared Gladstone's distaste for egalitarianism, democracy, and 'collectivism' though, like him, they were prepared to acknowledge that, in certain circumstances, these principles might have to be accepted as unpleasant necessities. The great Whig constitutional lawyer, Albert Venn Dicey, explained collectivism to his Oxford students in the following terms:

The Reform Acts, 1867–84, were carried in deference to the wishes and by the support of the working classes, who desired, though in a vague and indefinite manner, laws which might promote the attainment of the ideals of socialism or collectivism . . . By collectivism is here meant the school of opinion often termed . . . socialism, which favours the intervention of the State, even at some sacrifice of individual freedom, for the purpose of conferring benefit upon the mass of the people.

(*Lectures on the Relation Between Law and Opinion in England*, 1905)

Clearly, the socialism of which Dicey spoke was not the same as the dogmatic beliefs of Karl Marx or James Keir Hardie. For Dicey, it signified 'the denial that *laissez-faire* is in most cases, or even in many cases, a principle of sound legislation' and 'a belief in the benefit of governmental guidance or interference, even when it greatly limits the sphere of individual choice or liberty'. He pointed, in particular, to legislation which curtailed freedom of contract, which favoured collective action, or which fostered the 'equalisation of advantages' as proof of the practical application of collectivist theory, and he claimed that examples in all three categories were to be found among the measures sanctioned by Parliament during the last three decades of the nineteenth century.

The central dilemma of Liberalism was that it did not know how far it wanted to travel, or was capable of travelling, down the collectivist road. Gladstone's first ministry was preoccupied with a desire to advance individual freedom by attacking privilege, and its fruits won general applause from the Liberal faithful. The abolition of religious tests at Oxford and Cambridge appeased Nonconformity without interfering in the internal workings of the Oxbridge colleges. An Order in Council of June 1870 threw open to public competition all posts in the Civil Service, other than those in the Foreign Office. In July 1871 Gladstone persuaded Queen Victoria to issue a royal warrant abolishing the purchase of commissions in the army. The Queen had already, on Gladstone's advice, used the royal prerogative to bring the Commander-in-Chief of the army under the direction of the Secretary of State for War (and therefore under parliamentary scrutiny). The Judicature Act of 1873 put into effect a long-overdue streamlining of the administration of justice.

But other achievements of the first Gladstone government were more controversial, even within Liberal circles, because to a greater or lesser extent they fell within Dicey's definition of collectivism. Foremost among these was W.E. Forster's Education Act of 1870, the undisguised aim of which was to create enough school places to give every child between the ages of 5 and 13 the opportunity of full-time education. Acknowledging that the voluntary organisations had failed to create this provision, Forster's Act brought government grants for school buildings (but not building maintenance) to an end, and replaced them with a system of school boards in both municipal boroughs and county parishes. These boards, elected by male and female ratepayer suffrage, were empowered to levy a rate and to use the proceeds to build and maintain schools wherever, in their view, the voluntary system was deficient; they were further authorised to remit, in cases of poverty, the fees normally charged. Forster did not go so far as to make attendance at school compulsory; instead his Act gave the power of compulsion to the individual boards. In 1880, however, Gladstone's second administration did take the step of making education compulsory to the age of 13, with a provision that bright youngsters might leave earlier. By the turn of the century some 2,500 school boards were functioning in England and Wales, providing a full-time elementary education for two million pupils, though there were still more children in the voluntary system.

The 1870 Education Act represented a fairly massive state involvement in the re-ordering of society. By 1885 the Treasury was contributing roughly £4 millions annually to elementary education. Even so, Forster's conviction that the education rate would never exceed 3d in the pound proved wildly optimistic. There could be no doubt that compulsory schooling and the compulsory payment of a school rate were restrictions upon individual liberty (aggravated by the realisation that rates would have to be paid to schools where only non-denominational religious instruction would be given, and that rate-aid might reach voluntary schools); moreover, the Acts of 1870 and 1880 had, as their purpose— admittedly in a very crude way — 'the equalisation of advantages'.

In 1871 the Liberal government took a further step in the direction of collectivism. The Trades Union Congress (founded 1868) had been campaigning for some relaxation of the law on combinations, and a revision of the master and servant legislation. Gladstone, anxious to acknowledge in a modest way the support given to him by urban working-class voters at the polls, agreed to a measure which recognised the legal status of trade unions and gave their funds the benefit of legal protection. But a Criminal Law Amendment Act passed the same year was so tightly drawn as to make almost any form of strike action or picketing illegal.

The following year, 1872, there issued forth an enactment which interfered with individual liberty in a manner even more blatant than the establishment of the school boards or the legitimation of trade unions. The Licensing Act gave magistrates the power to license public houses (and hence to regulate and reduce their number) and also restricted the hours during which they might remain open. The Act was bitterly contested by the members of the drink trade (whom Gladstone subsequently blamed for his 1874 election defeat) and was denounced by many others as a quite unwarranted attack upon the freedom to drink when and for as long as one pleased. 'England free better than England sober', was how Dr W.C. Magee, the Bishop of Peterborough, attacked the measure in the House of Lords. The legislation was a modest victory for the temperance movement and, as such, one indication of the extent to which the Liberal party had already come under the influence of radical pressure groups — in this case the United Kingdom Alliance — just as the Education Act had been, partly at least, a response to pressure from the National Education League, founded at Birmingham in 1869 to advocate a national system of 'free compulsory and secular' education; prominent figures in the League included Chamberlain, John Morley and William Harcourt.

Gladstone's first ministry was not concerned solely with domestic British issues. He had come into office believing that he had a mission to pacify Ireland, and he was one of the very few statesmen of the period possessed of sufficient political courage to tackle some of the causes of Irish discontent at their roots. The famine of 1845–8, which had reduced the Irish population to 5.5 million by 1871, had made a deep impression upon him, and he had vision enough not to react to the outrages of the Irish-American Fenian brotherhood (formed in 1858) simply by urging yet more repression. In 1869 he removed one Irish Catholic grievance by disestablishing and disendowing the Anglican Church of Ireland, and the following year he made a first attempt at solving the Irish land question by making the payment of compensation for improvements obligatory in cases where tenants were evicted, and by endeavouring to enforce a scale of damages payable to tenants evicted for non-payment of rent. However, the Irish Land Act of 1870 was not a success; it did nothing to protect tenants against excessive rents, and the quarrels that ensued between landlords and tenants only led to further evictions, and hence to further agrarian disorder.

Believing, correctly, that most Englishmen did not understand the problems of Ireland, which were best dealt with by the Irish themselves, both Catholic and Protestant Irishmen turned, once more, to the prospect of internal self-government for Ireland. The Irish Protestant lawyer Isaac Butt, whose conversion to this view had come about as a result of defending Fenians in court, formed a Home Government Association (1870). Following his election to Parliament, in 1871, Butt became the acknowledged leader of a group of Irish MPs committed to Home Rule; at the election of 1874 the Home Rule League (successor to the Association) won 59 seats at Westminster, and embarked upon a policy of obstruction of parliamentary business until Ireland's needs, as the League perceived them, should be met. Butt himself opposed these extreme tactics; in 1877 he was succeeded in the leadership of the Home Rulers by Charles Stewart Parnell, a Protestant landlord whose hatred of England had developed into an obsession.

Parnell and his friends became acknowledged masters of the art of using the rules of procedure of the House of Commons to compel sittings of extraordinary duration ('filibustering'); their crowning achievement came on 2 February 1881, when they succeeded in prolonging for no less than 41 hours a debate on the passage of an Irish Coercion Bill, providing for the detention without trial of those suspected by the Lord Lieutenant of agrarian crimes. But Parnell's activities extended well beyond the parliamentary sphere. In 1879 the ex-Fenian Michael Davitt founded the Irish Land League; Parnell became its President. The League's ultimate purpose was to replace landlordism in Ireland with a true peasant proprietorship which, it was hoped, would lead inexorably to the ending of the legislative supremacy of the Westminster Parliament. Its more immediate aims were to secure fair rents (to be fixed by arbitration) for Irish tenants, fixity of tenure so long as rents were paid, and the freedom for a tenant to sell, without his landlord's permission, the right to occupy his land, thereby ensuring that the tenant, not the landlord, would recoup the cost of any improvements that might have been made. In pursuance of these aims, Parnell advised tenants to offer their landlords a fair rent and, should that offer be refused, to pay nothing at all. Davitt's League organised 'rent strikes' against landlords and burnt the ricks and maimed the cattle of those intent upon evictions. Some elements of the League went further, murdering landowners (for example, Lord Mountmorres, in February 1880) and those who informed against these clandestine activities.

Gladstone's response to the activities of the League was to grant some of its basic demands. His 1881 Land Act gave Irish tenants the 'three F's' (fair rents, fixity of tenure and freedom of sale), which were enforced by a Land Court composed of judges empowered to fix 'fair rents' for a period of 15 years; as a result, the rents paid by Irish tenants were reduced by about a quarter. Gladstone also recognised the strength of the argument for the creation of a peasant proprietorship, and so his 1881 Act also established Land Commissioners, able to lend up to three-quarters of the purchase price to tenants wishing to buy their holdings. But the Land League was not satisfied. The idea that the state should advance some of the money necessary to enable tenants to buy the land they farmed was attacked on the grounds that the three-quarters' limit was inadequate. Moreover, if the land belonged to the Irish, why should they have to pay the British Treasury for the privilege of possessing it?

In 1885 Lord Salisbury's short caretaker administration legislated to enable tenants to borrow the full purchase price (Lord Ashbourne's Act), the sums so advanced to be repaid over 49 years at 4 per cent interest. However, the total amount made available by the treasury (£5 millions) was exhausted within three years. In any case, Parnell and the League had long since shifted their ground, to demand complete Home Rule. In spite of Gladstone's concessions of 1881, the outrages had continued. In October 1881 the League was declared 'an illegal and criminal association', and suppressed; its leaders, including Parnell, were imprisoned in Kilmainham gaol. But the following April Gladstone and Parnell reached an apparent accommodation: Parnell and his associates would be released from prison, and would use their influence to curb violence in Ireland, while Gladstone would embark upon a policy of further conciliation and would, in particular, deal with the problem of rent arrears.

Whether anything constructive could have emerged from the so-called 'Kilmainham Treaty' must remain a matter for conjecture. Gladstone did attempt to keep his side of the bargain, by passing an Arrears Act. But in Ireland the initiative had, momentarily, passed out of Parnell's hands, and the murder, in Phoenix Park, Dublin, on 6 May 1882, of the newly appointed Chief Secretary for Ireland, Lord Frederick Cavendish, and of Thomas Burke, the Permanent Under-Secretary, seemed to confirm the worst fears of those who had warned Gladstone against appeasement. Cavendish had been appointed to replace W.E. Forster, who had resigned in protest against the 'concessions to law-breakers' embodied in the release of Parnell and others from gaol. Parnell himself was not implicated in the crimes in Phoenix Park. None the less, as a result of the public and parliamentary outcry that followed the murders, the Liberal government had to pass a Prevention of Crimes Act, authorising trials without juries and strengthening the powers of the Lord Lieutenant. But Gladstone himself, for whom the events in Phoenix Park represented a personal loss (Cavendish had been his nephew) drew a quite different conclusion: that Home Rule might, after all, solve the Irish Question.

These sombre events possessed an importance and a significance which extended beyond the problems of Ireland. For the solutions which the Gladstonian Liberal governments of 1868–74 and 1880–5 prescribed for Irish ills were heavily influenced by collectivist ideology. In 1865 Gladstone had declared the disestablishment of the Irish Church to be 'apparently out of all bearing on the practical politics of the day'. Yet his 1869 legislation carried out this very disestablishment in what seemed to be a particularly confiscatory manner, because although the property of the Irish Church was valued at £16 millions, only half this sum went to incumbents and curates by way of compensation; the rest was used for the public benefit — public works, education and the relief of poverty. Disraeli's comment, that the Act 'legalised confiscation . . . [and] consecrated sacrilege' fell upon many sympathetic ears. The 1870 Land Act clearly restricted the rights of landlords to evict tenants as they pleased, while the Act of 1881 instituted in Ireland a comprehensive scheme of rent control (the like of which was not to be seen on the British mainland until the First World War), so that the notion of the inviolability of contracts 'freely negotiated' between landlords and tenants was abandoned; the Duke of Argyll resigned from the Cabinet in protest. By 1885 the Duke of Bedford and the Marquess of Lansdowne, both, like Argyll, leading Whigs of the day, had also ceased to support Gladstone's administration.

The desertion of aristocratic landlords from the Liberal camp was hardly surprising. But it was not Irish legislation alone that had impelled them to leave, and those that left the party were by no means only landlords. We have already noted the collectivist strain within the domestic non-Irish legislation of Gladstone's first government. His second government took the process several stages further. An Act of 1880 allowed tenants to kill ground game, a privilege hitherto reserved for landlords. That same year a blow was struck at the rights of employers. During the 1870s the trade-union movement had mounted a campaign against the legal doctrine of 'common employment', by which a master was deemed not to be liable to his servant for any injury caused by the negligence of a fellow servant, with whom the servant injured was engaged in common activity. Thus, where one employee suffered injury or death because of the ineptitude, or perhaps lack of training, of another employee, any claim for damages had to be brought against the fellow employee, not the employer.

In great industrial concerns, in which the boards of directors could not exercise a personal supervision over every one of their workers, this doctrine provided a highly convenient method of denying all liability; but the prospects of a widow obtaining satisfactory compensation from the workmate of her deceased husband were, of course, exceedingly remote. In 1880 the trade unions found that the new Liberal administration included two powerful allies in their campaign to reform the law: Chamberlain, at the Board of Trade, and J.G. Dodson, President of the Local Government Board. Employers who appealed to Gladstone to follow Disraeli's example (1879) and resist reform, now found themselves outmanoeuvered. The Employers' Liability Act of 1880 made the employer liable in any case where a workman sustained an accident 'by reason of the negligence of any person in the service of the employer to whose orders or directions the workman at the time of the injury was bound to conform and did conform'. From the point of view of the unions this phraseology was not ideal. None the less, the way was now open for injured parties to litigate with some prospect of success and, though contracting out of the Act's provisions was not illegal, in practice it could only be requested in return for membership of a substantial insurance scheme.

The Act of 1880 went a long way towards abolition of the doctrine of common employment, and on the railways the restriction was especially severe; a Liberal backbench amendment to prevent railway companies from using the doctrine to ward off claims in respect of the negligence of signalmen and engine-drivers was carried without a division. The business community found the passage of this legislation thoroughly alarming, and with good reason. A workman accepted employment (so the argument went) knowing the risks involved. A contract was made. Now Parliament presumed to interfere with the terms of that bargain, and apparently had every intention of applying the philosophy of interference to other types of business activity. For in the same year in which the Employers' Liability Act was passed, Chamberlain secured legislation to regulate the carriage of grain cargoes by sea, and to abolish the widespread practice of paying merchant seamen by 'advance notes' — in effect, credit notes usually cashed by lodging-house keepers and pimps at a huge discount. In 1883 Chamberlain promoted the Cheap Trains Act, allowing railway companies exemption from payment of the railway passenger duty, but only if they agreed to provide workmen's trains and third-class accommodation of a type and at a level found satisfactory by the Board of Trade. The following year Chamberlain attempted, unsuccessfully, to enact further reform of the mercantile marine (which would have permitted judges to vary contracts of maritime insurance, to deal with the deliberate over-insurance of unseaworthy vessels), and he also proposed reforms in the system of railway charges and of railway safety.

Property, it seemed, was no longer safe in Liberal hands, and would become still more unsafe as the Whigs left the party and Gladstone grew too old to resist the radical onslaught. The wilder schemes of Chamberlain and his friends were worrying enough. When not at the Board of Trade thinking of new ways to undermine *laissez-faire*, Chamberlain was making speeches of unashamed boldness attacking those 'who toil not, neither do they spin' (30 March 1883). This crusade reached a climax on 5 January 1885, when he addressed a Birmingham audience:

But then I ask, what ransom will property pay for the security which it enjoys? What substitute will it find for the natural rights which have ceased to be recognised? Society is banded together in order to protect itself against the instincts of those of its members who would make very short work of private ownership if they were left alone. That is all very well, but I maintain that society owes these men something more than mere toleration in return for the restrictions which it places upon their liberty of action.

The Liberal radicals were not Marxists, though their rhetoric smacked of class warfare. They were, however, much influenced by the ideas of the American economist Henry George, whose *Progress and Poverty* (1879) had become a best-seller. George advocated punitive taxation of the rents derived from land, and he believed that such a revenue would meet all the government's financial needs. For the radicals, too, the taxation of land was a central element in a policy which included land reform, heavier direct taxation, free primary education, cheaper municipal housing, a modest social welfare programme, more representative local government, further disestablishment of the Anglican Church, manhood suffrage, and the payment of MPs.

This *Radical Programme* (published in July 1885) was not unlike the manifestos of a number of fringe groups — for instance, the Marxist Social-Democratic Federation, founded by Henry Hyndman in 1883, and the non-Marxist Fabian Society, established in January 1884 and whose early adherents included Sidney and Beatrice Webb, George Bernard Shaw and other middle-class social reformers. But whereas their political influence was — as yet — negligible, Chamberlain was in his prime, and made no secret of his desire to secure the return to Parliament of enough like-minded MPs to force Gladstone to legislate along radical lines. And he appeared to have the means to carry out this threat.

Building upon the experience of the National Education League in achieving sweeping victories in the school-board elections in Birmingham in 1873, Chamberlain had, in 1877, launched the National Liberal Federation which (he wrote to John Morley) would 'become a very powerful organization, and proportionately detested by all Whigs and Whips'. The Federation was based upon ward and constituency meetings, which chose parliamentary and local-government candidates and elected representatives to an Annual Council Meeting, at which resolutions aimed at the national leadership of the party were passed. Chamberlain's claim that his Federation had played a major part in the 1880 Liberal victory was certainly exaggerated, though Gladstone was sufficiently impressed to put him in the Cabinet. Throughout the 1880s the Federation, though loyal to Gladstone, proved a most effective vehicle for the advancement of radical ideas. At the

Council held at Newcastle-upon-Tyne in October 1891, Gladstone surprised his audience by abandoning the expected speech on Ireland and substituting instead a warm endorsement of the customary string of resolutions embodying radical ambitions. Thus was born the 'Newcastle Programme', which was to form the basis of the reforms instituted by the governments of Sir Henry Campbell-Bannerman and Herbert Henry Asquith in the years immediately preceding the First World War.

But the Liberal party of the 1890s was very different from that whose interests Chamberlain had advanced a decade before. As long ago as 1877 the *Annual Register* had prophesied that the time would come 'when the two great sections of Liberalism should fall definitely apart, and fuse on one side with the great Radical body . . . [and] on the other, with its natural opposite, the Conservatism of the time'. And so it was. The attacks upon property and, in particular, upon the sanctity of contracts, dissolved the ties that had once bound the business community to the Liberal party. Gladstone's espousal of Home Rule for Ireland, in his short-lived third ministry of 1886, proved the last straw. On 9 June 1886 a total of 93 Liberal MPs voted with the Conservatives to prevent the second reading of the Home Rule Bill. They did so, not merely or even primarily because of the threat allegedly posed by the Bill to the unity of the Empire ('Home Rule' had already been given to Canada, Australia and New Zealand), but because the enactment of Gladstone's Bill would, in their view, have opened the floodgates to a radical deluge upon both landed and industrial wealth in Great Britain.

The irony was that Chamberlain was one of the leaders of this Liberal Unionist revolt. Chamberlain agreed with Gladstone that Ireland should enjoy a large measure of self-rule, but objected to the 1886 proposals because they envisaged the complete cessation of Irish representation at Westminster. In Chamberlain's view this would have resulted, eventually, in Irish independence, which was something quite other than Home Rule. He would have preferred to have satisfied Irish demands for internal self-government within the context of a much wider reform of local government throughout the United Kingdom, verging upon devolution. Indeed, Gladstone's Cabinets of 1880–85 had been much concerned with this question, and the establishment of the Scottish Office, in 1885, was one result of their labours.

Beyond this, however, one can detect in Chamberlain's break

with Gladstone the growing impatience of an ambitious radical politician, then 50 years of age and at the height of his powers, with the Celtic obsessions of an old man who was clinging to the leadership of the Liberal party only in order to be able to regain office and enact Home Rule. 'If he [Gladstone] retired', Chamberlain wrote to his close friend Jesse Collings in July 1886, 'all would come right pretty quickly.' But Gladstone would not go. His embrace of the Newcastle Programme was widely regarded as a calculated move to maintain his popularity in readiness for the next general election. However, it would be wrong to regard the Liberal preoccupation with Home Rule at this time, in the 1890s, as having been Gladstone's fault alone. When Salisbury did go to the polls, in July 1892, the Liberal share of the vote actually fell, from 44.9 to 44.2 per cent; though the number of Liberal MPs increased, compared with 1886, the government Gladstone formed was a minority one, dependent on Irish Nationalist support. Of necessity, therefore, this last Gladstone government (1892–4) was dominated by the second Home Rule Bill. This measure, which made provision for continued Irish representation in the Imperial Parliament, was approved by the Commons but rejected by the Lords (September 1893). Gladstone resigned, for good, the following March, to be succeeded as Liberal premier by Lord Rosebery, chosen not by the Liberals themselves but by Queen Victoria.

These last Liberal administrations of the nineteenth century were generally unproductive, and disappointing from the radical point of view. Asquith, the Home Secretary, proposed to widen still further the concept of employers' liability, but Gladstone withdrew the Bill to give effect to this reform when the Lords insisted on allowing workmen to contract out of its provisions. A Local Government Act (1894) set up rural and urban district councils to administer the poor law and to act as sanitary authorities, but the much vaunted parish councils, established by the same legislation, were never funded at a level commensurate with their obligations. The introduction, by Sir William Harcourt, of a single graduated succession (i.e. death) duty, payable on both real and personal property, in his 1894 budget, fulfilled a long-standing radical ambition. However, the revenues produced thereby were to be applied, not to the funding of social reform, but to the building of extra warships, so that the 'two-power standard' — the policy that the fighting strength of the Royal Navy should equal that of the combined navies of any two other countries — might be maintained.

A number of Bills designed to implement other parts of the Newcastle Programme (especially Welsh disestablishment and the institution of local vetoes on the sale of alcoholic drinks) came to grief in the Upper House, so that it was clear that the key to the enactment of radical reform lay, not just with the electorate, but in fundamental constitutional change, to subordinate the Lords to the Commons. In November 1894 Campbell-Bannerman, then Secretary of State for War, raised the matter with the Queen at Balmoral. It was clear at once where her sympathies lay. Campbell-Bannerman noted her view that she 'could never agree to taking from the Lords their power to alter or reject measures . . . [She] quite admitted that the H.[ouse] of L.[ords] might require reform . . . But we must have a check against the H.[ouse] of Commons which [was] too strong, and had been ever since Lord Beaconsfield's most unfortunate Act [i.e. the 1867 Reform Act]'.

So that was that. Victoria would never agree to the creation of sufficient Liberal peers to restrict the Lord's veto and, with their veto intact, the Lords would continue to sabotage Liberal policies. There seemed little point in the continuation of the government. Rosebery remained in office for another six months, and then used the excuse of an accidental defeat in the Commons (a 'snap' vote on a motion of censure arising from a shortage of cordite) to call an election. In Scotland, Wales, London and the agricultural constituencies of south-west England and the west Midlands there was a heavy anti-Liberal vote; farming communities revolted against free trade, and urban working-class voters demonstrated their disappointment at the apparent sterility of Liberal ideas on social reform. The Conservatives, with their Liberal-Unionist allies, emerged with a parliamentary majority of 152 seats. Chamberlain accepted Lord Salisbury's offer of the Colonial Office, and the Liberal party entered upon a decade of parliamentary opposition, marked for the most part by feuding over the leadership and squabbles between the imperialist and anti-imperialist wings of the party concerning the Boer War.

Chamberlain's agreement to enter a thoroughly Conservative administration was only partly opportunistic. He was already beginning to see in the expansion of the Empire a means of increasing national prosperity, perhaps making social welfare provision less urgent. 'We desire [he told an audience in May 1895] . . . to develop that commerce and that enterprise upon which I am convinced the happiness of the population depends much more than it does upon any legislative action.' It was clear that the electoral base of Liberalism had been substantially eroded. Its preoccupation with Celtic issues had alienated English working-class voters, to whom imperial themes seemed increasingly attractive. But its inability to legislate on matters such as further temperance reform and disestablishment damaged its standing in Scotland and Wales, while its abhorrence of tariffs deprived it of support in hard-pressed English rural areas. In terms of the popular vote the electoral history of the Liberal party between 1885 and 1910 was one of almost unmitigated decline, as the following table shows:

Table 4.2: Liberal Share of the Total Vote, 1885–1910 (per cent)

1885	49.0
1886	44.9
1892	44.2
1895	45.8
1900	45.9
1906	45.9
1910 (Jan)	43.1
1910 (Dec)	43.8

Source: M. Kinnear, *The British Voter: An Atlas and Survey since 1885* (2nd edn, 1981).

The Liberal election victory of 1906, when the party was returned to Parliament with an overall majority of 84, was a 'landslide' in terms only of seats, not votes, and must really be seen as a Unionist defeat (deriving largely from the internal antagonisms over tariff reform) rather than as a Liberal triumph. At the two elections of 1910 the Liberals lost their overall majority; they have never regained it.

These trends were, if only in outline, clearly discernible in the 1890s. Chamberlain, the radical Liberal, chose alliance with the Conservatives in 1895 for much the same reason that had persuaded Gladstone, the free-trade Conservative, to join the Liberals in 1859: any other choice would have meant exile into a political void. But one other factor weighed with him, and that was the possibility that the Conservatives might be persuaded to embark upon a programme of social reform. Historically, nineteenth-century Conservatism had been associated with opposition to unfettered industrialism and the single-minded pursuit of commercial ends. Under Peel it had acquired the reputation of a party that cared about the welfare of the people. Disraeli had seen himself as the heir to this tradition, but also to the Palmerstonian tradition of a brash foreign policy that put Britain's interests first, even if this meant (as it most certainly did with respect to support for the decaying Ottoman Empire) constricting the growth of genuine nationalist movements in Europe. The enfranchisement of male heads of households in 1867 was, as we have seen, largely an accident, over which Disraeli had little control. But he was quick to grasp the new electoral reality, and to conjure up a vision (as *The Times* of 18 April 1883 put it) of 'the Conservative working man as the sculptor perceives the angel imprisoned in the block of marble'.

The Liberal victory of 1868 was, in this respect, misleading: it did not mean that the working-class electors had turned their backs on Conservatism. Hodgkinson's amendment had enfranchised those occupiers who agreed to pay their rates personally; but many artisans either could not or would not adopt this practice, and so were unable to vote in the 1868 election. In 1869 the law was amended to enable tenants to forgo personal payment but still retain the right to a vote — though, of course, they had to wait until the election of 1874 in order to do so.

None the less, contained within the 1868 election outcomes were some results of great significance for the future of urban conservatism. In Lancashire the Conservatives won 21 seats, as compared with the Liberals' 13, and were particularly successful in capturing heavy industrial constituencies such as Salford, Blackburn, Preston and Bolton. Conservative victories in solid middle-class areas, such as the former radical strongholds of Westminster and Middlesex, attested to the arrival of middle-class suburban Toryism. Indeed, in 1868 the party was successful in no less than 34 boroughs with populations in excess of 20,000 each. Thus, although the basic strength of Conservatism was still to be found in the English rural heartlands (in 1868 the Conservatives held three-quarters of the English county seats), the party was already putting down roots in the towns and winning support from within the aristocracy of labour.

To assist in the gathering of this harvest, Disraeli concocted a hotch-potch of high-sounding generalities which, in their definitive forms, were articulated at a meeting of the National Union of Conservative and Unionist Associations at the Crystal Palace on 24 June 1872. After having assured his audience that the first duty of the Conservative party was 'to maintain the institutions of the country', and that the second was 'to maintain the Empire of England', Disraeli declared his belief in the importance of what he termed 'the elevation of the condition of the people'. But the major burden of the speech (as of one delivered at Manchester the previous April) was an appeal to those sections of society most under attack from Liberalism, whose 'tone and tendency', Disraeli said, was 'to attack the institutions of the country under the name of Reform'.

When the Conservatives obtained their parliamentary majority, in 1874, Disraeli's overriding concern was with the Empire. His government purchased a half-share in the Suez Canal, and so established itself in Egypt. Victoria was made Empress of India. Ignoring Gladstone's crusade against the 'Bulgarian Horrors' (1876), and without waiting for parliamentary authority, Disraeli sent a fleet forwards and backwards across the eastern Mediterranean, and despatched (upon the authority of the Crown) an army of some 7,000 Indian troops to Malta, in order to force the Russians to submit to the Great Powers (at Berlin, 1878) the results of their unilateral intervention against the Turks; Russia was, as a result, compelled to agree to the division of Bulgaria, while the United Kingdom obtained control of Cyprus. Between 1878 and 1880 Disraeli (by now Earl of Beaconsfield) pursued a 'forward' policy in Afghanistan, annexed the Transvaal, and consented to the conquest of Zululand.

These flamboyant and expensive policies horrified the Liberals; Gladstone felt compelled to emerge from retirement (1879) to launch his Midlothian campaign against 'Beaconsfieldism'. But their effect upon the electorate was almost certainly far less repulsive. At the election of 1880 the Conservatives lost 118 seats. But in terms of popular support the Conservative vote in 1880 increased by over 30 per cent compared with 1874, while in those seats that were contested in both elections the increase was about 8 per cent. The main feature of the election, and the true cause of Gladstone's victory, was the proportionately greater increase in support achieved by the Liberals: in all seats this increase was about 43 per cent, and in seats contested in both elections it was about 36 per cent. In the 72 seats won by the Liberals in which

Conservative candidates came within 10 per cent of the Liberal vote, the total number of votes separating the two parties was a mere 4,054!

In absolute terms, therefore, Conservatism had lost neither its popularity nor its fascination. Working men were genuinely patriotic, even jingoistic, and believed that imperial policies would benefit their own standard of living. Many were employed making munitions, or in the dockyard towns; many others hoped that trade with expanding colonial markets would make their jobs more secure and their purses fatter. Disraeli caught this mood, but he was exceedingly careful not to alienate middle-class support by adopting too generous an attitude towards domestic reforms. On the morrow of his 1874 victory, he had to confess that he had not really thought out what these reforms might be. In a private memoir printed in 1903 his Home Secretary, Richard Assheton Cross, revealed that the Prime Minister had 'had to rely entirely on the various suggestions of his colleagues'. Chief among these was Cross himself, whose Factory Act (1874) finally established the ten-hour day, by reducing the 60-hour week embodied in the 1850 Act to 56 hours (10 hours a day from Monday to Friday and six hours on Saturday), and whose Artisans' Dwellings Act (1875) empowered but did not oblige local authorities to undertake slum-clearance in order to build houses for working people.

Three pieces of legislation, also passed in 1875, affected the trade-union movement. Gladstone's Criminal Law Amendment Act was repealed, thus allowing peaceful picketing. An Employers and Workmen Act removed the possibility of criminal proceedings against workmen for breach of contract. The Conspiracy and Protection of Property Act placed peaceful strikes beyond the reach of the conspiracy laws. At the time, these enactments were hailed as victories for the trade-union movement, which they undoubtedly were, in the sense that they represented the acceptance by the state of the legitimacy of trade unionism and of peaceful trade-union activities. The Parliamentary Committee of the Trades Union Congress, which had campaigned hard in 1874 for the enactment of such reforms, declared that 'the work of emancipation' was 'full and complete'. It was not. The Conservative government had not gone so far as to endow the unions with immunity from civil proceedings, either by way of injunctions to prevent picketing or by means of claims for damages in respect of strikes.

Other pieces of social reform were largely cosmetic. The Public Health Act (1875) simply codified existing legislation (principally the Acts of 1866 and 1872) in this area of public administration. The 1875 Unseaworthy Ships Act, a piece of emergency legislation made permanent by the Merchant Shipping Act of the following year, was altogether fraudulent. Enacted in response to the hysterical campaign of the Liberal MP for Derby, Samuel Plimsoll, the Acts of 1875 and 1876 did indeed provide for a maximum load-line to be put on every ship's side, to prevent overloading, but did not say where the line was to be painted. Within a short time it became clear that in many cases the load-line was being positioned at such a height (*The Times* of 25 November 1875 revealed) 'as to ensure its being well out of the water under any circumstances of loading'. Plimsoll was justified in telling his constituents that the legislation was 'lamentably, and I believe, designedly inadequate'. The deficiencies of the Act were not put right until 1890.

When we add to the above list the 1876 Education Act (which established school attendance committees in those areas where there were no school boards), a Sale of Food and Drugs Act, which permitted but did not oblige local authorities to appoint public analysts, and a timid Rivers' Pollution Act, we arrive at the sum total of Disraelian social reform. Apart from the genuine, but limited, concessions to the trade unions, the legislation was not collectivist at all, merely permissive. After 1876, and his translation to the Upper House, Disraeli lost all interest in working-class reforms; the subject of employers' liability, for example, was shunted onto a Select committee, and a modest Bill introduced in 1878 by the Attorney-General, John Holker, was withdrawn in the face of opposition by business interests.

But there were those within the Conservative party who continued to hope that it might be turned into an instrument for radical reform, and they found a leader in Lord Randolph Churchill, a son of the seventh Duke of Marlborough, who had been elected for the family constituency, Woodstock, in 1874. Churchill has often been compared to Joseph Chamberlain; a famous *Punch* cartoon of 19 September 1885 depicted them both as polo players, each attempting to gain possession of the ball (labelled 'votes'). Their backgrounds could not have been more dissimilar: Chamberlain, the Unitarian screw-manufacturer, Churchill the Anglican aristocrat educated at Eton and Oxford.

Yet both had come to recognise the centrality of the working classes to the post-1867 political system. In a speech delivered at Birmingham in October 1883 Churchill explained:

> The great bulk of the Tory party throughout the country is composed of the artisans and labouring classes . . . The Conservative party will never exercise power until it has gained the confidence of the working classes . . . Our interests are perfectly safe if we trust them fully, frankly and freely: but if we oppose them, our interests, our Constitution, and all we love and revere, will go down.

To match the Radical Programme, Churchill constructed his own 'Dartford Programme', so-called after a speech he delivered at Dartford in 1886, when Chancellor of the Exchequer in Salisbury's second administration. The essentials of the Dartford Programme were: the appointment of four Royal Commissions on Irish affairs; reform of the procedure of the House of Commons; the granting of powers to local authorities to acquire land for allotments; reform of the tithe laws and of railway rates; legislation to facilitate and make less costly the transfer of land; comprehensive local government reform; and reduced taxation.

These proposals comprised 'Tory Democracy' as Lord Randolph Churchill conceived it. The problems of late-Victorian urban society did not figure very prominently in his schemes which, Ireland apart, were heavily angled towards rural reforms. But Tory Democracy had another side to it. Churchill was as ambitious to become a future Conservative leader as Chamberlain was to succeed Gladstone and, just as Chamberlain used the National Liberal Federation to further his own political ambitions, so Churchill exploited the potential of the National Union of Conservative and Constitutional Working-Men's Associations. Founded in 1867, the National Union held annual conferences but, more importantly, allowed access to the local Conservative constituency parties independently of Conservative Central Office (established in 1870). Both organisations had played a prominent part in the 1874 election victory, but had then been allowed to languish. In the early 1880s Churchill used the apparatus and annual conferences of the National Union to preach the gospel of Tory Democracy, at the same time furthering his own claim to 'Elijah's Mantle' — the leadership of the party after Disraeli's death in 1881. In addition, Churchill himself founded the Primrose League (November 1883), which was designed to widen constituency support for the party by allowing non-voters (including women) as well as voters to become members. By 1886 membership of the League had reached 237,000, and by 1891 the figure exceeded one million.

Gladstone never succeeded in buying off Chamberlain, who cared too deeply for his own principles to admit of any compromise, even after 1886, when it was clear that the great bulk of the Liberal radicals, and the National Liberal Federation, were going to remain loyal to the party leader. But Lord Salisbury recognised the ambition that lay behind the rhetoric of Churchill and his 'Fourth Party' in the Commons. In 1884 Churchill, then just over 35 years of age, accepted the promise of office in a future Conservative administration. He became Secretary of State for India in 1885, and Chancellor of the Exchequer and Leader of the House of Commons the following year.

Then, in December 1886, he made a gross error of political judgement, either through youthful impetuosity or perhaps as a result of the brain disease which was beginning, slowly, to kill him. Churchill intimated that he would resign from the Cabinet unless his demands for economy in the War Office were met; what is more, he told *The Times* what he intended to do. Salisbury (to whose authority this was, of course, a direct challenge) stood firm and, rather than lose face, Churchill left the government. The National Union was quickly brought under Central Office control. Churchill's rapid loss of influence in the party accompanied his physical deterioration. He died, of what was termed 'General Paralysis of the Insane', on 24 January 1895. Five months later, Joseph Chamberlain and three other Liberal Unionists (G. J. Goschen, Lord James of Hereford and the Duke of Devonshire) accepted Cabinet posts in Salisbury's third government.

Although Churchill's personal influence within the Conservative party effectively ended in 1886, his insistence upon the importance of a broad popular base for the party and, therefore, of embarking upon a programme of social and political reform, left a legacy which was not without solid achievement. The spirit of Dartford was clearly reflected in the legislation of the second Salisbury administration. Two Irish Land Acts were passed: that of 1887 extended to leaseholders the benefits of Gladstone's Act of 1881, while Balfour's 1891 Land Purchase Act established a Congested

Districts Board to deal with areas in which there was not enough land to turn every tenant into a viable peasant proprietor. A Tithe Act transferred the payment of tithes in England and Wales from tenants to landlords. Other reforms included the 1888 Local Government Act; 'whisky money' for technical education; comprehensive reform of railway rates (1888); the right to free elementary education (1891); and an ambitious Factory Act (1891) which raised the minimum age for factory workers to 11, and extended sanitary regulations to workshops in which only adult males were employed.

The enactment of such measures seemed to indicate that Tory Democracy was no mere phantom. Indeed, the results of successive general elections between 1885 and 1895 demonstrated quite clearly the relentless urban advance of Conservatism, which could only have been achieved through attracting working-class votes. In west and south Lancashire (especially Liverpool) the tensions that existed between English Protestants and Irish Catholics, cleverly exploited by local Conservatives, were certainly part of the explanation. But in Birmingham and the west Midlands the influence of the Chamberlainites was matched by the rising popularity of tariff reform within industries hard-hit by foreign imports. In London the growth of Conservatism was spectacular. In 1874 there were Conservative MPs in only 10 of the capital's 22 seats. In 1885, when London's parliamentary representation was increased to 59, Conservatives were returned in 35 seats; the following year the number reached 47; in 1892 it fell to 36 but in 1895 (and again in 1900) it rose to 57. The poorest East End constituencies (including five out of the seven Tower Hamlets' seats and two of the three in Southwark) all returned Conservative MPs in 1895; at Bethnal Green North-East George Howell, former secretary of the TUC's Parliamentary Committee, standing as a Liberal, was defeated by an Indian, Sir M. M. Bhownaggree, whom the Conservatives had put up and who thus became the country's second coloured MP (the first, D. Naoroji, had sat as a Liberal for Central Finsbury from 1892 to 1895).

The obvious importance of the urban seats in the electoral horserace, and the consequent need to address working-class interests, taken together with the apparent attractions of Tory Democracy, seemed in 1895 to indicate that a future Conservative administration would have to devote some of its energies to social reform. But the domestic achievements of the Salisbury and

Balfour governments (1895–1905) were limited and disappointing. The two centrepieces were the Workmen's Compensation Act of 1897 and the Education Act of 1902. The former, inspired by Chamberlain, finally did away with the doctrine of common employment, and with contracting-out, by placing the onus for compensation in respect of accidents at work squarely on the shoulders of employers. In practice, and as was intended, this meant that henceforth all employers had to insure against the cost of industrial injuries.

Balfour's Education Act abolished the school boards, and made the education committees of the various local authorities in England and Wales responsible for elementary, secondary and technical education. The demise of the directly elected school boards was not achieved without protest, and though the advantages of placing the three levels of education under the control of one management were clear enough, the 'one authority' objective was not actually attained, since the larger urban districts and most municipal boroughs won the right to control their own elementary education. Still, the provision of public secondary education was a veritable leap forward in state educational provision, and its importance can scarcely be overestimated. But a much more contentious part of the 1902 Act gave the local authorities some control over the voluntary (i.e. denominational) schools, in return for which these schools were to receive more aid from the rates. Nonconformists were furious that public moneys should support denominational religious instruction, and there were 'Passive Resisters' who refused to pay rates on this basis. Yet the principles of the Balfour Act (extended to London in 1903) have never been overturned. The Act established the principle of local-authority involvement in education, and has proved to be one of the foundations of the present-day educational system in Britain.

Some other domestic initiatives of the period are worthy of note. The 1900 Prevention of Accidents Act endowed the Board of Trade with sweeping powers to compel the adoption of safety measures on the railways. The 1901 Factory Act raised the minimum working age to 12. But we may also detect in these initiatives an unimaginative, Disraelian approach. The 1896 Conciliation Act allowed the Board of Trade to intervene in industrial disputes, but only at the behest of both sides. The 1904 Licensing Act was a genuine attempt to control drunkenness by giving magistrates the power to quash the licenses of public houses deemed to be surplus to requirements. Compensation was to be paid from funds made available by the drink trade itself, a reasonable provision which was, however, attacked by the Liberals, who did not see why compensation of any kind should be forthcoming. It was certainly true that the Act linked the reduction of licenses to the size of the compensation fund, rather than to considerations of broad public interest. Walter Long's Unemployed Workmen's Act of 1905 permitted the establishment of local 'Distress Committees', empowered to find jobs for those 'genuinely' seeking work; the Committees could also provide work and, in suitable cases, arrange for emigration. But these schemes were not to be financed wholly from the rates; in practice most of the money came from voluntary contributions — that is, private charity. The 1905 Aliens Act was, as we have already noted, a sop to working-class xenophobia and antisemitism.

In the domestic field, therefore, some very important proposals were enacted, but the overall achievement was marred by a lack of vision, a refusal to contemplate (save in exceptional cases, such as the railways) any dramatic extension of state power, and an almost total unwillingness to commit Treasury money to the cause of reform. In Ireland it was clear that Conservative politicians were too closely involved with Ulster Protestantism (ironically, another Churchillian legacy) for them to be able to contemplate bold initiatives. It was true that an Irish Land Purchase Act of 1903 set aside the sum of £10 millions to further facilitate the transfer of estates to the peasantry. But matters had, by now, definitely passed beyond the stage at which the creation of a peasant pro- prietorship might have solved the Irish Question. The Irish parliamentary party, led, after Parnell's disgrace and death (1890–1) by John Redmond, expressly repudiated total separation, and would have settled for Gladstonian Home Rule. But this party no longer represented the Irish people.

On the one hand, there were the proponents of a new militant Catholic nationalism, epitomised in the establishment of the Gaelic League (1893) and the formation in November 1905 of Sinn Fein, whose constitution declared ominously that 'we are a distinct people'. Arthur Griffith, Sinn Fein's founder, did not at first demand total independence, but favoured rather a revival of Grattan's Parliament of 1782. On the other hand, the period following the Lords' repudiation of the 1893 Home Rule Bill witnessed the complete alienation of Ulster Protestants from the

Irish nationalist movement. The year which saw the beginnings of
the Gaelic League also saw the establishment of the Ulster Defence Union, closely linked to Liberal Unionism and, hence, to the
Conservative interest at Westminster.

The tragic consequences of this politico-religious polarisation
were soon evident. Following the passage of his Land Purchase
Act in 1903, George Wyndham, the Irish Secretary, gave his
consent to the discussion, in 1904, of a scheme of devolved
administration in Ireland put forward by his Permanent Under-
Secretary, the distinguished Roman Catholic civil servant, Sir
Antony Macdonnell. Ireland had been given elected local authorities in 1898, and there were some influential Irish landowners
(notably Lord Dunraven) who felt that an agreed scheme of devolution might be accepted by the Nationalists and Unionists
alike. In fact, Ulster Unionists vied with each other in denouncing
the proposal — 'a weak and silly attempt to grant home rule on
the sly', according to the Irish Attorney-General, John Atkinson.
Such was the Protestant reaction that Balfour determined to
sacrifice his Irish Secretary as an act of appeasement: on 6 March
1905 Wyndham resigned, his political career at an end. The Ulster
Unionist Council, charged with the duty of defending Ulster from
Home Rule, was formed the same year.

So it was that those who believed that radical social and political
reform, of which the late-nineteenth-century Liberal party had
proved ultimately incapable, might be achieved through Conservatism, saw these hopes gradually evaporate. The major
achievements of the Unionist administrations of 1895–1905, and
the principal channels for their energies, lay in the field of foreign
affairs: the extension of Empire in Africa and Asia; a full-blooded
military alliance with Japan (1902) to safeguard that Empire in the
Pacific; a settlement of colonial differences with France (the 1904
Entente Cordiale) which confirmed British control of Egypt; a war
in South Africa to establish equal rights for British settlers (but not
for native Africans) in the Boer Republics, leading to the conquest
of these territories.

This vigorous approach to Imperial problems contrasted sharply
and unmistakably with the tempo of Unionist social policy. As
early as 1891 Chamberlain, impressed by Bismarck's scheme of
sickness benefit and old-age pensions (1889) had formulated
similar proposals for implementation in the United Kingdom.
Salisbury's government ignored these, and shunted the matter

onto a Committee on Old Age Pensions, presided over by Lord Rothschild (1896–8). In 1899 a Select Committee (of which David Lloyd George was a prominent member) recommended that a state pension of five shillings per week be paid to the needy and deserving poor over 65 years of age; the scheme was vetoed by the government on the grounds that the cost of the South African War precluded its implementation.

Perhaps it did. But it is worth noting that the Conservative party which endorsed these postponements was very different from that which had supported the principle of nationalisation, under Peel, and of the legitimacy of peaceful trade-union activity, under Disraeli. The revolt of property which had split the Gladstonian Liberal party had had profound repercussions upon Conservatism. Most of the Liberal Unionists were not radicals, but landowners and businessmen profoundly distrustful of any attack upon wealth. Although the fusion of the Conservative and Liberal Unionist parties was still some years away, the two groups had formed, from at least 1895, if not earlier, a coherent political force dedicated to the protection of capital in any form, and to the maintenance, in so far as it was possible, of the *status quo*. In the House of Commons the number of Liberal Unionists steadily fell, from 79, in 1886, to just over 30, in 1910; the formal merger took place two years later.

The business community looked to Conservatism for its defence. By 1900 less than half the Conservative MPs were drawn from the ranks of the landed classes; 53 per cent of the parliamentary party in the Commons had industrial and professional backgrounds. The party was, even then, still heavily Anglican and led by a landed aristocrat who sat in the Lords. A dozen years later its leadership was entrusted to Andrew Bonar Law, an iron merchant from Glasgow and the son of a Presbyterian minister.

Conservatism had thus been reconstituted, and was now unlikely to favour heavy public expenditure to finance schemes of social provision. Nor could it any longer be expected to facilitate the development of trade-union activity, particularly when such activity acted as a vehicle for the propagation of socialism. The demands of labour were to form a central theme of British social and political development in the early twentieth century. It remained to be seen whether they could be accommodated within the post-Gladstonian Liberal consensus.

5 A REVOLUTION OF VALUES

The deaths of monarchs are of very limited interest to political and social historians of the recent past, and a study of modern British history bounded by such events is likely to be artificial in its treatment. Queen Victoria's death, on 22 January 1901, was of no special significance in itself. Though the unpopularity of the monarchy that had characterised the middle years of her reign (when, following Albert's death in 1863, she seemed to have retired into a state of permanent mourning), had long since been replaced by popular reverence bordering on adulation, this was directed less at Victoria herself, as a person, than at the imperial achievement of which the Queen-Empress was the ultimate symbol. The jubilees of 1887 and 1897 — particularly the latter — were lavish celebrations of the Victorian age; Victoria remained a sombre, authoritarian figure, known to be possessed of political opinions far to the right of those espoused by the late Lord Beaconsfield.

When Victoria died, it was said that an era had come to an end. When Edward VII passed away this feeling was widespread. Paradoxically, Edward was a truer exponent of Victorian values than his mother. An affable extrovert, fond of the good life and of the company of wealthy men and accommodating women, Edward none the less had a social conscience; he had been a member, under Sir Charles Dilke's chairmanship, of the Royal Commission on Housing in 1884, sitting alongside Cardinal Manning, Lord Salisbury, G. J. Goschen, R. A. Cross, Jesse Collings and Henry Broadhurst. Kept away from all official business by a jealous mother, Edward had, it is true, patronised the turf and the casinos, but he had also educated himself in some at least of the nation's problems. He was far closer to his people than his mother had ever been, and he had met more of them.

Edward VII died on 6 May 1910. The remnants of Victorian certainty and confidence died with him. To the young Virginia Woolf it seemed that in 1910 'all human relations have shifted — those between masters and servants, husbands and wives, parents and children. And when human relations change there is at the same time a change in religion, conduct, politics and literature'. A revolution was taking place in the values by which society regulated itself. The social fabric of the nation, no less than the political and economic, was being reworked. In particular, two bastions of Victorian middle-class culture — the church and the family — were under attack.

It is clear that during the last quarter of the nineteenth century religious observance and identity became less important. The decline did not happen suddenly. The religious census of 1851 had shocked contemporaries by its revelation that only about half the population of England and Wales went to church, and that only a half of these were Anglican. Even so, the reform of abuses in the Church of England (and especially the establishment in 1836 of the Church Commissioners, to manage the Church's property) had paved the way for a substantial programme of church building and rebuilding, so that by 1901 there were over 17,000 Anglican churches and chapels, whereas 50 years earlier there had only been 14,000. Yet, despite this improvement, the proportion of the population identifying with the Church of England continued to fall. In 1854, 84 per cent of all marriages had been performed according to Anglican rites; by 1904 the figure was only 64 per cent. There is some evidence of a rise in marriages performed in Nonconformist churches (from 6 per cent of the total in 1854, to 13 per cent 50 years later), but even the Roman Catholic church experienced a downward trend (from 5 per cent of all marriages to 4 per cent over the same period), in spite of a substantial Irish immigration to Britain at this time. Civil ceremonies, however, rose dramatically. In 1854 they had accounted for 5 per cent of all marriages, but a half-century later the proportion was 18 per cent.

Although, therefore, we are justified in talking of a modest expansion in Nonconformist identity, at least at the time of marriage, overall the picture is one of a relentless contraction in religious observance, especially in urban areas. An inquiry carried out in Sheffield in 1881 revealed that only one person in every three who could have attended church actually did so. In 1882, in the cities of Nottingham, Liverpool and Bristol, church attendance averaged only 27 per cent. In London the extent of the decline may be measured by comparing two surveys of Sunday church attendance, one carried out by Robertson Nicoll for the *British Weekly* in 1886, the other by R. Mudie Smith for the *Daily News* in 1902–3. Between the dates of these two investigations the population of London (the London County Council area) increased by some 500,000 souls; but church attendance, in absolute numbers, actually dropped from 1,167,312 attendances to 1,003,361 — that is, by 14 per cent. Mudie Smith was further able to demonstrate that, in a population in the nation's capital of about 4.5 millions at the turn of the century, less than one-fifth bothered to attend any sort of institutional church service on a Sunday.

Truly did a clergyman remark in 1896 'It is not that the Church of God had lost the great towns: it has never had them'. People who moved into the towns from the countryside seem to have lost the habit of public worship, while the urban-born proletariat were never possessed of it. To the town-dwelling working classes the disputes between the anti-intellectual Evangelicals and the reverential anglo-catholic Tractarians appeared as a total irrelevance. Nor had the Established Church done itself any good by prosecuting, under Disraeli's Public Worship Regulation Act of 1874, clergymen accused of Anglo-Catholic practices. In 1888 the Church Association brought the Bishop of Lincoln, Dr Edward King, to trial before the Archbishop of Canterbury on seven charges of illegal practices in divine worship. Dr King was found guilty on only two counts, and did not have costs awarded against him.

Thereafter, prosecutions dwindled in frequency and the public lost interest in them. The churches, as institutions, ceased to occupy a central place in the life of most men and women; religion, in its turn, lost its role as a social cement, except, perhaps, among some sections of the middle classes, for whom (if only for appearances' sake) church-going retained a certain status-value. In general, if people turned to the church at all, it was only in public celebration of the most important or solemn occasions: birth, marriage and death. In 1914 the total number of Easter communicants within the Church of England was just 2.2 millions, or 10 per cent of the population over 15 years of age.

We hear no more of the great 'revivals' that had shaken the Protestant churches in Britain in the first half of the nineteenth century, such as the Oxford Movement. The Welsh Revival of 1904 did have a transitory impact, a protest by rural chapel-going (and Welsh-speaking) Wales against the sins of city life. But the popularity of this Revival was due largely to its social content, its emphasis upon the evils that emanated from urban squalor and, in particular, from appalling housing conditions. Significantly, too, the only Christian movement to make any impact upon the urban proletariat in England in the late-nineteenth and early-twentieth centuries was the one that abandoned 'the church' and busied itself with the fundamentals of mere existence in the towns: the Salvation Army. Founded by the Reverend William Booth in 1878, the Army was originally conceived simply as a revivalist organisation to aid him in his evangelical mission in the East End of London. But it grew into a highly respected social-work agency. To establishment circles (even the Methodist ones whence he sprang) 'General' Booth, in military uniform accompanied by a brass band and selling his newspaper, *The War Cry*, did not appear at all like a man of God. But his publication in 1890 of *In Darkest England and the Way Out* shocked church and secular society alike by its brutal exposure of the conditions under which 'The Submerged Tenth' of the population lived, 'those who have gone under, who have lost their foothold in Society, those to whom the prayer of our Heavenly Father, "Give us day by day our daily bread," is either unfulfilled, or only fulfilled by the Devil's agency: by the earnings of vice, the proceeds of crime, or the contributions enforced by the threat of law':

> The denizens of Darkest England, for whom I appeal, are (1) those who, having no capital or income of their own, would in a month be dead from sheer starvation were they exclusively dependent upon the money earned by their own work; and (2) those who by their utmost exertions are unable to attain the regulation allowance of food which the law prescribes as indispensable even for the worst criminals in our gaols.

It is very doubtful whether the Salvation Army succeeded in converting large numbers of working people to Christianity. It is equally certain that Booth demonstrated, by his example, how Christianity might be practised without even setting foot in a church.

Undoubtedly, the most dramatic manifestation of the decline in religious observance was the demise of the Victorian Sunday. But the very manner of its death serves to underline the strength of secularist tendencies. If the masses did not attend church or chapel on Sundays (so the argument went) other activities must be organised for them, lest they turn to idleness and immorality. The

National Sunday League had already persuaded the railway companies to run cheap Sunday excursions, and now campaigned for the Sunday opening of museums and art galleries. In 1896 its efforts were crowned with success, when, following a resolution passed by the Conservative-dominated House of Commons, the state-owned art galleries and museums were opened to the public, free of charge, on Sunday afternoons.

Parallel with the decline of religious observance there took place a fatal erosion in the sanctity and status of the family. At the beginning of Victoria's reign middle-class families of between six and nine children were commonplace. Some of these children would in all probability die in infancy, but around them, perhaps living in the same house and equally part of the family, there would have been gathered an assortment of grandparents, maiden aunts and other dependants. The Victorian family was a compact self-contained unit, making its own entertainment, living near to the place of employment of the principal breadwinner.

With the growth of surburban railways, of horse-drawn and later of electric trams, and later still of motorised bus services, this pattern of life was bound to alter. Tramways, in particular, had a significant impact upon the pre-1914 working classes, for they were cheaper than buses but often more accessible than the nearest railway system. At the time of the outbreak of the Great War Britain was still a horse-drawn society. However, during the first decade of the twentieth century omnibus services succumbed to the lure of the internal combustion engine. In 1905 London had only 20 motor buses; by March 1908 the figure had exceeded 1,000 and by 1913 only 6 per cent of passenger vehicles plying for hire in the metropolis were still horse-powered. Although, therefore, car ownership was still the prerogative of the wealthy few (in 1914 only one person in every 232 in Great Britain owned his or her own motor vehicle), the benefits of motor transport were much more generally available. In addition, there had taken place a considerable expansion of the electric street tramway, about 2,300 miles of which had been built by 1909.

These developments enabled families to live some distance from the fathers' place of work, and brought within the grasp of many a range of entertainments not previously available, such as the music-hall, the theatre and the cinema. Music-halls dated from the 1840s. The first variety theatre in London, the Coliseum, opened its doors in 1904. Britain did not acquire its first 'picture palace' until 1910, but by 1914 some 3,700 cinemas had been constructed. The playing and watching of games also increased. The Rugby Union had been founded in 1871, eight years after the establishment of the Football Association. The first visit by an Australian cricket team to England took place in 1878, just as Dr W. G. Grace was embarking upon an (amateur) career that was to turn cricket into a highly popular spectator sport. Attractions such as these acted as powerful solvents of the Victorian family unit, and their impact was sharpened not only by the secularisation of Sunday, but by shorter working hours generally, the spread of the 'free' Saturday afternoon, and the custom of giving holidays. At first, in the late-nineteenth century, such holidays were invariably unpaid. Towards the end of the century some groups of workers secured a holiday entitlement without loss of earnings. The first group of manual workers to secure such holidays were some employees of Brunner-Mond, the chemical conglomerate, who were granted an annual week's holiday, with pay, in and from 1884.

However, none of these developments wrought such a revolutionary change in the nature of family life as did the spread of birth control. We must distinguish here between the postponement of a marriage, on economic grounds, and the limitation of the number of children born of the marriage. Late marriages were a feature of Victorian middle-class values; around 1850 the average age of marriage within the professional classes was 30 but, once the marriage had taken place, large families were the norm. At that time the birth-rate in England and Wales was about 35 per 1,000. After 1875 the rate fell dramatically so that, just prior to the outbreak of war in 1914, it stood at only 24 per 1,000. The number of children per family, which had stood at 6 in 1870, dropped to 4.3 in the 1890s, and by 1915 was just 2.3.

Although this fall in the birth-rate did in time exhibit itself within all sections of society, there can be no doubt that it started in the upper and professional classes, whose incomes had in general remained stationary in the last quarter of the nineteenth century, and who now, in any case, had more to do with their money. With respect to all couples married between 1890 and 1899, the average number of children per family among professional people was 2.80, among salaried 'white-collar' workers 3.04, among manual wage-earners 4.85, and among labourers 5.11. By 1914 the comparable figures for each group were: 2.05;

1.95; 3.24; and 4.09. As a result, although the population continued to increase, the rate of increase was appreciably lower than
in the early- and mid-nineteenth century. While the death-rate (in
England and Wales) fell from 20 per 1,000, in 1881, to about 12
per 1,000 in 1911, and the rate of infant mortality from 140 to 110
per 1,000 over the same period, the rise in population was only
from 26.0 to 36.1 millions — a rate of increase, that is, of about
1.3 per cent per annum, whereas in the preceding 30 years
(1851–81) the rate had been about 1.5 per cent per annum.

The First World War added its own sombre impetus to this
downward trend. Between 1911 and 1921 the population of England and Wales increased by only 1.8 millions (and of Great
Britain as a whole by 1.9 millions, to 47.2 millions); the annual
rate of population increase in England and Wales in the first two
decades of the twentieth century was a mere 0.8 per cent.

But if we confine the discussion to the period before 1914, and
note that there is no evidence either of a decline in fertility or of a
decline in the frequency of sexual intercourse, we must conclude
that the major reason for the fall in the birth-rate, and hence in the
rate of population increase, was the growing popularity of birth
control. At the height of the industrial revolution, as we have
observed, a large number of children was a family asset. But by the
close of the nineteenth century the various prohibitions on child
labour and the enforcement of compulsory education prevented
children from contributing more than small amounts to the family
income; large families had become a financial liability.

It is possible that the falling away of religious observance played
a part here, by casting doubt on the view that all children were
God-given. At all events, during the 1870s there was a great deal
of public discussion of the notion of family planning. In 1877
Charles Bradlaugh and his disciple, Mrs Annie Besant, were prosecuted for republishing in England a pamphlet written in 1832 by
the American Charles Knowlton, which described how douching
after intercourse might prevent conception. Bradlaugh and Besant
were sentenced to be fined and imprisoned, punishments later
quashed on technical grounds. However, as invariably happens in
obscenity trials, the legal action boosted sales of the work, in this
case from 700 a year to 125,000 in three months. In the same year
that the trial took place the Malthusian League was formed, to
persuade medical practitioners to give their patients advice on
birth control; between 1879 and 1921 the League issued some

three million pamphlets and leaflets on the subject, and in 1913 produced its own practical guide, *Hygienic Methods of Family Limitation*.

By the time of the Great War, popular women's magazines were commonly carrying advertisements for contraceptives (mainly pessaries and douches) under the discreet title of cures for 'female ailments'. In Gorton, Manchester, in 1914 it was said that the subject of birth control was 'freely talked about and openly discussed in the workshops where any girls and young women work'.

Abstention from sexual activity remained the only form of family planning approved by the church; in 1916 the Anglican National Birth Rate Commission condemned all other methods. But the use of pessaries (often home-made) and the practice of *coitus interruptus* (withdrawal) were widespread even among the working classes. As a last resort, recourse could always be had to back-street abortionists (abortion remained a criminal offence until 1967) or to abortion-inducing medicaments; one estimate produced in 1914 alleged that 100,000 women each year took drugs to induce miscarriage. By 1914, too, reliable rubber contraceptive sheaths were to be had from barber shops and newspaper advertisements. The development of the rubber contraceptive was undoubtedly hastened by the Great War, when it became commonplace to issue sheaths to the troops to prevent the spread of venereal disease; in 1919 a reasonably efficient diaphragm was marketed for female use. The previous year, 1918, the botanist Dr Marie Stopes had published two books that were to revolutionise public attitudes towards family planning; *Married Love* was a guide to sex and marriage, while *Wise Parenthood* argued that family planning was essential to the maintenance of a happy marriage. Both books became best-sellers. In 1921 Dr Stopes opened Britain's first birth-control clinic, in London's Holloway Road, and in 1930 she and others formed the National Birth Control Council, later (1939) to become the Family Planning Association.

The evident widespread demand for birth-control advice, which Dr Stopes and her colleagues sought to satisfy, was, in its turn, the outcome of a much deeper change in attitudes towards the role of women in society. One may, of course, cite early proponents of greater equality between the sexes, such as Mary Wollstonecraft's *A Vindication of the Rights of Women* (1792), the socialist William Thompson's *Appeal of One Half of the Human Race* (1825) and

John Stuart Mill's *The Subjection of Women* (1869), and one may point to a few individual women who pursued successful careers during the nineteenth century, such as Harriet Martineau and Florence Nightingale. None the less, until the 1880s the view commonly held in Victorian society was that women were subordinate to men, and that their role must be confined within the domestic household. In part this view derived from prevailing theories concerning the effect which the physiology of women was supposed to have upon their intellectual capabilities. In 1896 the antifeminist James MacGrigor Allan instructed the Anthropological Society upon the subject of the menstrual period, as follows:

> At such times women are unfit for any great mental or physical labour. They suffer under a languor and depression which disqualify them from thought or action, and render it extremely doubtful how far they can be considered responsible beings while the crisis lasts . . . Michelet defines woman as an invalid. Such she emphatically is, as compared with man . . . In intellectual labour, man has surpassed, does now, and always will surpass woman, for the obvious reasons that nature does not periodically interrupt his thought and application.

The supposed physical and intellectual inferiority of women was reinforced by a battery of legal enactments. Upon marriage, a woman's property passed completely to her husband; divorce was impossible except by way of an expensive private Act of Parliament; and, most notably, the 1832 Reform Acts had specifically excluded women from their provisions. Although there was some change to the legal position of women during the second half of the nineteenth century, these changes were not always for the better. Married Women's Property Acts in 1870, 1882 and 1893 bestowed upon a wife the same rights in property as were enjoyed by an unmarried woman. The establishment of the Divorce Court through the passage of the Matrimonial Causes Act in 1857 made divorce easier (though it still remained very expensive), but in a most discriminatory fashion, for it was provided that whereas a wife might not obtain a divorce on the sole grounds of her husband's adultery, but was obliged, additionally, to prove cruelty or desertion, he could obtain a divorce on the grounds of her adultery.

This inequitable state of affairs (not rectified until 1923) was a perfect reflection of the double standard of morality in common usage at the time: a wife was expected to be sexually faithful to her husband, but his extra-marital liaisons might be overlooked. The same double standard also informed the Victorian attitude towards prostitution, which, broadly speaking, condemned wholeheartedly the women (generally working-class) who lived by it, but much less so the men (generally middle-class) who sought their services. Between 1865 and 1869 a series of Contagious Diseases Acts had attempted to check the spread of venereal disease in garrison and dockyard towns by permitting the arrest, enforced medical inspection and, if necessary, detention in hospital of infected prostitutes. Proposals to extend this system to the entire civilian population of the country led to the establishment of a Ladies' National Association for the Repeal of the Contagious Diseases Acts, in which the leading parts were played by the Liberal politician James Stansfeld and the formidable Mrs Josephine Butler. The Contagious Diseases Acts, declaimed Mrs Butler, 'violated the feeling of those whose sense of shame is not wholly lost', and she pointed out how unjust it was 'to punish the sex who are the victims of a vice, and leave unpunished the sex who are the main cause, both of the vice and its dreaded consequences'.

The repeal of the Acts, in 1886, following so soon upon the passage of the 1882 Married Women's Property Act (in the campaign for which Mrs Butler had also played a prominent role), marked a new phase in the political awareness of Victorian middle-class women. It has often been observed that the origins of the English feminist movement were bourgeois. The women who supported Mrs Butler were not working-class, but well-to-do mothers who, from the comfort of their drawing-rooms, contemplated with horror the prospect that their law-abiding daughters might be arrested by plain-clothes police officers and subjected to intimate medical examination. It is true that even in the mid-nineteenth century women were very often to be found working as shop assistants, clerks and elementary school teachers; but their remuneration was invariably lower than that of men in similar employments. The Victorian pioneers of equal rights for women were concerned, in the main, with entry into the professions, not with equality of opportunity in, say, the railway industry or as dock labourers. Elizabeth Garrett Anderson and

Sophia Jex-Blake fought long battles in order to get women admitted into medical schools. By the beginning of the twentieth century, daughters from middle-class families might pursue their studies at Oxford or Cambridge as well as London and provincial universities, and so enter the civil service, or become librarians, dentists, nurses, journalists or — above all — teachers; in 1851 there were over 70,000 women teachers, but by 1901 the figure had reached 172,000.

Politically, too, some progress had been made. Women who owned property in their own right had been able to claim for some time that, where the franchise depended upon a property qualification, they should be entitled to exercise it. But this argument excluded married women, who were supposed to be represented by and through their husbands. The right of single women to vote in municipal elections was granted in 1869, and propertied women were subsequently permitted to vote for School Boards (1870), Poor Law Guardians (1875), County Councils (1888) and Parish and District Councils (1894). Women were also elected to Schools Boards, Boards of Guardians and Parish and District Councils, though it was not until 1907 that the right of women to sit upon county councils was established in law.

The claim that women should be allowed to vote in municipal and national elections irrespective of what property they might possess was, in one sense, part of a much wider discussion of the basis upon which the franchise was to be granted; the triumph of person over property did not take place until 1918. But, quite apart from these considerations, it is clear that Victorian politicians drew a sharp distinction between the rights of women to be concerned with matters of local government, such as welfare provision, education and public health, and the right to vote for and sit in the Westminster Parliament. The former were considered to be legitimate matters of female concern, and merely an extension of the domestic role of womankind. But to deal with questions of high policy, of law-making, foreign affairs, the nation's finances — this was the preserve of men. The art critic and author John Ruskin had put the matter succinctly in his book *Sesame and Lilies* (1865): 'The man's work for his own home is to secure its maintenance, progress and defence; the woman's to secure its order, comfort and loveliness'. Idealised — one might almost say sanctified — by the Pre-Raphaelite painters, but at the same time exploited (as, for example, domestic out-workers) by large numbers of employers, the female population of Victorian Britain (there were 1,068 women for every 1,000 men in England and Wales according to the 1901 census) could not count even upon the Sovereign for support in the matter of the suffrage. Sir Theodore Martin recorded in 1908 how, in 1870, Queen Victoria had told him that she was:

> most anxious to enlist everyone who can speak or write to join in checking this mad, wicked folly of "Women's Rights," with all its attendant horrors, on which her poor feeble sex is bent, forgetting every sense of womanly feeling and propriety.

The campaign for women's suffrage began in earnest two years after Victoria's death, with the formation of the Women's Social and Political Union (WSPU) by the widow of a Manchester barrister, Mrs Emmeline Pankhurst, and her two daughters, Sylvia and Christabel. The late Mr Pankhurst had been active in Keir Hardie's Independent Labour Party, and it is worth noting that of all the political parties in Britain in the early-twentieth century only the Labour Party adopted women's suffrage as part of its programme, within the context of a wider demand for universal adult suffrage. The Conservative and Liberal parties were split on the issue. Against the straightforward egalitarian demand of the WSPU, that the parliamentary franchise be granted to women on the same terms as it was granted to men (a demand which must be distinguished from that for the enfranchisement of all adult women), the Unionist Sir Austen Chamberlain argued in 1910 that 'the sex of a woman is a disqualification in fact, and we had better continue so to regard it in law'. A Liberal MP, Julius Bertram, had told the Commons the previous year that 'so long as this country is constituted as the directing power of a huge Empire . . . it is of vast importance that our policy should be directed in the same masculine, virile way'. Asquith himself resorted to the delaying tactic which was a hallmark of his premiership; he feared enacting universal suffrage, for that would have brought into existence an electorate dominated by women, yet if only propertied women were enfranchised, the Conservatives would be sure to benefit.

Political considerations apart, however, the arguments of those who opposed women's suffrage were frankly sexist. In his autobiography (*Fate Has Been Kind*, 1943), Lord Pethwick-Lawrence put the matter succinctly:

The principal motive of men's opposition to women's suffrage was undoubtedly fear of the use to which women would put the vote if they got it. Men, it was said, were governed by reason, women by emotion. If once the franchise were thrown open to women, they would speedily obtain a majority control and force an emotional policy on the country to the detriment of the public weal.

The tactics of the WSPU did not help matters. At first these were largely constitutional, and were confined to the holding of political meetings and the heckling of politicians. But in 1909 a section of the movement took to destroying property, slashing paintings, arson, bombings and even, in the case of Emily Wilding Davison, who threw herself in front of the King's horse at the 1913 Derby, to martyrdom. Many suffragettes were imprisoned and, while in prison, went on hunger strike. In reply, the Liberal adminstration authorised force-feeding and, in 1913, passed the 'Cat and Mouse' Act, which allowed the Home Secretary to release hunger strikers whose health was in danger, and to order their re-arrest once they had recovered.

It is probably true that the response of the Asquith government to the suffragette campaign helped undermine public confidence in the ethical foundations of Liberalism itself. On the other hand, the resort to violence and illegality seemed to confirm the arguments of those who warned against female irrationality. Moreover, to concede the suffragettes' demand now might be taken as a capitulation to force. In December 1911 the Prime Minister declared that 'the grant of parliamentary suffrage to women would be a political mistake of a very disastrous kind'. The descent into illegality also split the suffragette movement. In 1912 Mrs Pethwick-Lawrence, one of the founders of the WSPU, withdrew in protest against the Pankhurst hegemony. Early in 1914 Emmeline and Christabel quarrelled with Sylvia, who had attempted to link the suffrage campaign to wider issues of socialist trade-unionism in the East End of London.

When the Great War broke out Sylvia spoke against it, but Christabel returned from exile in Paris to preach the dangers emanating from the Kaiser's Germany; most suffragettes agreed with her. One must not, however, suppose that the female suffrage movement suspended its activities during the hostilities. Rather, the war gave the feminist movement an unprecedented opportunity to meet the arguments of its detractors. The employment of women in industrial and commercial occupations had been growing before 1914; by the outbreak of war just over three million women were so employed, out of a total female population of 23.4 millions. But, as a result of the conscription of men to the fighting front (March 1916) many more women were drawn into occupations previously thought of as male preserves, such as engineering and munitions, transport and clerical work, and over 150,000 women joined auxiliary branches of the armed services. By 1918 the number of women employed in commerce and industry had reached almost five million. Although many of these lost their jobs once the troops came home, we know that between the censuses of 1911 and 1921 the number of employed females rose by approximately 230,000.

More important from the point of view of the suffragettes was the fact that the wartime experience proved that women were as capable as men of performing even the most arduous tasks. Middle-class women were liberated from the cloying domesticity prescribed by pre-war social convention, while working-class women were able, albeit temporarily, to forsake the badly paid occupations of sweated labour and domestic service for better jobs in munitions factories; during the war years the number of domestic servants in Britain fell by a quarter. During the war, too, women earned wages undreamt of before 1914; what is more, with so many husbands conscripted, many women were in charge of the family wage-packet and budget for the first time.

A revolution in social values had taken place, and its existence was cautiously recognised by the passage of two pieces of legislation in 1918. The Representation of the People Act lowered the voting age for men to 21 and gave the vote in parliamentary elections to women of 30 years of age and over who were or whose husbands were local government electors, or who possessed a university degree or its equivalent. In this way six million women were enfranchised. However, women were not given the vote on the same terms as men until 1928, when the female voting age was reduced to 21. In November 1918, in time for the general election that was about to take place, the Lloyd George Coalition legislated to allow women to stand for Parliament. The honour of being returned as the first woman MP belonged to the gun-toting Sinn Fein member Constance Gore-Booth (Countess Markievicz) who, following the policy of her party, declined to take her seat;

the first woman to sit in Parliament was Nancy Lady Astor, returned at the Plymouth (Sutton) by-election a year later.

The general election of 14 December 1918 was no less remarkable for the fact that it saw the emergence as a separate electoral force in British politics of the Labour Party, whose 2.4 million votes represented approximately 22 per cent of the total votes cast. Whereas the First World War had witnessed the breaking of the Liberal Party it had been the making of the organised Labour movement. In December 1910 the Labour Party had polled less than 372,000 votes and had returned only 42 MPs; 13 years later (6 December 1923) its total vote was higher than that of the Liberal Party (4.4 as against 4.3 millions) and its parliamentary representation — 191 MPs — enabled it to form a minority government. The rise of Labour, no less than the advances of the feminist movement, represented a complete break with Victorian norms. But in order to understand how these events were made possible, we must examine the Labour movement in the closing decades of the nineteenth century.

In the previous chapter we briefly noted the spread of socialist ideas in Britain in the 1880s. Marxism was brought to the attention of the British public by a most untypical enthusiast, the Cambridge-educated stockbroker and ex-radical Tory Henry Mayers Hyndman, who had read a French translation of *Das Kapital* while on a business trip to the USA. In 1881 Hyndman published *England for All*, in which he sought to popularise Marxist economics, and in the same year he formed a Democratic Federation, designed to bring together London radical clubs whose members might wish to campaign against government repression in Ireland and for more working-class representation at Westminster. Early in 1884 the Federation became openly Marxist, and was renamed the Social-Democratic Federation (SDF).

The SDF never became a 'mass' movement. In the year of its inception it had about 400 members in London and little influence elsewhere, though branches were established in Lancashire, Edinburgh and Glasgow. Its importance lay in the fact that it attracted and educated a new generation of socialist activists, such as the artist and poet William Morris and the engineers' leaders John Burns and Tom Mann. In 1885 the SDF suffered the first of a series of splits that within three years or so were to relegate it to the fringes of the Labour movement. Hyndman's growing

addiction to violence (he had been at the head of riotous demon-
strations in Hyde Park in February 1886 and at Trafalgar Square in
November 1887) alienated middle- and working-class radicals
alike, but it was his dictatorial nature and his total lack of political
realism that ultimately told against him. At the general election of
1885 he accepted money from Conservative Central Office ('Tory
Gold') to fight the solidly middle-class seats of Hampstead and
Kennington, which the Tories were certain to win, as they did.

This adulteration of socialist principles outraged Hyndman's
colleagues. Morris left the SDF to form the Socialist League, and
took with him the newspaper *Justice*, which was his personal
property; he was soon joined by Marx's daughter, Eleanor, and
her lover Edward Aveling. In 1888 Burns and Mann also walked
out of the SDF. In company with Harry Champion, a former
Army officer who had been one of Hyndman's staunchest
supporters, they carried the socialist message into the London
docks, with hopes of results more practical than Hyndman could
ever have achieved. The Socialist League soon fell into anarchist
hands. But Burns, Mann and Champion nurtured the belief that
their missionary work, if successful, might lead to important political initiatives within the Labour movement. Indeed, Champion at
once launched a new journal, the *Labour Elector,* to advocate the
establishment of a separate political party to represent the working-classes in Parliament. It was clear that Hyndman could never
lead such a party, and that the Fabian Society (also founded 1884)
was exactly what its name implied, a fellowship of evolutionary
social reformers and a radical 'think-tank', but one without any
parliamentary pretensions. Instead Champion's call was taken up
by the first secretary of the Scottish Miners' Federation, James
Keir Hardie.

At this time, as we have seen, the representation of working
people at Westminster meant 'Lib-Labism' — the election of
moderate trade-union officials, like Henry Broadhurst, as Liberal
MPs. Hardie could see no future in such an arrangement, partly
because it could never have resulted in the triumph of socialist
policies but, more pragmatically, because a Liberal party
dominated by Gladstone and his Irish preoccupations was finding
it extremely difficult to deliver radical social reforms. Hardie also
believed that, given the right conditions, working-class electors
(which meant, principally, the aristocracy of labour) could be
induced to vote in sufficient numbers for a socialist candidate to

ensure victory. In 1892 he put up at West Ham South, a constituency of dockers, gas workers and general labourers, and fought and won (though without having to face Liberal opposition) on a platform of land nationalisation, the statutory eight-hour day, and municipal workshops to combat unemployment. The following January, at Bradford, Hardie summoned a conference of those interested in order to bring into being the Independent Labour Party (ILP). Its programme was blatantly socialist: the use of the taxation system to redistribute wealth; comprehensive welfare provision; and the collective ownership of all land, industry and of the means of distribution and exchange.

Hardie had been fortunate in the circumstances of his election, which had come at a time of great ferment within the trade-union movement. The social composition of West Ham made it peculiarly sensitive to the changes that were afoot. The most dramatic of these, and the one which most impressed itself upon contemporary observers, was the spread of trade-union activity among unskilled workers. This tendency had been observed in the strike of London matchgirls in 1888, which Mrs Besant had helped plan, and further evidence of its progress was provided by the organisation the following year of the gas stokers in the National Union of Gas Workers and General Labourers, which was able, without recourse to strike action, to win the eight-hour day. But it reached a new level of public awareness at the time of the great London dock strike, in the summer of 1889, when a dockers' leader, Ben Tillett, joined forces with Burns, Mann, Champion, Eleanor Marx, Annie Besant and — an unlikely but most powerful ally — Cardinal Manning, to organise the mass of casual dock labourers in London in a demand for the 'dockers' tanner': an increase of wages from fivepence to sixpence per hour. The demand was conceded. Out of this five-week struggle, which aroused very strong public sympathy, was born the Dock, Wharf, Riverside and General Labourers Union, of which Tillett became full-time secretary and Mann the president. By 1890 it boasted 40,000 members, while the Gas Workers, organised by a child of the SDF, Will Thorne, had no less than 60,000.

Such were the beginnings of 'New Unionism'. But if we wish to grasp the essential characteristics of this movement we must look beyond the narratives of 1888–90 and, indeed, beyond the New Unions themselves. New Unionism was nothing less than a rebellion against the *laissez-faire* philosophy with which the mid-

Victorian trade-union leadership was saturated. This philosophy, which emphasised the importance of the sickness benefit and the emigration fund rather than that of the strike fund and political agitation, appeared to have served the trade-union movement well in the years of plenty. Now that the rate of economic growth was slowing down, and with unemployment rising, it seemed less relevant, and was, in truth, viewed with scepticism by the mass of unskilled workers, who had never had the advantages of a strong trade-union system behind them.

Yet the new mood of militancy originated from within this system, and was itself a product of the prosperity that now seemed to be on the wane. When manufacturers sought to adjust to falling prices by cutting wage rates, workers accustomed to a certain standard of living naturally became resentful. This resentment was compounded by the fact that levels of economic expectation had risen, especially with regard to the length of the working day. By the 1870s many employees enjoyed a working day of about nine hours, and looked forward to the state-enforced eight-hour day. This became generally accepted as a legitimate goal of trade-union activity, even though the old-guard trade-union leadership was openly critical of any legislative interference with the hours of work of adult males. At the 1892 Trades Union Congress Charles Fenwick, a Northumberland miner and a Liberal MP, who had succeeded Henry Broadhurst as secretary of the TUC's Parliamentary Committee, was heavily criticised for having failed to support the eight-hour day in the Commons; in 1894 he voted against the second reading of a Miners' Eight Hours Bill.

The economic and Social fatalism of the old guard was revealed at its starkest when applied to the relationship between prices and wages. In the mining communities of Durham, Northumberland and Yorkshire, for example, there was a remarkable identity of views between mineowners and mineworkers, that 'prices should rule wages' — that is, that wages should be linked to the selling price of coal rather than to any consideration of the standard of living. In the Northumberland and South Wales coalfields intricate 'sliding scales' had been developed, to make this linkage absolutely formal: take-home pay varied according to the state of the market.

This struck the Webbs as particularly amoral. 'We see [they wrote] the sturdy leaders of many Trade Union battles gradually and insensibly accepting the capitalist axiom that wages must necessarily fluctuate according to the capitalists' profits, and even with the variation of market prices.' As wage rates fell between 1870 and 1880 (from a little over nine shillings a day to just over four shillings for a Northumberland miner), the sliding scale came under attack from within the mining unions, whose members were increasingly attracted by proposals to restrict output, through a reduction of working hours, in order to maintain the selling price of coal at a level that would preserve wage rates from further erosion. In 1889 representatives of many mining unions met at Newport, Monmouthshire, and agreed to form themselves into the Miners' Federation of Great Britain, which was from the outset committed to a policy of collective wage increases (to prevent coalfields being played off against each other) and the statutory eight-hour day, and which was committed also to the abolition of the sliding scale.

Here, therefore, a number of policies characteristic of New Unionism — the statutory regulation of working hours, industry-wide wage bargaining, and an end to the production free-for-all — were to be observed coming to maturity within 'established' trade unions. The railway industry provides another example. The Amalgamated Society of Railway Servants had been founded in 1871 on the initiative of the brewer and Liberal MP for Derby, M.T. Bass. In its early years it never succeeded in attracting into membership more than about 17,000 of the 200,000 or so railway employees in Britain; it was a glorified friendly-society that set its face firmly against trade-union action. This gentility evaporated in 1888, following the dismissal by the Midland Railway of 189 railwaymen who had gone on unofficial strike. At its annual general meeting that year, the Society resolved to alter its rules to permit strike action, a move in the direction of industrial militancy that clearly anticipated the New Unionism of the 1890s.

The philosophy underlying New Unionism was much more important than the 'new' unions themselves. Born in the euphoria that had accompanied the London dock strike, the new 'general' unions, catering for the unskilled as well as the skilled, and intent upon breaking through the craft sectionalism of the working classes, enjoyed a brief moment of glory and then faded away as the depression deepened after 1891 and as employers were emboldened to resist radical demands. The dockers' union proved unable to attract the stevedores into membership, and its hold upon the London docks was broken by the shipowners scarcely a year after its great victory over them; by 1910 its membership had fallen to 10,000. Will Thorne's Gas Workers' Union also survived, and put down new roots in provincial centres; but by 1892 it had less than 23,000 members remaining on its books. In order to retain their memberships the New Unions had to offer precisely the sort of social benefit schemes that had been the hallmark of the older craft unions. It is perfectly true that a marked increase in total trade-union membership took place in the 1890s, so that by 1900 about two million workers were union-organised. But of this total the New Unions accounted for — at most — ten per cent.

The true measure of the impact of New Unionism is to be found in the attitude of mind which it represented. If strike action was to be successful it needed to be total: there had to be picketing and there had to be a closed shop. New Unionism was, in the words of George Howell (1902) 'an aggressive militant unionism, which said, not *let them* all come, but *you must* all come, into the union'. Tillett and Mann were utterly frank in their desire to enforce the closed shop, and so make the strike weapon omnipotent. But, in so doing, two risks were run. The first was that there might be a backlash from more traditionally-minded trade unions; the second, that employers might adopt counter-measures, and be supported by sections of the working classes. George Shipton, secretary of the London Trades Council, warned in June 1890 that, 'If the men support an appeal to force, to compel their fellows to belong to a union, the employers are equally justified in appealing to force to prevent men from joining a union'.

A quarter-century of bitter and unprecedented industrial strife was inaugurated in August 1890, when shipowners, meeting in London, decided to form the Shipping Federation, whose avowed purpose was to break the National Amalgamated Sailors' and Firemen's Union by issuing 'tickets' of employment only to those seamen who pledged themselves to carry out their agreements whether or not the remainder of the crew were union men. In this way strikes, like that in London in the winter of 1890–91 and at Hull in 1893, were defeated without difficulty, and the ticket system, having proved itself so successfully, did not disappear until 1912, when the Liberal government announced that it was no longer prepared to give blacklegs unconditional protection.

Almost three years after the establishment of the Shipping Federation, on 16 May 1893, there was formed at Aldgate, in London's East End, an organisation whose existence posed an even greater threat to New Unionism, because its founders all had impeccable trade-union credentials. The National Free Labour Association was a formal expression of opposition by anti-socialist working men to New Unionism in general and, in particular, to the way in which (as it appeared to them) Tillett, Mann and others were exploiting the plight of the unemployed to further their own dogmatic ends. The leading figure in the Association was William Collison, a former trade-union organiser in east London, bitterly opposed to the closed shop, who regarded strike-breaking as a perfectly legitimate means of fighting the 'tyranny' of New Unionism.

In the 20 years following its inauguration (so Collison claimed in his autobiography, published in 1913), the Association had 'fought and been successful in no less than six hundred and eighty-two pitched battles with aggressive Trade Unions in different parts of the United Kingdom'. Most of these interventions appear to have been small-scale, mainly involving skilled or semi-skilled workers in dockland. Collison's value to the craft unions was very limited; the use of his 'free labourers' by engineering firms during the great lock-out of 1897, for example, had a minimal impact on the dispute. But in the year 1900 the National Free Labour Association scored a momentous victory. Collison had just been asked to organise a supply of railwaymen for a strike anticipated by the directors of the Great Eastern Railway, when a dispute broke out on the Taff Vale Railway in south Wales. The free labourers were transferred there instead, but not before each one of them had signed a contract to enter into the service of the Taff Vale company. When officials of the Amalgamated Society of Railway Servants tried to turn back Collison's men, and to persuade them not to break the strike, the company sought damages from the union for inducement to breach of contract. After a series of protracted legal hearings the Taff Vale Railway (December 1902) was awarded compensation amounting to £23,000, plus costs.

The impact of the Taff Vale judgement upon the trade-union movement was profound. In the decade following the 1889 London dock strike a passionate controversy had taken place within the movement, not merely over the industrial tactics advocated by New Unionists, but also concerning the socialism that underpinned the New Unionist approach to labour questions. For New Unionism was primarily a political movement which declared that trade unions had purposes which far transcended the immediate goals of wage bargaining and improvements in conditions of work. In *The 'New' Trades Unionism* (1890) Mann and Tillett declared:

> the real difference between the 'new' and the 'old' is, that those who belong to the latter, and delight in being distinct from the policy endorsed by the 'new', do so because they do not recognise, as we do, that it is the work of *the trade unionist to stamp out poverty from the land.* They do not contend, as we contend, that existing unions should exert themselves to extend organisations where they as yet do not exist. . . . Clannishness in trade matters must be superseded by a cosmopolitan spirit . . . Our ideal *is a Co-operative Commonwealth.*

As the New Unions themselves suffered defeat and underwent transformation, the New Unionists placed ever greater emphasis upon this political dimension: if industrial activity could not better the lot of the poor and the underprivileged, then political solutions must be tried. The result was a series of attempts to push the trade-union movement into espousing socialist ideals, but these attempts were fiercely resisted by the old leadership, most of whom were Liberal and a few of whom (such as James Mawdsley, General Secretary of the Amalgamated Association of Operative Cotton Spinners) were Conservatives.

Socialism was resisted for a number of reasons. The atheism of many of its proponents repelled those trade unionists who were committed Christians. The idea that the unions might create for themselves an independent political role, as Continental trade unions were doing, seemed to be a recipe for protracted internal strife. The egalitarianism upon which socialists placed so much emphasis was not generally supported. We have already noticed the deeply ingrained hierarchical structure of the Victorian working classes. Differentials were highly regarded. Besides, a levelling-up in conditions of employment for some groups might mean a worsening of the terms of employment of others: it was for this reason that the statutory eight-hour day was fiercely contested in some quarters at the TUC. Finally, socialism preached state intervention, and, therefore, a strengthening of the organs of central government. Many trade unionists regarded such a prospect as highly damaging to working-class interests, for the power of the state was a double-edged weapon: it could be used to better the lot of the poor, but it could also be used (and had been, frequently, since 1799) to restrict trade-union activity.

The fortunes of the ILP at the 1895 general election, when all 28 candidates, including Hardie himself, were defeated, seemed to bolster these arguments, by apparently demonstrating that working-class electors saw no need for independent labour representation in Parliament. Anti-socialist forces within the trade-union movement at once exploited these reverses, by persuading the 1895 TUC to agree to rule changes designed to curb socialist influence; the 'block' vote was introduced (one vote per thousand members) and it was stipulated that henceforth TUC delegates must either be working within their respective trades or be permanent officials of their unions. The 'professional socialist', offering his services to a trade union in return for the right to become a delegate, was therefore excluded henceforth.

Hardie was not only out of Parliament; he was out of the TUC as well. 'The Unions', he exclaimed, 'must be won.' And won they were, but the credit lay with the capitalists, not the socialists. The employers' counter-attack against New Unionism was conducted at several levels. Alongside the strike-breaking strategy there was a legal offensive, one object of which was to push to whatever limits the judges might set the civil liabilities of trade unions, liabilities with which Disraeli had been careful not to interfere. At the same time, employers asked the courts to intervene in the conduct of industrial disputes where it seemed possible that violence might otherwise erupt. In Temperton *v.* Russell (1893) the Court of Appeal held that a third party could sue a union for damages alleged to have resulted from industrial action. In Lyons *v.* Wilkins (1896–9) the Court of Appeal supported the decision of a lower court to grant an injunction to prevent picketing, in spite of the apparent provisions of the 1875 Conspiracy Act.

While Lyons *v.* Wilkins was being pursued through the legal machinery, the Engineering Employers' Federation inflicted (July 1897-January 1898) a most humiliating defeat upon Britain's premier union, the Amalgamated Society of Engineers, by imposing a national lock-out to counter the union's demand for the eight-hour day and its opposition to technical change. By 1899, therefore, the feeling had become widespread within the trade-union movement that the effectiveness of industrial action had been heavily circumscribed, and that this effectiveness could only be restored by a political initiative. The Conservative party was now so very different from that over which Disraeli had presided that, evidently, not much sympathy could be expected from it. The Liberal party was in disarray; moreover, it had become clear that (often under the influence of Nonconformist employers) local Liberal associations were reluctant to adopt working men as parliamentary candidates. Herbert Gladstone, the future Liberal Chief Whip, admitted in January 1892 that, 'The long and short of it is that the constituencies, for social, financial, and trade reasons are extremely slow to adopt Labour candidates'. In 1894 T.R. Threlfall, secretary of the Labour Electoral Association, confessed that it was 'a waste of time to advise the working classes to attend and make the [Liberal] caucus what they want it to be. The fact is they distrust it — they regard it as a middle-class machine . . . it is too narrow and too much hampered with class prejudice to be a reflex of the expanding democratic and labour sentiment.'

But the reluctance of the Labour movement as a whole to take the route so eagerly commended by Hardie may be gauged from the fact that the famous resolution put forward by the Railway Servants at the 1899 TUC, asking the Parliamentary Committee to convene a conference 'of all co-operative, socialistic, trade union, and other working organisations . . . to devise ways and means for securing the return of an increased number of labour members to the next parliament' was only approved by 546,000 votes to 434,000. The conference, which took place in London on 27 February 1900, decided to establish, through the instrumentality of a Labour Representation Committee (LRC), 'a distinct Labour group in Parliament, who shall have their own whips and agree upon their policy, which must embrace a readiness to cooperate with any party which for the time being may be engaged in promoting legislation in the direct interests of labour, and be equally ready to associate themselves with any party in opposing measures having an opposite tendency'.

At the October 1900 general election two candidates were returned to Parliament under LRC auspices: Hardie for Merthyr Tydfil and Richard Bell, Secretary of the Railway Servants, for Derby. Bell was really a Liberal, and had chosen to fight a seat where the votes of railwaymen were very significant. Hardie had been returned for a constituency dominated by the mining vote. However, Ben Pickard, the President of the Miners' Federation, was an anti-socialist and strongly opposed the use of miners' money to return non-miners to the House of Commons; the

Federation did not affiliate to the Labour Party until 1909. Most other unions were, to begin with, deeply suspicious of the LRC; in the first year of its existence only 29 per cent of all unions affiliated to the TUC agreed to support it. Lib-Labism was still a healthy animal, with plenty of trade-union admirers. But the future of the LRC was assured by the Taff Vale case and its awesome implications for industrial action. James Ramsay MacDonald, the LRC's secretary, told the trade-union movement that, 'The recent decisions of the House of Lords . . . should convince the unions that a labour party in Parliament is an immediate necessity'. Within the space of two years the proportion of TUC-affiliated unions supporting the LRC rose to over 56 per cent.

A number of by-election successes for LRC-sponsored candidates (especially the victory of Arthur Henderson, an ex-Liberal, in a three-cornered contest at Barnard Castle, in July 1903) convinced the Liberal leadership that an accommodation with the new party was highly desirable, if only to avoid splitting the anti-Conservative vote at the next general election. Under the terms of a secret agreement concluded between MacDonald and Herbert Gladstone in August, the LRC was to be given a free run against the Conservatives in 30 seats and, in return, would support Liberal candidates in the other seats and a Liberal government should one be voted into office. At the 1906 election 29 LRC-sponsored candidates were, in this way, elected to Parliament. The Labour Party had been born.

In trying to understand the relationship between the Labour and Liberal parties in the period 1906–14 it is important not to be influenced by hindsight. We know that the MacDonald-Gladstone pact bore some responsibility for future Liberal decline. But in August 1903, before Tariff Reform had crippled the Balfour government, the pact seemed full of common sense, and certainly saved the Liberals a great deal of money when the general election was called. We know that a major element in the destruction of the Asquithian Liberal party was the Great War. Liberalism was simply not equipped to fight a 'total war', in which state control of society and interference with individual liberties reached unprecedented levels, and during which conscription had to be introduced. Such policies were the exact opposite of what pre-war Liberalism had stood for. Asquith's indecisive leadership was blamed for the deterioration in the military situation on the western front in 1915–16, and his downfall (December 1916) and replacement by Lloyd George marked the very death throes of the Liberal state. But in 1906 these events would have seemed a piece of science fiction. The Liberal party had won, in parliamentary terms, a magnificent victory at the polls; its future seemed totally assured. The 29 Labour MPs were no more than a pressure group destined, for the time being, to dance to the Liberal tune.

The early Parliamentary Labour Party (PLP) had no distinctive ideology, save that of representing and furthering working-class interests. Hardie was its first chairman (1906–7), but his election to this office was little more than a gesture; no-one understood better than he how suspicious the trade unions were of socialist influence. A number of the Labour MPs depended on Liberal votes in the constituencies they represented; Richard Bell had already (1904) defected to the Liberal party. The affiliation of the miners' MPs in 1909 underpinned the Liberal traditions within the PLP, and these traditions were strengthened further when MacDonald became chairman in 1911. A former Liberal, MacDonald had developed a 'socialist' philosophy which was highly emotional and which appealed to moral sentiment rather than to intellectual conviction. His views were certainly neither revolutionary nor utopian; they were, on the contrary, heavily elitist, not to say patronising:

> Socialism [he wrote in 1911] is not to be found in the slummy and most miserable quarters in towns, but in those quarters upon which the sun of prosperity manages to shine. It is the skilled artisan, the trade unionist, the member of the friendly society, the young workman who reads and thinks, who are the recruits to the army of socialism.
>
> (*The Socialist Movement*)

and in 1920 he observed:

> the growth of the Labour Party has been owing to the rise within Labour organisations of an intellectual class of work-men.
>
> (*A Policy for the Labour Party*)

The early Labour Party behaved as the political arm of the trade-union movement — for this is what it was. It was concerned almost exclusively with the redress of trade-union grievances: the reversal of the Taff Vale decision (1906); the establishment of the eight-hour day in the coal mines (1908); the creation of wage boards for sweated industries (Trade Boards Act, 1909). But the enactment of these reforms was not really due to the Labour Party. They were major ingredients in the 'New' Liberalism which the 1906 election victory had brought to power. The reversal in 1913 of the 1909 Osborne judgement that had prevented trade unions using their funds to sponsor parliamentary candidates was a more clear-cut case of Labour influence on Asquith's government. The Coal Mines Minimum Wage Act (1912) was hurriedly passed in response to the calling of a national coal strike by the Miners' Federation.

The Labour Party could, of course, do no other than support, to a greater or lesser extent, the major welfare reforms enacted by the Liberal administrations, such as the provision of school meals (1906; a measure that originated from the Labour benches) and school medical inspections (1907), the establishment of a modest scheme of old-age pensions (1908) and of labour exchanges (1909), as well as the National Insurance Act of 1911, which gave very modest financial help (on a contributory basis, of which some sections of the Labour movement disapproved) to the sick and the unemployed. Labour gave wholehearted support to the Liberal government following the refusal of the House of Lords to pass Lloyd George's 1909 budget. Lloyd George proposed to meet some of the escalating defence costs (especially in respect of the provision of 'Dreadnought' battleships) by raising £16 millions in new taxes: a super-tax on incomes over £5,000 per annum; a tax of 20 per cent on the 'unearned increment' in land values; and taxes on mineral royalties and on undeveloped land. These proposals had never been placed before the electorate and the Conservative peers argued that, therefore, the Liberal government could not claim a specific mandate to put them on the statute book. For Asquith, however, the issue was very different. He observed on the second reading of the Parliament Bill in February 1911 that:

> the assumption which lies at the root of representative government [is] that the House of Commons, itself a product of popular election, is, under normal conditions, a trustworthy organ and mouthpiece of the popular will.

This was a view of the constitution with which (in spite of the limited franchise then in operation) Labour was bound to agree.

But it struck a disconcerting note with many middle-class voters, who were distinctly uneasy about the prospect of an elected dictatorship.

It was in order to meet these fears that Asquith consented to the insertion of a provision in the Parliament Bill allowing the House of Lords to exercise a power of total veto over any Bill passed by the Commons to postpone the date of a general election beyond the statutory term, which was reduced from seven years to five. The Lords lost their power to reject 'Money' Bills, and could henceforth only delay other Bills for two years. But the Parliament Act did not cover delegated legislation (rules and regulations made by Ministers under powers given by Parliament), which the Lords may also reject outright. In fact, the Upper House still retained, after 1911, very formidable constitutional authority. Moreover, it had won its original point twice over. Asquith was forced to call a general election in January 1910, on the question of the budget, and another, the following December, on the question of the Lords' veto powers. Balfour's announcement (November 1910) that, if returned to power, he would not introduce tariffs without a referendum, reassured many Conservative free-traders. As compared with January 1906, in December 1910 the Liberals suffered a net loss of 107 seats, and the Conservatives and Liberal Unionists registered a net gain of 118 seats; the average percentage vote per opposed Liberal candidate fell from 52.6 to 49.5 per cent. Asquith governed thereafter only with Irish Nationalist and Labour support.

But if the elections of 1910 witnessed a severe electoral reverse for the Liberal party, they amounted to a disaster for Labour, in several respects. First, although the Labour vote rose, as between January 1906 and December 1910, from 5.9 to 7.1 per cent of the total votes cast, and although the number of Labour MPs increased from 29 to 42, this was only because of the accession of the miners. In December 1910 Labour polled 154,388 votes fewer than in 1906 — a drop of 29 per cent. In real terms not only had no headway been made, but such electoral successes as were forthcoming were due almost entirely to the continuation of the electoral pact with the Liberals. Not one of the 40 Labour MPs returned in January 1910 had been opposed by an official Liberal candidate, and only two of the 42 returned in December had been so opposed. By August 1914 the Labour contingent at Westminster had been reduced to 36, as a result of by-election losses; three of these had occurred in mining seats, while two miners' MPs were expelled from the party for persistently ignoring the Labour whip.

Secondly, given the political facts of life at Westminster after December 1910, and the parlous state of Labour finances (which made its leaders most unwilling to face yet another general election so soon) the PLP had, perforce, to support Asquith's administration, but in an atmosphere very different from that of 1906. The Irish Nationalists, as the price for their support, demanded the enactment of Home Rule, which the Lords could now only delay. A Bill to re-establish an Irish Parliament was introduced in 1912 and became law two years later (but was suspended on the outbreak of war). 'The conspiracy of Home Rule', as Sir Edward Carson called it, led directly to the Ulster Revolt and the formation in Ireland of two opposing private armies, Carson's Ulster Volunteers and the Nationalists' Irish Volunteers.

Under Balfour the Conservative party had made unashamed use of the House of Lords to thwart the will of the House of Commons. Now the Conservatives sided, naturally, with the Ulstermen and encouraged armed resistance to the will of Parliament. Bonar Law declared that he could imagine 'no length of resistance to which Ulster will go, which I shall not be ready to support and in which they will not be supported by the overwhelming majority of the British people'. This recognition of the unpopularity of forcing Ulster to accept Home Rule was soundly based. Although Labour supported Home Rule, it was not popular with all sections of the British working classes (particularly on Merseyside and Clydeside) and its immediate relevance to purely working-class needs was obscure. No less peripheral was the disestablishment of the Anglican Church in Wales (1914), a measure long sought after by Welsh Nonconformists but which was also delayed (for a year) by the Upper House.

For the Labour movement the central feature of the years 1910–13 was the industrial unrest, marked by major disputes on the railways and in the docks and the coalfields; in 1912 alone over 40 million working days were lost through industrial stoppages. We should discount at once any suggestion that syndicalism — which advocated the employment of political strikes in order to overthrow the parliamentary system and replace it by the rule of industrial unions — played anything more than a minor role in this time of troubles, even in south Wales, where syndicalist ideas did indeed take temporary root. Each of the disputes had its own specific origins: payments for working 'abnormal' seams in south Wales (1910–11); recognition of railway unions by the companies (1911); rates of pay for seamen, dockers and transport workers (1911–12); minimum wage levels in the mining industry (1912).

But it is surely no coincidence that all these strikes occurred following and not during the period of high unemployment which had reached its peak in 1908, when it had stood at 7.8 per cent of the total workforce, nor that the unrest began after real wages had ceased to rise. In 1910 real wages stood at 98 per cent of their level the previous year, and in the years 1911–13 at 97 per cent of their 1909 value; only in 1914 was the 1909 level restored. The period 1911–13 saw renewed growth and self-confidence within the trade-union movement; membership of unions rose from 1.7 to 2.7 millions. Yet trade-union membership of the Labour Party stagnated at around 1.6 millions, partly, no doubt, owing to the operation of the Osborne judgement, but also from a feeling of frustration at the inability of Labour in Parliament to achieve politically the victories that had to be won on the picket lines. To be sure, the use of troops and the shooting dead of strikers did nothing to enhance the reputation of the Liberal administration with the working classes. But the prospects of betterment through parliamentary activity seemed to be no brighter.

The experience of the First World War marked a watershed in the history both of organised labour and of the Labour Party. Like the Liberals, Labour was divided over the morality of the war; its pacifist wing, which was particularly strong within the ILP, argued not merely that war was wrong but that the war which the British and German working classes were being asked to fight was an imperialist one and therefore contrary to socialist principles. However, when it became clear that the British workers were inclined to follow General Kitchener rather than James Keir Hardie, the Labour Party made a tactical volte-face: now that the war had begun, Labour would not obstruct the war effort, but would work to secure peace at the earliest possible moment, and would use the opportunities provided by the war to further working-class interests. MacDonald's pacifist convictions would not allow him to remain chairman of the PLP. He resigned and was succeeded by Arthur Henderson who, in May 1915, joined the Coalition government which Asquith had been obliged to form following a national outcry over shortages of ammunition.

In this way the war, which brought about the downfall of the country's last Liberal administration, made it possible for the Labour Party to share for the first time in the government of the country. The war also benefited the trade-union movement. The agreement of the TUC (in July 1915) to forsake the strike weapon for the duration of hostilities and to accept compulsory arbitration and the 'dilution' of labour (that is, the introduction of semi-skilled and female labour into jobs hitherto the preserve of craftsmen) did lead to an alienation of the 'shop floor' from the trade-union leadership, and to the growth in importance of the shop stewards. Rank-and-file militancy was especially in evidence among the railwaymen, the metalworkers and the south Wales miners, who in 1915 conducted a successful strike for a wage increase. In May 1917 the Clyde Workers' Committee led a national strike against dilution of labour. In the winter of 1917–18, fired by the example of Bolshevik Russia, munitions and engineering workers agitated against the removal of craftsmen's exemptions from conscription, but also for a peace with Germany without annexations or indemnities.

It is tempting to see in this undoubted militancy the seeds of a revolutionary working-class movement in Britain. Seeds there may well have been, created by inflation (the cost of living rose by about 27 per cent each year between 1914 and 1920) and encouraged into growth by legislative measures, such as the 1915 Munitions Act, which had as their avowed purpose the direction of labour by the state. Yet, if the plant did begin to put down roots, it was destroyed by the very war which had called it into existence. Wartime collectivism witnessed many of the changes for which socialists and trade unionists had agitated in vain during the pre-war years of peace. The railways were taken under state control in 1914. The gold standard was suspended. All shipping came under state control in December 1916, as did the coal industry early the following year. There were stringent import controls, to ensure the optimum use of scarce maritime resources. As Chancellor of the Exchequer, 1915–16, Reginald McKenna introduced import duties, made substantial increases in the rates of income tax and super tax, and brought in an excess profits tax. Basic food commodities, such as bread and potatoes, were subjected to price control (1917) and later rationed.

Class barriers were not removed. However, there was somewhat less inequality of wealth at the end of the war than at the beginning. During the war wage rates roughly doubled, while the average working week fell from 55 to 48 hours. Penalised by high taxation and death duties, many landowners were forced to sell up. At the same time the peerage was diluted by Lloyd George's sale of honours to self-made businessmen willing to contribute to his personal political funds. In order to run the war the government needed professional managers and bureaucrats; between the censuses of 1911 and 1921 the proportion of the working population represented by those in receipt of salaries rose from 12 to 22 per cent.

Above all, the common experience of war, and especially of conscription and bereavement, had led to a greater democratic spirit. Lloyd George had recognised and caught this mood. Although his accession to the premiership had been the result of careful and calculated manoeuvering, in which he had allied with the very Conservatives whom he had denounced during the constitutional crisis of a few years previously, there was no denying that Lloyd George had the very qualities of leadership, organisation, energy and innovation which were so desperately needed at the time. His former Cabinet colleague R.B. Haldane observed that:

> Lloyd George cares nothing for precedents and knows no principles, but he has fire in his belly, and that is what we want.

Yet, in becoming Prime Minister as he did, Lloyd George paid a penalty which was to lead to his ultimate downfall. He permanently alienated a section of the Liberal party, loyal to Asquith and thoroughly disgusted at the Welshman's lack of scruple. At the same time, Lloyd George was forced to distance himself from the Labour Party, a development symbolised in his refusal to allow Henderson to attend the peace conference which neutral socialists had called at Stockholm in 1917. Henderson resigned from the government (11 August), became reconciled with MacDonald and other Labour pacifists, and set about redesigning the party on a mass basis and with distinct domestic and foreign policies. Lloyd George had also become a prisoner of the Conservatives. Bonar Law spoke frankly when he declared, at a Conservative party meeting in November 1918:

> By our own action we have made Mr. Lloyd George the flag-
> bearer of the very principles upon which we should appeal to the

country. It is not his Liberal friends, it is the Unionist Party which has made him Prime Minister, and made it possible for him to do the great work that has been done by this government.

For the moment Lloyd George was the undisputed war hero; he could not be cast aside, nor did the Conservatives wish to do so. They urged him (against his own better judgement) to join France in imposing a vindictive peace settlement upon Germany, knowing that 'making Germany pay' would be popular with the British public. They supported the great franchise reform of 1918. Hitherto the suffrage had been linked to the payment of rates. Henceforth universal manhood suffrage was bestowed on the basis of six months' residence and, as we have seen, there was a limited grant of female suffrage; the university franchise was extended to graduates of provincial universities, and an additional vote was given to occupiers of business premises worth at least £10 per annum. This extension of the franchise was revolutionary in its implications. The total electorate jumped from 7.5 millions, in 1910, to nearly 20 millions, or approximately three-quarters of the adult population. When the voting age for women was reduced to 21, a decade later, the electorate embraced over 90 per cent of all adults. Although the business and university votes survived until 1948, the principle of the representation of individual citizens, regardless of wealth, was thus largely accepted; representation was no longer based on taxation. It is noteworthy that, as a result of the 1918 Act, the receipt of poor relief ceased to be a voting disqualification.

Without this massive increase in the enfranchised population, it is difficult to see how the growth of the Labour Party in the 1920s could have been achieved. As it was, Labour was particularly well placed to appeal to the newly enfranchised. At the outbreak of war the party was, as it had been created, a federal organisation without individual membership. Henderson, working in collaboration with Sidney Webb and MacDonald, formulated a new constitution which was accepted by the party conference in February 1918. This provided for a network of local Labour Party branches, which non-trade unionists (and especially, it was hoped, members of the middle classes) would feel able to join, and a National Executive of 23 members elected by the Annual Conference, which, because of the operation of the block vote, the trade unions dominated. At the same time the new Constitution contained a statement of 'Objects' which (Clause 3(d)) committed the party:

> To secure for the producers by hand or by brain the full fruits of their industry, and the most equitable distribution thereof that may be possible, upon the basis of the common ownership of the means of production and the best obtainable system of popular administration and control of each industry or service.

This could hardly be construed as a statement of full-blown socialism since (for example) it said nothing about state control of the private banking and financial systems. In an article in the *Observer* of 21 October 1917, Webb had already explained that the socialism of the Labour Party would be 'no more specific than a definite repudiation of the individualism that characterised all the political parties of the past generations and that still dominates the House of Commons'. The programme he had in mind was spelt out in greater detail in *Labour and the New Social Order*, largely written by him and published in June 1918, which talked about the necessity for a 'National Minimum' (full employment, minimum wages and conditions of work, and the maintenance of a basic level of income for those out of work); the 'democratic control of industry' (public ownership of the railways and canals, the coal mines, the insurance companies and — 'as suitable opportunities occur' — the land, as well as systems of administration and control, in particular services and occupations, that would promote 'not profiteering, but the public interest'); redistributive taxation, including a progressive income tax and a capital levy; and public expenditure on social services, leisure and education. The document proclaimed:

> We of the Labour Party . . . must ensure that what is presently to be built up is a new social order, based . . . in industry as well as in government, on that equal freedon, that general consciousness of consent, and that widest participation in power which is characteristic of Democracy.

But even in this document, upon which Labour fought the 1918 general election, the shopping-list of activities proposed for public ownership was composed mainly of those which were already under state direction. What the party set before the electorate was, therefore, merely the continuation on a permanent footing of wartime emergency measures. Capitalism was not to be overthrown and there was to be no shift to 'workers' control'; rather, the economic system was to be made to function more efficiently in the interests of the nation as a whole.

The mildness of this typically Fabian approach outraged the socialist left and acted as an encouragement to the formation of the British Communist Party in 1920. Negotiations for the affiliation of the Communists to Labour foundered on the refusal of the former to renounce revolution, and on the determination of the latter to be, and to be seen to be, a non-revolutionary and a parliamentary organism. Labour's emphasis upon managerial efficiency, and its condemnation of profiteering, attracted (as was intended) many formerly Liberal middle-class voters; at the same time its distinctive break with Liberal radicalism appealed to the newly enfranchised working-class electors.

There could, of course, be no question of a renewal of the pre-war electoral pact with the Liberals. In 1918, as a totally independent party, Labour fielded 388 candidates, of whom 63 were successful. In 1922 (411 candidates) 142 Labour MPs were returned, and in 1923 (422 candidates) 191 were successful. However, in assessing the growing popularity of the Labour Party, it is more constructive to examine the total votes obtained, absolutely and as a proportion of the total votes cast, and to compare these with the corresponding Liberal figures:

Table 5.1: Electoral Performance of the Labour and Liberal Parties, 1918–1929 (votes in millions)

	Labour Party		Liberal Party	
	votes	% of total vote	votes	% of total vote
Election				
1918	2.40	22.2	1.32[a]	12.2[a]
1922	4.24	29.4	4.18	29.1
1923	4.44	30.5	4.31	29.6
1924	5.49	33.0	2.93	17.6
1929	8.39	37.1	5.31	23.4

Note: a. non-Coalition Liberals.

By 1922 the Labour Party was already more popular than the Liberal, and by 1924 could claim the allegiance of a third of the voters. The decline of the Liberal party must evidently not be pre-dated. In 1929, indeed, the Liberals polled their highest ever number of votes. But it is a well-known feature of the British 'first-past-the-post' electoral system, which gives victory in a con-stituency to the candidate with the highest number of votes, irrespective of the total of votes cast for the other contestants, that it abhors third parties. Once Labour began to attract a third or more of the votes cast, this system imposed a disproportionate punishment upon the Liberals, whose parliamentary represen-tation fell from 159 MPs in 1923 to 40 in 1924, and rose to only 59 MPs five years later. Neither as a party of government nor as a party of opposition did the Liberals any longer possess credibility.

Historians have argued passionately over the relationship be-tween the decline of the Liberal party and the rise of Labour. In its appeal both to working- and to middle-class voters, the Labour Party became in the 1920s what the Liberal party ought to have become in the 1890s, had the younger radical members of it had their way. Many of the issues to which the Liberal party had addressed itself in the late-nineteenth century were confronted in the early twentieth, and solutions (some, admittedly, more permanent than others) had been found. The Lloyd George Coalition won an overwhelming victory in 1918; armed with the 'Coupon' (a letter of recommendation signed by both Lloyd George and Bonar Law),no less than 478 Coalition candidates (335 of them Unionists but only 133 Liberals) had been returned. The Coalition had legislated (1918) to raise the school-leaving age to 14 or, at the discretion of local authorities, to 15; had provided government subsidies for local-authority housing projects (1919); and had extended unemployment insurance cover to almost all employees earning over £250 per annum (1920). The Irish Question had been solved, at least for the foreseeable future, by a treaty (1921) with the leaders of the Irish Republican Army, leading to the establishment of a southern 'Irish Free State', with its own Parliament in Dublin and Dominion status, and an inter-nally self-governing Northern Irish province, represented by 12 MPs at Westminster.

In the field of social reconstruction the Coalition could have achieved more. But, quite apart from the domination of it by the Conservatives, it was overtaken by economic problems. In 1921 a period of post-war boom came to an end, ushering in 18 years of high unemployment, the level of which rarely fell below 10 per cent. The government had already relinquished control of most industries taken under wartime management; in 1921 the railways were 'grouped' into four large companies and returned to private ownership, and the coal mines were also 'decontrolled'. Rather than take measures to deal with the causes of poverty, Lloyd George was content to abandon many workers to the mercy of their new employers, and seemed willing at this stage to accept the phenomenon of unemployment as a permanent feature of the social landscape. In 1922, following the advice of a committee of businessmen under the chairmanship of Sir Eric Geddes, cuts of £64 millions were made in public spending, including a reduction of £6.5 millions in spending on education. The excess profits tax had been repealed in 1921; the following year the rate of income tax was reduced by a shilling to five shillings in the pound.

Yet, in spite of implementing a broadly Conservative economic policy — to the extent of imposing, under the Safeguarding of Industries Act of 1921, a duty of 33.3 per cent on a range of selected imports, mostly from Germany — Lloyd George was unloved and distrusted by the Conservative back-benchers. Some were scandalised by his personal lifestyle, others by his sale of honours, many resented his dictatorial methods in government, most came to see him as a liability. With the departure of the Sinn Fein MPs following the Irish treaty, the House of Commons was now reduced from 707 to 615 seats. On the basis of the 1918 results there was a very good chance that the Conservatives could command an outright majority, because it was obvious that the major effect of the 'Coupon' had been to save about 120 Lloyd George Liberals from having to face official Conservative opposition. Yet at East Fife, where Asquith had had no 'coupon' issued against him, a rebel Unionist, Colonel A. Sprot, had easily won the seat. Lloyd George had already destroyed the Liberal party (so the argument went); might he not destroy the Conservative party as well?

The opportunity for a break with Lloyd George was provided by the Chanak crisis of September 1922, when he had seemed obstinately determined to go to war with Turkey over Kemal Pasha's demand for the return of territory garrisoned by Britain since 1920. The British general in charge of the garrison declined to deliver Lloyd George's ultimatum for a withdrawal of Turkish forces, the Turks themselves refrained from attacking and the matter was solved by negotiation. On 10 October the Cabinet was persuaded by Lloyd George, supported by Austen Chamberlain, to call an immediate general election. The prospect of a 'Khaki' election victory that would put the Prime Minister back in Downing Street for another five years was too much for the Conservative back-benchers. At a fateful meeting at the Carlton Club on 19 October the Conservatives gave notice that the Coalition was at an end. And at the general election the following month they won an overall majority of 71 seats.

Andrew Bonar Law remained Prime Minister only until May 1923 when he resigned through ill health (he died of cancer on 30 October) and was succeeded by the Chancellor of the Exchequer, Stanley Baldwin, a shy Worcestershire iron master then in his late 50s but with just 15 years' parliamentary experience, only the last two of them at Cabinet level. Baldwin had made the key speech at the Carlton Club meeting that had brought down Lloyd George, of whom he was, in every way, the complete antithesis: a caring industrialist, interested in simple country pleasures, who had, during the war, donated one-fifth of his private fortune to reduce the War Loan.

Lloyd George had a first-class mind; Baldwin was, by common consent, in the second division. He demonstrated this limitation almost at once by calling a general election on the issue of protection (6 December 1923). Although the Conservatives remained the single largest party they lost their outright majority. Asquith and Lloyd George became temporarily reconciled in order to defend free trade; but, as we have seen, Labour was the chief beneficiary. Since there was now not the remotest possibility of a Liberal-Conservative coalition, Asquith, the nominal leader of the Liberal MPs, decided to offer very limited support in the division lobbies to a minority Labour government.

The previous October Baldwin had admitted to the National Union conference at Plymouth that he was 'not a clever man', and that he knew 'nothing of political tactics'. His blundering, Asquith's principles and Lloyd George's lack of them had now combined to give the premiership to James Ramsay MacDonald, whom, on 22 January 1924, George V appointed as Prime Minister. The King noted in his diary that 'Today 23 years ago dear Grandmama died. I wonder what she would have thought of a Labour Government!'

A NATION DIVIDED AND A NATION UNITED

In tracing the political no less than the social and economic de-velopment of Britain in the 1920s and 1930s, the historian is compelled so often to focus upon the grim thread of un-employment that it is tempting to regard it as the one central feature that dominated people's lives. For those who were un-employed, or who lived their daily lives in the expectation that they might lose their jobs, and for their families, the centrality of this issue was total; it ceased to be so only after the onset of war in September 1939. The barest statistics tell their own story. During the brief recovery that followed the slump of 1920–2, the monthly average number of registered unemployed persons (a statistic that excluded public employees, railway workers, domestic servants, agricultural workers, white-collar employees earning more than £5 per week and the self-employed) fell (1924) to 1.1 millions, or just over 6 per cent of the civilian workforce. Between 1925 and 1929 the number fluctuated, but never exceeded 1.4 millions. However, in 1930 it rose to 1.9 millions and by 1932 had reached 2.7 millions (15 per cent of the workforce). In spite of the economic upturn in 1934 the monthly average did not drop below 2 millions again until 1936, and even in 1939 it still stood (at 1.5 millions) above the 1924 figure.

These statistics relate merely to the overall national picture; they conceal enormous variations, which in turn reflect fundamental differences in the pattern and — ultimately — the causes of unemployment around the country. In South Wales levels of unemployment were very high indeed. In 1934 the town of Brynmawr experienced rates of unemployment as high as 74 per cent of the male workforce; at Dowlais the proportion was 73 per cent, and at Merthyr 66 per cent; even in 1935 over 45 per cent of the coalminers in the Rhondda valley and over half those at Merthyr were out of work. In 1934 one could travel across Eng-land and observe unemployment rates as high as 68 per cent of insured workers in Jarrow and 57 per cent at Maryport, but as low as 8 per cent at Luton and just over 5 per cent in the cities of Oxford and Coventry. A survey undertaken by the Pilgrim Trust

(*Men Without Work*, 1938) found that in Deptford, south London, in 1936 only 7 per cent of the industrial workforce were unemployed, and that in the south-east of England as a whole the rate of unemployment was about 6 per cent of insured workers; in the north-west, however, the proportion stood at 18.6 per cent, in the north-east it was over 21 per cent, while in Wales it exceeded 32 per cent.

Not only were there glaring regional differences in the pattern of unemployment; there were also major differences in the type of unemployment. Seasonal unemployment continued to be a feature associated with some occupations, particularly in the building and construction industries and the hotel and catering trades, but also in some of the newer industries; sales of motor cars were invariably greater in the summer than the winter, when car workers were commonly 'laid off' or made subject to short-time working. However, the national burden of unemployment was made much more severe by two other factors: the effects of the war, and the decline of the Victorian 'heavy' industries.

The Great War imposed direct and indirect costs upon the British economy. The ranks of the permanently unemployable had been swollen as a result of the war. About 1.6 million ex-soldiers were sufficiently disabled to be able to claim government pensions, which were calculated according to the extent of each injury; formerly skilled men who had lost a limb were still expected to work, but, of course, could often only undertake light duties or find only casual employment. The shabbily dressed limbless ex-serviceman, sporting his war medals as he sold matches or bootlaces on the street corner, was a common sight in many towns and villages of inter-war Britain.

The destruction of physical resources during the war had not, in fact, been that great; the largest single loss was about one-third of the merchant fleet, though by the end of hostilities these losses were being more than made good, and shipowners were complaining that they had too much tonnage on their hands. But the loss of manpower was very great indeed. The British war dead amounted to 616,382. In 1920 the American economist E.L. Bogart estimated that each dead British serviceman represented a loss to the National Product of $4,140 (about £1,190). This estimate was necessarily based upon a number of hypotheses: what might the soldiers have achieved had there been no war? What might their earning power and the level of their savings have been?

And so on. Assumptions must also be made about other effects of the war. Assets (for example, railway equipment, plant and machinery in the coal industry, and the national housing stock) had been allowed to deteriorate; their repair or replacement after the war obviously cost much more than would otherwise have been the case.

The liquidation of overseas investments must also be put into the equation. On government orders (so as to maintain the value of the pound against the American dollar), about one- eighth of all private investments abroad had been sold off. These losses were not made good until the late 1920s; meanwhile, invisible income in the form of interest payments remitted from abroad was lost. The war itself had wrought havoc with Britain's international trade. Between 1913 and 1923 exports of cotton goods to India declined by over 50 per cent, and there was a fall of about a third in the value of exports to South America. More dramatically, the National Debt had increased from £650 millions to £7,000 millions, while about £850 millions was owed to the United States. The size of the Debt haunted the Treasury and struck those brought up on principles of strict Victorian economy as wicked and immoral, though in fact money used to buy the War Loan was infinitely more secure than funds invested in Russia and South America, where international obligations as to repayment were soon repudiated.

At the end of the war the Labour Party had suggested a once-for-all capital levy to eliminate the National Debt; Beaverbrook and Churchill warmed to the idea, but it was rejected by the then Chancellor of the Exchequer, Bonar Law, who feared its employment as a precedent by some future socialist administration. The servicing of the National Debt absorbed almost half the proceeds of taxation, as against about 14 per cent before the war, and the obligation to those who held War Loan was given a priority that ranked above the claims of social policy. In 1918 the standard rate of income tax stood at 30 [old] pence in the pound; though by 1930 this proportion had fallen by a third, there was no question of the rate ever reverting to its pre-war level of sixpence. High levels of income tax were obviously more popular with working people than indirect taxation, but they probably acted as a disincentive to investment. Government borrowing during the war also affected interest rates; the rate of interest offered on gilt-edged stock remained above 4 per cent until 1932.

As we shall see, for those in work the inter-war period saw substantial improvements in the standard of living, as higher wages chased higher prices and real wage levels rose as a result. But for the unemployed these years witnessed a grim struggle merely to survive.

The destruction and depreciation of capital during the Great War was reckoned by some observers to have been responsible for the unemployment of the 1920s. In his book *Some Economic Consequences of the Great War* (1930), A. L. Bowley estimated the loss of wealth sustained by Britain as a result of the conflict to have been the equivalent of between two and four years' normal accumulation of capital resources. But, even if accurately computed, such losses do not explain the most important single cause of unemployment in the 1920s and 1930s, namely the severe contraction experienced by the 'old staples', cotton, iron and steel, shipbuilding and coal.

In the case of cotton, dislocation of trade during the war is only a partial explanation of the catastrophe that followed the peace. The Lancashire cotton industry shared in the immediate post-war boom; new spinning mills were constructed in the hope that pre-war production levels might now be exceeded and the Japanese ousted from the markets they had managed to penetrate. In fact, the Japanese were less of a threat than the perfectly natural — and foreseeable — rise of a domestic manufacturing sector within the Indian sub-continent, able to produce cotton goods at prices with which Lancashire could not compete. Tariffs and boycotts made the export of cotton to India increasingly difficult; the Lancashire industry, burdened with outdated machinery and outmoded work practices, gradually fell into the hands of the banks. The world slump in trade after 1929 intensified an already desperate situation. Cotton production fell by a quarter between 1910 and 1920, but by almost half again in the following decade; by 1940 production stood at only 3,500 million square yards, compared with 6,000 million square yards in 1920. In 1932 the rate of unemployment in the cotton industry was 31.1 per cent of the workforce, and in 1938 was still as high as 27.7 per cent, over twice the national average.

The production of iron and steel was closely geared to the building of ships, the need for which was related to the demands of world trade and to the supply of credit. We have already noted the over-production of merchant ships by 1918. In this sector, too, there was an unwise speculation at the end of the war that world shipping needs would increase. World ship construction did indeed rise in the immediate post-war years, but then collapsed as interest rates and trading conditions worsened. Again, outdated plant and machinery, restrictive work-practices and unsuitable yards had a predictable effect upon the British shipbuilding sector. In 1914 Britain's shipyards had launched three-fifths of world shipping tonnage; by 1938, in the face of strong competition from Japan and the USA, the British share had fallen to just one-third. After 1918, steel replaced iron as a basic ingredient of ship construction and in civil engineering. In 1920 British mills produced 9 million tons of steel, of which roughly a quarter was exported. By 1930 steel production in Britain had fallen to 7 million tons and represented only 8 per cent of world steel output, though by 1937, heavily protected by tariffs and benefiting from the demands of the motor industry and of re-armament, output had increased a return to about 13 million tons.

These economic difficulties were made more serious still by the failure of world trade to revive in the 1930s. In the previous decade, world trade had grown by a mere 8.5 per cent. In the aftermath of the Wall Street crash of 1929 world trade contracted (1929–33) by over a third. During the war Britain had remained on the Gold Standard, but the Treasury had been authorised to issue paper currency, in the form of the one-pound and ten-shilling notes, which could only be exchanged for gold at the pre-war rate of $4.86. But in 1919 the Gold Standard really had been suspended, temporarily. During the early 1920s pressure grew in the City of London for its complete restoration. Of the 26 members of the Court of Governors of the Bank of England (still a private, self-appointed corporation), at least 15 were involved primarily in overseas banking, and five more were connected with shipping and insurance; only two were industrialists. The Court believed that the re-establishment of 'the City' as the financial centre of the trading world demanded a return to Gold, at the pre-war rate, choosing to forget that before the war Britain's position had been that of a net creditor, whereas now much of the money invested in City institutions was 'hot' — attracted by relatively high interest rates but deposited for short periods, and easily withdrawn.

In his first budget speech (28 April 1925) as Chancellor of the Exchequer in Baldwin's second government, Winston Churchill announced that the suspending Act of 1919 would not be renewed. This did not mean that the Gold standard was restored on quite the same terms as it had existed in 1914. Gold coinage ceased to be used for domestic purposes; paper currency was happily accepted in its stead. What was restored was the gold-exchange standard for international transactions, and what was of crucial importance was the re-establishment of that standard at the pre- war level of $4.86 to the pound sterling.

City bankers almost certainly exaggerated the importance of international financial transactions in the national economy. Their zeal for the prestige of the City, and their relative lack of concern for the effects which a return to Gold, at the pre-war level, could have reasonably been expected to have had upon the domestic industrial sector seem, in retrospect, the epitome of short-sightedness and of callous indifference to the social consequences of economic decisions. At the time, however, the return to Gold was not unpopular. It is true that there were some important dissentient voices. Consulted by Churchill, Reginald McKenna (by now chairman of the Midland Bank) and the Cambridge economist John Maynard Keynes both advised against a return. But the weight of informed opinion was not with them. In the *Economic Consequences of Mr. Churchill*, Keynes subsequently declared that Churchill took the decision

> Partly, perhaps, because he had no instinctive judgement to prevent him from making mistakes; partly because, lacking this instinctive judgement, he was deafened by the clamorous voices of conventional finance; and, most of all, because he was gravely misled by his experts.

Yet Keynes' own objections were directed less to the return to Gold itself than to the re-establishment of the pound at $4.86. Since 1919 the sterling-dollar exchange rate had been edging closer to the pre-war level; in 1924 it stood, at its highest, at $4.694. The City argued that the difference between prices in the USA and Britain was — at most — 2.5 per cent in favour of American producers, and that a return to the $4.86 level would act as an incentive to industrial efficiency. British producers would have to lower their prices, and hence British workers would have to accept lower wages, but the reduction would not be very great and would be counterbalanced by cheaper imports both of food and raw materials. At the same time, London's international standing as a financial centre would be enhanced.

Beyond these considerations, however, one may detect the deep-seated and widely shared yearning for a return to pre-war 'normalcy' which was such a central feature of social discourse in the 1920s. The return of Gold, at the pre-war parity, was a symbol, misconceived without doubt but of immeasurable psychological significance, that in so far as was possible all the distorting effects of the Great War had been rectified. Speaking to the Institute of Bankers in November 1921 Sir Felix Schuster had exhorted,

> Let us have done with short cuts and by-paths and return to the old standard. The road may be long and painful but our fathers trod it before us and we know the way.

Keynes did not agree with the optimistic prophecies of those, like Schuster, who were successful in persuading Churchill to take his 1925 decision. Keynes had calculated the difference between American and British prices at 10 per cent, and argued that the maintenance of $4.86 would entail nothing less than the deflation of domestic prices by precisely that percentage — leading inexorably to unemployment, wage reductions and industrial strife.

Keynes was right, though at the time it did not seem so. For a brief moment London regained its position as the centre of the world's money markets. However, even this benefit was largely illusory. As Sir Alfred Mond pointed out during parliamentary discussion of Churchill's policy, by tying the pound to a particular level against the dollar, the fortunes of the City had in reality been made dependent upon the whims of Wall Street. When the New York Stock Exchange 'crashed', in October 1929, the City of London was unable to protect itself from the consequences.

Montagu Norman, the Governor of the Bank of England, later accepted that the 1925 return to Gold had had damaging effects upon employment prospects. But at the time he had voiced the opinion that 'in connection with a golden 1925, the merchant, manufacturer, workman, etc., should be considered (but not consulted any more than about the design of battleships)'. In the past, governments had been afraid to engineer wage reductions and to aggravate either the level of unemployment or the privations of the unemployed. In the immediate aftermath of the Great War, and with the Bolshevik Revolution as a constant reminder, there was genuine fear of the revolutionary consequences of social unrest; in 1919 even the police had gone on strike. A Cabinet Minute of October 1921 had warned:

A very large proportion of the unemployed today are not the usual type of unskilled or workshy men, but are very largely people who all their lives have been used to regular work at good wages and many of whom are still making every effort to avoid having to apply to the Poor Law Guardians for relief. A very large percentage of these men fought in the War and they are not prepared to see their families endure misery and want without a serious struggle and even disorder.

This was the view of a Conservative-dominated Coalition. But in 1925 the Conservative Prime Minister, Baldwin, declared publicly that 'All the workers of this country have got to take reductions in wages to help put industry on its feet'. A number of factors had led to this change in attitude towards the standard of living of the working classes. Threats of civil disorder had proved largely illusory. The provision of sickness and unemployment benefit undoubtedly acted as a safety net. There was much deprivation but little actual starvation. The growth of new industries gave employment to many and hope to many others and — significantly — prevented (to the extent that it could ever have existed) the growth of nationwide working-class solidarity. But of prime importance in convincing the politicians of the right that the politics of the left could be contained was the development of the post-war trade-union movement and the experience of a Labour government in 1924.

The depression which began to affect trade and industry in the summer of 1920 had led to a reduction rather than an intensification of industrial militancy. At first this was not apparent. The decontrol of the mines and the railways came as a great disappointment to the unions, particularly since the Royal Commission set up in 1919, under the chairmanship of Sir John Sankey, to enquire into the future of the coal industry, had recommended 'that the principle of State ownership of the coal mines be accepted'. Politically, this was something to which Lloyd George was not in a position to agree. The miners huffed and puffed, but remained quiescent. In September 1919 there was a national strike of railwaymen, provoked by the determination of the President of the Board of Trade, Sir Auckland Geddes, to foist wage reductions upon them. A national strike was called, but lasted only seven days. The manner of its settlement was significant. A stoppage of the railway system affected, at once, many other workers. The Transport and General Workers' Union (TGWU) acted immediately, by setting up a Negotiating Committee with other unions affected by the strike, and persuading the government to maintain existing wage levels for a further twelve months.

The railwaymen's leader was J. H. Thomas, the Labour MP for Derby who, in 1918, had become General Secretary of the National Union of Railwaymen (NUR). Thomas was a shrewd negotiator and, within limits, a loyal servant of the trade-union movement. But he had too great a liking for alcohol and gambling, and too limited an understanding of politics. In 1921, in the course of a libel action he had brought against *The Communist*, he denied on oath that he was a socialist. Ten years later he joined Ramsay MacDonald in the National government, and was expelled both from his union and from the Labour Party. The leader of the transport workers was Ernest Bevin, since 1910 secretary of the Docker's Union, who in 1921 brought together 50 unions to form the TGWU, of which he remained General Secretary until 1940. Bevin was totally loyal to the Labour Party, and an accomplished advocate of his members' grievances. But he regarded the strike as a weapon of the very last resort; in 1919 he had achieved substantial gains for the dockers in an arbitration (conducted under the Industrial Courts Act of the previous year) by the results of which both he and the employers agreed to be bound.

Jimmy Thomas and Ernie Bevin were not the stuff of which revolutionaries are made. On the day upon which government control of the coal mines ended (31 March 1921), and in the face of the coalowners' determination to enforce reductions in wages, the miners struck, invoking at the same time the much vaunted Triple Alliance of miners, railwaymen and transport workers that had lain dormant since its conception in 1914. The NUR and the TGWU had no option but to pledge their support. 'If you carry out your threat and strike [Lloyd George told the Triple Alliance leaders] then you will defeat us. But if you do so have you weighed the consequences?' Thomas had, and was appalled. He was in no way afraid of the government, but he feared deeply the left-wing advocates of Direct Action. On 15 April ('Black Friday'), just 24 hours before the railwaymen were due to strike in sympathy with the miners, Thomas demanded that they return to the negotiating table; the NUR and the TGWU then cancelled their proposed industrial action. 'From that moment on', the Miners' Federation President, Robert Smillie, later confessed, 'we were beaten and we knew we were.' The miners continued to strike for three months and then returned to work on the coalowners' terms. The Triple Alliance was dead; so was Direct Action.

In defence of the policy of Thomas and Bevin it needs to be said that not only did they sincerely not believe in the use of general or sympathetic strikes for political ends; they feared also that such action, whether successful or not, would damage the electoral prospects of the Labour Party. The fact that MacDonald was able to form a Labour administration in 1924 seemed to vindicate this approach. The first Labour government operated under severe political as well as economic constraints. Not ónly did its parliamentary majority depend upon Liberal support in the division lobbies. Its reserve of administrative experience was severely limited, so that MacDonald had to call upon the services of ex-Liberals such as Viscount Haldane (Lord Chancellor) and C. P. Trevelyan (President of the Board of Education). Philip Snowden became as orthodox a Chancellor of the Exchequer as the Treasury and the Bank of England could have desired. The one concession that MacDonald made to the socialist wing of the party was the appointment of the Clydesider, John Wheatley, to the Ministry of Health.

MacDonald accepted the responsibility of office for three reasons. First, he did not fear the constraining hand of Liberal support; the fact that there could be no question of implementing Clause 3(d) of the Labour Party's Constitution did not worry him. Secondly, he believed that Labour needed to show it was ready to assume the burdens and responsibilities of office; its credibility in the eyes of the electorate would be strengthened as a result. Third, MacDonald's primary interest was in foreign affairs (he appointed himself to the Foreign Office), and one did not normally need a parliamentary majority to conduct the foreign policy of the United Kingdom. MacDonald was able to negotiate the French withdrawal from the Ruhr, and to obtain the subsequent agreement of France (at the London Conference, over which he presided) to the implementation of the Dawes Plan for the more sensible payment of reparations by Weimar Germany. He personally attended the Assembly of the League of Nations and was one of the architects of the Geneva Convention (repudiated later by Baldwin) which pledged its signatories to accept arbitration in the settlement of international disputes. He gave diplomatic recognition to the Soviet Union, and proposed to grant a loan to the Bolshevik regime in return for vague promises from Moscow to repay Tsarist debts.

On the domestic front the achievements of the Labour government were limited. In 1919 the Liberal President of the Local Government Board, Christopher Addison, had legislated so as to require local authorities to rectify housing deficiencies; Addison also instituted a Treasury subsidy to help in this task, plus a lump-sum subsidy to private builders. The Addison scheme was terminated in 1921, but in 1923 Neville Chamberlain had instituted a new subsidy of £6 a year for 20 years, mainly to assist private builders to construct houses for sale. Now, in 1924, John Wheatley increased the subsidy to £9 a year for 40 years, on houses built, either privately or by local authorities, for occupation at controlled rents. Wheatley also reached agreements with the building unions to increase the number of apprentices and to shorten the period of apprenticeship, and he promised the building industry that the scheme would last for 15 years. By the time the programme was abandoned, in the wake of the economic crisis in 1932, over 500,000 council houses had been built under the terms of the Wheatley Act; these accounted for half the total number of houses built by local authorities between the wars. Wheatley had, moreover, established the principle that the provision of working-class housing was an obligation falling upon local authorities to fulfil; it was a duty devolving upon society as a whole.

MacDonald's government achieved some other successes. At the Board of Education Trevelyan repaired some of the damage done by the Geddes Axe; the number of free places in secondary schools was increased and state scholarships to assist university students from poorer homes were re-established. County Agricultural Wages Committees were set up. There was some amelioration of the conditions under which unemployment benefit was paid. But the government showed little capacity for bringing constructive thought to bear upon the ways in which the problem of unemployment might be solved. Snowden paid lip-service to the idea of public works (in July he announced government support for road building and other construction programmes), but introduced a free-trade budget that included the repeal of the corporation profits tax.

In September the government's term of office was brought to an abrupt end. Ever since the overthrow of Tsarism the press had been obsessed with the idea that Bolshevik agents were at work fomenting revolution within Britain. The formation of the British Communist Party seemed to corroborate this theory, and the hand of Communism was seen at work in the militancy of 'rank-and-file' movements in South Wales and on the Clyde. At the general election of 1922 the Communists gained their first parliamentary seats, with the victories of J. T. W. Newbold at Motherwell and S. Saklatvala at Battersea North. Newbold, a former Quaker, owed his victory to the absence of Labour opposition, and Saklatvala owed his to his endorsement as official Labour candidate.

Communists had, meanwhile, been instrumental in establishing, in 1921, the National Unemployed Workers' Movement (NUWM). Under the inspiration of its secretary, Wal Hannington, who had led the engineering shop stewards' movement in London during the war, the NUWM embarked upon a campaign of violent civil disobedience, organising resistance to evictions, occupying council offices and workhouses, raiding factories where overtime was being worked, and proclaiming that it would 'never cease from active strife against this system until capitalism is abolished'. Observing its relatively sophisticated organisation, and the prominent part played in its activities by ex-servicemen, the Director of Intelligence at Scotland Yard warned that 'in the event of rioting, for the first time in history, the rioters will be better trained than the troops'. The NUWM also organised hunger marches and gave advice and assistance to claimants seeking higher national insurance and poor-law payments. Between 1922 and 1925 there was limited support from the TUC for some of its activities.

In right-wing circles the Labour Party appeared as the Trojan horse, by means of which Communism would exert an ever greater influence upon the nation's affairs. MacDonald's policy of friendship with the Soviet Union was therefore highly suspect, and the failure of the government to prosecute the Communist J. R. Campbell, who had published an appeal to troops not to 'turn your guns on your fellow workers', led the Conservatives to put down a vote of censure against the Labour administration. The Liberals supported the motion, and MacDonald's government fell. At the consequent general election, on 29 October 1924, much was made of the publication in the *Daily Mail* of a letter alleged to have been written by Grigory Zinoviev, the President of the Communist International, to the British Communist Party, praising the proposed Anglo-Soviet treaty as a means of assisting in 'the propaganda of ideas of Leninism in England and the Colonies'.

This episode quickly entered the mythology of the Labour Party as an example of the evil power of the Conservative press: Labour, it was said, had been robbed of electoral victory by a trick. The Zinoviev letter may have been genuine. But there is nothing to support the Labour complaint. Labour ran 90 candidates more than in 1923 and suffered, as we noted in the previous chapter, a net loss of only 40 seats. The Liberal Party was shattered. Baldwin reaped a rich harvest. He returned to Downing Street at the head of a government which could command a majority of 223 votes in the House of Commons.

The massive Conservative victory of 1924 did not demoralise Labour, though the circumstances of the election did lead the party to take steps to bar Communists from membership. Nor did it induce Baldwin to abandon free trade, to which the banking fraternity still clung as another example of the return to pre-war economic orthodoxy. Baldwin had other reasons for not raising again the spectre of protection. It was not, on the evidence of 1923, a vote winner. Baldwin had already made his peace with those Conservatives who had been opposed to the termination of the Lloyd George Coalition; Austen Chamberlain and Lord Birkenhead, the leading members of this group, both entered his Cabinet as, respectively, Foreign Secretary and Secretary of State for India. By setting his face against tariff reform, Baldwin now reassured the Conservative free-traders. There was an additional bonus. Winston Churchill, who had left the Tory party over free trade in 1904, was enticed back into it and, as we have seen, given the Chancellorship of the Exchequer; a public guarantee, so to speak, that free trade was inviolable and that the Treasury would continue to worship at the altar of *laissez-faire*.

Churchill was by no means the only Liberal to turn or return to the Conservative fold. The atmosphere in which political debate was conducted became, during the late 1920s, heavily charged with the vocabulary of class warfare. Some radical Liberals, including Addison, Benjamin Jowitt, Trevelyan, Josiah Wedgwood and William Wedgwood Benn, had already deserted to the Labour benches. The rump Liberal party still contained within its membership a wealth of experience and expertise, but the inability of the party to win votes (symbolised by the defeat of Asquith by the Labour candidate at Paisley in 1924, even though the Conservatives did not contest the seat) seemed to call for a change of tactics. In January 1926 the Liberal Land Conference, while rejecting the idea of land nationalisation, endorsed a policy of taxation of land values; many Liberals regarded this as nationalisation by the back door. On 26 January Sir Alfred Mond announced his intention of leaving the party and of joining the Conservatives. In the *Saturday Review* (30 January) he explained why:

> Shorn of all sham and pretence . . . that policy . . will remain, unadulterated Socialism . . In Socialism I see today, as I have always seen, the degradation of the individual, the deterioration of the community, and the downfall of the State . . . I have come to the conclusion that the Conservative party, under its present direction, is the national anti-Socialist party.

Mond's defection was quickly followed by others, less prestigious, perhaps (though they included the former Lloyd George Chief Whip E. Hilton Young), but of great significance as reflecting support for Mond's view that, in a society dominated by the struggle between Socialism and Capitalism, there was no room for a third force that tried to mediate between the two. By the summer of 1926, therefore, Baldwin's government could claim even greater public support than at the moment of its election victory. The success of Churchill's return to Gold depended upon a fall in the costs of production and presumed that workers would agree to lower wages; on this issue the government was not in a compromising mood.

Of all the industries hit by the depression, none was being affected so drastically as coal. At times, higher rates of unemployment were to be found in other sectors of the economy. In 1924 the proportion of miners out of work was a mere 7 per cent, compared with 16 per cent of workers in the cotton industry, over 20 per cent in iron and steel and 28 per cent in shipbuilding; even in 1932, arguably the worst year of the depression, the rate of unemployment in the coal industry (41.2 per cent) was still less than in shipbuilding (59.5 per cent) or iron and steel (48.5 per cent). But the coal industry was affected by factors from which, by their very nature, recovery was either not possible at all, or possible only by means of a capital investment programme which governments did not wish to fund and which the coalowners were incapable of funding.

In explaining the decline of the coal industry, we may distinguish two sets of causes. On the one hand, there were those resulting in falling demand. Coal output declined from a record 287 million tons in 1913 to an average of about 237 million tons in the early 1920s and 220 million tons annually between 1930 and 1934. After 1919 the industry faced stiff competition from the Polish coalfields and from Germany, whose coal was cheap because labour costs were lower. The demand for home-produced coal was also affected by the contractions of the iron, steel and shipbuilding industries. If less coal was dug out of the ground, fewer trains were needed to transport it, and consequently less coal was needed to drive the steam locomotives. An additional factor of increasing importance was the substitution of oil for coal as the fuel used in ship propulsion.

The second set of causes derived from the organisation of the industry. British coalmining was notoriously overmanned and grossly under-mechanised. In 1913 only 8 per cent of coal had been extracted mechanically. By 1925 the proportion had risen to 20 per cent, and by 1932 to 38 per cent. In that year only a quarter of the tonnage was transported by mechanical conveyor; the rest was carried away from the coal face by horse-drawn wagons, cable-hauled tubs, or simply by the human hand. The Royal Commission of 1926 (chaired by the Liberal statesman Sir Herbert Samuel) found that although there were 2,481 mines, owned by 1,400 companies, most of these were very small in terms of their productive capacity; over 80 per cent of total output was produced by just 323 colliery companies. Too many mines were extracting coal from very thin seams located at great distances from the surface. Output per man had stood at an annual average of 247 tons in the period 1910–14; by 1920–24 it had fallen to just 199 tons. There was some improvement in productivity in the 1930s. By 1936, output per manshift in British coalmines had risen by 14 per cent compared with 1927; but, over the same period, output in the coalfields of Poland had increased by 54 per cent, and in the Ruhr by 81 per cent.

The Lloyd George Coalition had rejected nationalisation, and left the miners to the mercy of the coalowners. Although some rationalisation of the industry took place, this proved to be a slow process; by 1944 some 750 companies still controlled over 1,500 mines. The return to Gold accelerated the decline of the industry, by raising the price of British coal destined for export. Before the Great War Britain produced about a quarter of the world's coal; by 1927 this proportion had fallen to a fifth. In 1925 British coal output stood at approximately 243 million tons, of which 67 million tons were exported; in 1938 output had fallen to 227 million tons, of which only 46 million tons were sold abroad. The solution most favoured by the owners was to press for wage reductions coupled with an increase in the hours of work. But, having been obliged, by the failure of the Triple Alliance in 1921, to accept cuts in wages, the miners were in no mood to accept meekly a further erosion of their already low standard of living. A national strike was only averted, on 31 July 1925 ('Red Friday'), by Baldwin's agreement to continue the government subsidy to the coal industry while the Samuel Commission set about its work.

Those who led the Miners' Federation were of a temperament quite different from that of Jimmy Thomas and Ernie Bevin, whom they distrusted for obvious reasons. The Federation's Secretary was A. J. Cook, a leading figure in the pre-war syndicalist movement in South Wales, and a fiery speaker. In August 1925 he told his members:

> Next May we shall be faced with the greatest crisis and the greatest struggle we have ever known, and we are preparing for it. . . . I don't care a hang for any government, or army or navy. They can come along with their bayonets. Bayonets don't cut coal.

In fact, neither the miners nor the TUC made any preparations for a general strike, unlike the government, which laid its plans with meticulous care and (October 1925) had twelve Communist leaders (including J. R. Campbell) arrested and tried under the Incitement to Mutiny Act of 1797; they were all imprisoned after refusing the judge's offer to set them free on condition that they left the party. The Royal Commission, in its report the following March, rejected the idea of nationalisation and called for immediate wage reductions in the coal industry. The miners stood firm and, to make amends for the betrayal of 1921, the TUC's General Council pledged its support. On 30 April 1926 the miners were locked out; the General Strike began three days later.

Although there was a great deal of government propaganda to the effect that the strike was political, and had as its purpose the overthrow of parliamentary democracy, this was neither the intention of the TUC nor the aim of the Miners' Federation. The General Council did not call out every trade unionist, only those involved in transport, printing and the press, iron and steel, electricity and gas, building (but not workers involved in constructing houses and hospitals), and the metallurgical and heavy chemical industries. The hope was that the government would be persuaded to intervene and bring pressure to bear upon the coalowners, just as the General Council itself was attempting to moderate the miners' demands; Cook's famous declaration 'Not a penny off the pay, not a minute on the day' was widely regarded within the trade-union movement as a piece of wild obstinacy.

The strike was in reality nothing more than a large-scale industrial dispute. It suited the government not to portray it as such. But the remarkable response of millions of workers to the General Council's call first elated and then frightened the leadership of the trade-union movement. There undoubtedly were elements among the working population who still believed in the legitimacy of industrial action for political ends; Churchill's condemnation of the strike as a 'deliberate, concerted, organised menace', and his warning of the possibility that 'a Soviet of Trade Unions' might take charge of the nation's affairs, struck a chilling cord with the middle classes, from whose ranks most of the strike-breakers were drawn. Whatever else might happen, Labour's popularity with the electorate was likely to suffer; on Bevin's advice, MacDonald played no part in the dispute.

A majority on the General Council rapidly came to fear the power of the weapon they had unleashed. If the strike proved successful, there would be demands for its more frequent use, perhaps for non-industrial purposes. Thomas began searching for excuses to withdraw TUC support from the Miners' Federation. He found a helpmate in Herbert Samuel, who drafted a Memorandum calling for some wage reductions to be imposed in the coal industry, but only when the reorganisation called for by the Royal Commission had been 'effectively adopted'. The Samuel Memorandum did not in any way commit the government, which was not a party to it. But it was seized upon by the General Council and, when the miners rejected it, the strike was called off (12 May) 'unconditionally', just as Baldwin had demanded. Six days later Thomas wrote privately to Samuel expressing thanks for 'all that you have done towards averting what I am satisfied might easily have developed into a revolution'.

The General Strike was a watershed in the social and political development of Britain between the two world wars, and its repercussions have continued to be felt. The miners were abandoned to a hopelessly unequal struggle against the coalowners. By the autumn of 1926 a drift back to work had begun, and in October the Federation capitulated: the working day was lengthened; wages were drastically reduced; the industry was not reorganised and the Samuel Memorandum was forgotten.

Baldwin emerged as the valiant defender of what he called (in the government's newspaper, the *British Gazette* of 6 May) 'the British Constitution'. In reality the toughness of the government was not due to him, but to a group of ministers, led by Churchill and William Joynson-Hicks, the Home Secretary, who reflected in the Cabinet the views of the Tory backbenchers. In May 1927, in deference to their wishes, the government introduced a bill designed to make illegal any general or sympathetic strike; civil servants were henceforth prohibited from joining a TUC-affiliated union; and the principle of 'contracting out' of the political levy collected by trade unions was replaced by 'contracting in'. It was hoped that this last provision would result in a drastic fall in Labour Party membership, which it did: one million members were 'lost' in this way, and Party income dropped by over a third.

The major provisions of the 1927 Trade Disputes Act had nothing to do with the General Strike; they were inspired by political spite. The public noted this. Baldwin's determination to starve the miners into surrender after the collapse of the General Strike also lost him support. A relief fund set up by public conscription collected over £300,000, including a donation of £10 given by the Prince of Wales because (the covering letter made clear) 'it would be an unsatisfactory end to any dispute that one side should have to give in on account of the sufferings of their dependents'. In spite of heavy-handed attempts by the Conservatives to brand Labour as an anti-democratic force, the Labour Party began to win seats from the Conservatives at by-elections. Between the end of the General Strike and the general election of 30 May 1929 eight constituencies changed hands in this way. And at the general election the Conservative share of the vote fell by almost 10 per cent compared with 1924. Labour completed its conquest of most of the industrial areas which had been held by the Liberals in 1923; two-thirds of the borough seats in England were won by Labour, and ten of the eleven borough seats in Wales. The Conservatives remained strong only in agricultural and middle-class constituencies.

Labour emerged, for the first time, the largest party in the House of Commons, with 288 seats to the Conservatives' 260. But the Liberals had done better than expected. They had fought a vigorous campaign on an adventurous platform dominated by the need to counter unemployment, in contrast to the Conservative slogan of 'Safety First'. In those constituencies which they contested, the Liberal share of the vote fell (from 30.9 per cent, in 1924, to 27.7 per cent), but they put up more candidates (513) than at any time since 1910, and though their parliamentary representation increased to only 59 seats, it was enough to give them the balance of power at Westminster. Baldwin was urged by some within the Conservative party to try for a Conservative-Liberal coalition to prevent the formation of a Labour government; but his suspicion of Lloyd George ran too deep to permit such a stratagem and, besides, since 1926 the Liberal party had adopted policies which in some respects were more left-wing than those of the Labour Party. The 'Liberal Yellow Book' of 1928 (*Britain's Industrial Future*) was heavily influenced by Keynesian interventionism: the use of a managed economy to bring down unemployment and stimulate industrial recovery. These doctrines ran counter to the philosophy embodied in the return to Gold, and had no place in Conservative thinking. On 4 June Baldwin resigned, having advised George V to send for MacDonald.

The second Labour government was more right wing than the first. MacDonald gave the Foreign Office to Arthur Henderson; Philip Snowden returned to the Exchequer. Wheatley was deliberately excluded. The only left-winger in the Cabinet was the pacifist George Lansbury, who, as leader of Poplar Council in 1921, had spent 41 days in prison (together with 29 other councillors) for refusing to agree to the payment of an excessive rate to the London County Council. But Lansbury was now tucked away at the Ministry of Works, where he could do no harm. Jimmy Thomas, with the title of Lord Privy Seal, was put in charge of tackling unemployment; but those younger men whose ideas might have contributed positively to the formulation of constructive employment policies — such as Hugh Dalton and Oswald

Mosley — were given only junior posts. The Ministry of Labour was put in the care of Margaret Bondfield, the first woman to become a Cabinet Minister and to be sworn of the Privy Council.

In 1924 Labour's inability to implement socialist policies could be excused simply by reference to its parliamentary impotence. The same excuse cannot be offered to explain away the failures of 1929–31. True, Labour still depended upon Liberal votes to sustain its authority in the Commons. But the Liberal party was now much more radical than it had been under Asquith; indeed, on issues such as unemployment and the nationalisation of mining royalties it was more radical than Labour. MacDonald was probably right to reject Lloyd George's call for a coalition, in that he shared Baldwin's distrust of the Liberal leader and knew that such a coalition would not have been acceptable to the left of the party, represented by the ILP. But the Liberals never made formal coalition a precondition for supporting radical policies.

The second Labour government took the view that there was nothing fundamentally wrong with the economic system. Most members of MacDonald's Cabinet distrusted Keynesian economic theory, perhaps because they could not understand it. The view which prevailed in the Cabinet was that the economic system was basically sound, but that it needed better self-regulation. To achieve this, what was needed was not confrontation with capitalism, but co-operation. Thomas warned that 'all that government can do, when all is said and done, is infinitesimal compared with what business can do for itself'. There was to be no control of financial and banking institutions, no direction of private investment, certainly no public ownership, and most certainly no departure from free trade and Gold. Above all, there was to be a balanced budget.

Snowden's reappointment as Chancellor was a public acknowledgement of the government's determination to adhere to Treasury orthodoxies; for it ruled out any possibility of the adoption of deficit budgeting, protective tariffs, import restrictions and public control of bank investment. Mosley had put forward these ideas as a member of the unemployment committee chaired by Thomas, but became in turn angry and exasperated at the failure of his colleagues to comprehend them. In January 1930 he presented his proposals to the Cabinet, only to have them rejected (May), and the Labour Party Conference in October refused to have the 'Mosley Memorandum' discussed by the National Executive Committee. In March 1931, having already left the government, Mosley resigned from the party to form a New Party. This was a tragedy for Mosley personally; none of his candidates was successful in the 1931 general election, and the following year he founded the British Union of Fascists, thus perverting his undoubted talents to the furtherance of overtly Hitlerite and anti-semitic ends. But it was also a tragedy for Labour. The policies enumerated in the Mosley Memorandum became associated with Mosley himself; the policies were rejected along with the man.

The major achievements of the government lay in the field of foreign affairs: its support of the Young Plan (August 1929) for rearranging German reparations payments and securing the withdrawal of Allied troops from the Rhineland; the London Naval Treaty of 1930 between Britain, the USA and Japan; the resumption of diplomatic relations with the Soviet Union. At home it proved totally — and deliberately — unadventurous. Its most ambitious piece of legislation was the Coal Mines Act of 1930, which reduced the working day in the mines from eight hours to seven and a half, but gave the mine-owners the authority to fix minimum prices and production quotas. The Act also set up a Coal Mines Reorganisation Commission, but without powers to force owners to close inefficient pits and amalgamate others its impact was bound to be muted.

Christopher Addison, who became Labour's Minister of Agriculture in 1930, pushed through an Agricultural Marketing Act, which established boards of producers to market and fix the price of agricultural produce; another practical application of the philosophy of helping capitalism to help itself. A Housing Act of 1930 provided subsidies for slum clearance. Herbert Morrison's Bill to reorganise London's private bus and underground railway services under a public corporation, the London Passenger Transport Board, was a casualty of the government's fall from office in 1931, but it was enacted, in a substantially unaltered form, in 1933; the transport unions were denied any representation on the Board, whose members were appointed by a group of five 'trustees', mainly bankers and accountants. The government made an attempt to placate the trade-union movement by introducing legislation to restore 'contracting out' and to give back to civil servants the right to union membership. This Bill, which was given a second reading in the Commons in January 1931, would also have legalised a sympathetic but not a general strike; it was wrecked by a Liberal amendment, defining a general strike, which was carried at the committee stage with the apparent approval of the Cabinet and the Attorney-General. C.P. Trevelyan, once more in charge of the Board of Education, attempted to fulfil an election promise to raise the school-leaving age to 15; the Bill was effectively destroyed in the Commons by an amendment, put forward by Roman Catholic Labour MPs, that would have delayed its implementation until satisfactory provision had been made for voluntary schools, and was then thrown out by the Lords (March 1931). Trevelyan resigned, though less over the fate of this particular measure than over the general weakness of the government in the face of the economic crisis by then clearly visible on the horizon.

This crisis destroyed the Labour administration, in a manner as breathtaking as it was graceless. As the world depression deepened in 1930, and Britain's trading position grew worse and foreign investment diminished and unemployment rose, MacDonald and Snowden became ever more anxious to secure all-party agreement on questions of economic strategy. To this end, in February 1931, a committee had been appointed under the chairmanship (appropriately) of Sir George May, secretary of the Prudential Assurance Company. Its report, published on 31 July, declared that the repayment of the National Debt was sacrosanct, and the payment of unemployment relief was not. To shoulder both these burdens would entail a deficit of £120 millions, only £24 millions of which ought to be met by increased taxation; to eliminate the deficit there would have to be a number of economies, including a reduction of 20 per cent in payments to the unemployed.

At this point events intervened which had nothing whatever to do with the balancing of the budget. A banking crisis in Austria and Germany had led the German government, wisely, to impose a block on the outflow of funds. Foreign investors therefore turned to Britain, and asked the Bank of England to repay deposits in gold, a request with which it complied; the loss of gold amounted to £4 millions per day. This haemorrhage could have been stopped by the suspension of the gold standard and the imposition of exchange controls. Instead, the City bankers argued that foreign confidence in sterling would be restored, provided the government repudiated any prospect of a budget deficit. Arriving back in London from his Scottish holiday on 11 August, MacDonald announced, 'We are of one mind; we intend to balance the budget'.

But the Cabinet was not of one mind. Between 20 and 23 August it agreed to cuts in the pay of the police, teachers and other public servants. However, nine of the twenty Cabinet members, led by Henderson, would not countenance a proposed cut of 10 per cent in the standard rate of unemployment benefit. It was evident that the government could not continue. On the evening of Sunday 23 August MacDonald asked all his Cabinet colleagues to place their resignations in his hands, which they did, thinking that a Conservative-Liberal administration would follow. But when the Labour Cabinet met for the last time, at noon the following day, MacDonald calmly announced that he had agreed to head a National Government, in which Baldwin and Herbert Samuel would serve under him. That evening it became clear that three other members of the Labour Cabinet had agreed to follow him: Lord Sankey, Philip Snowden and Jimmy Thomas.

MacDonald had, of course, betrayed the Labour Party and the Labour movement. Behind the backs of his Labour Cabinet colleagues he had intrigued with Samuel, Baldwin and Neville Chamberlain. Samuel, upon whom the leadership of the Liberal party had devolved owing to Lloyd George's ill health, believed that the formation of a National Government would enhance the prestige of the Liberal Party, which would participate in government for the first time since 1922. It was he who planted the idea of such a Government in MacDonald's mind. MacDonald warmed to it, but not because it fell in with some deep-laid plot; there was none, though the Labour Party may be forgiven for believing subsequently that such a conspiracy had indeed existed. MacDonald genuinely believed that the severity of the times called for a National Government, and that loyalty to party must remain a secondary consideration. His socialism had always been of the weakest. The events of the General Strike had reinforced his distrust of trade unions. Observers noted how, during the 1920s, he had removed himself from that contact with the grass-roots of the Labour movement which he had used to such good effect in building up the early Labour Party before the First World War. In 1926 Beatrice Webb made this prophetic observation to her diary:

My general impression is that J.R.M. feels himself to be *the* indispensable leader of a new political party which is bound to come into office within his life-time . . . He is no longer *intent* on social reform — any indignation he ever had at the present distribution of wealth he has lost; his real and intimate life is associating with non-political aristocratic society, surrounded with the beauty and dignity which wealth can buy and social experience can direct.

In accepting the King's invitation to form and be head of a National Government, MacDonald, like Peel and Gladstone, Joseph Chamberlain and Winston Churchill, put Country before Party. Sankey and Snowden joined the Government to defend the idea of a balanced budget. Jimmy Thomas followed MacDonald because (inveterate punter that he was) he liked to back a winner. His gambling instincts did not deceive him. At the general election held on 27 October the National Government won 67 per cent of the votes cast and 90 per cent (554) of the seats. Labour's vote fell to 6.6 millions; it was represented in the House of Commons by just 52 MPs, its worst result since December 1910.

It is important to separate out the personal tragedy that befell MacDonald from the trauma that enveloped the Labour Party. From the experience of 1931 Labour emerged a leaner, but healthier, animal. Party activists seized the opportunity provided by the betrayal and the subsequent electoral disaster to urge the adoption of policies far more radical than anything Labour had espoused hitherto. They were assisted by the fact that, of those members of the government who had opposed MacDonald in August 1931, only Lansbury, Clement Attlee and Richard Stafford Cripps retained their seats. Lansbury became nominal leader of the parliamentary party; Attlee, his deputy, succeeded him in 1935. Cripps was the acknowledged leader of the militant left wing, but Lansbury and Attlee were equally left of centre, receptive to the ideas now coming forward at party conferences and on the National Executive Committee.

In 1932 the annual conference resolved that 'the main objective of the Labour Party is the establishment of socialism', and that 'the common ownership of the means of production and distribution is the only means by which the producers by hand and brain will be able to secure the full fruits of their industry'; the party was also committed to the nationalisation of the joint-stock banks, and to public control of the finance and merchant-banking houses. At the 1933 conference the next Labour government was further committed to the nationalisation of land, transport and electricity generation and distribution. Moreover, in an astonishing rebuff to Morrison, the conference pledged itself in favour of the direct representation of trade unions on the boards of management of nationalised undertakings. 'Workers' control', Attlee declared in 1935, 'is . . . an essential part of the new order'.

Labour's definitive programme, *For Socialism and Peace*, was approved by the party conference in 1934; it added water supply, coal, iron, steel 'and other key industries' to the list of activities to be taken under public control, talked about the 'public direction and control' of agriculture, and the 'public regulation . . . of industries and services not under public ownership'. This programme formed, in its essentials, the basis of the policy initiatives undertaken by the Labour government that came to power in July 1945.

But the 1930s did not belong to Labour. At the general election of 14 November 1935 Labour regained most of the votes it had lost in 1931; indeed, its share of the vote increased marginally compared with 1929, and 154 Labour candidates were returned to Westminster. The losers in 1935 were the Liberals, reduced to 21 MPs, only six of them representing urban constituencies; the Liberal Party was confined henceforth to a parliamentary impotence from which it has rarely emerged. The 1935 contest defined British politics in terms of the Conservative-Labour dichotomy within which it was to remain until 1970. The two parties drew their electoral strengths from well-defined areas of the country: Labour from South Wales, inner London, the west Midlands, south Yorkshire, Merseyside, north-east England and mid-Scotland; the Conservatives from southern England, East Anglia, the agricultural counties of the Midlands and the north. Within these areas were to be found constituencies of reasonably uniform social composition. Those seats in which the social composition was more fluid formed the real electoral battleground. During the 1930s this battleground fell to the Conservative party.

The National Governments which ruled Britain from 1931 to 1940 were in reality Conservative governments. In 1931 the Conservative party alone obtained 55.2 per cent of the votes cast, and returned 473 MPs. Baldwin could have formed a purely Conservative government, but it suited him not to. He had given his word that he would serve under MacDonald; besides, it was useful to be able to share the blame for the unpleasant medicine that was to be administered in an attempt to revive the economy. The 'National Labour' MPs numbered no more than 13, but as long as MacDonald, their leader, remained Prime Minister the term

'National Government' had a veneer of truth to it. On 7 June 1935 MacDonald stepped down from the premiership and took Baldwin's place as Lord President of the Council, a post he held until 1937, the year of his death. At the 1935 election the conservatives won 53.7 per cent of the votes cast, and though they suffered a net loss of 36 seats, their dominance of the Commons was still overwhelming. The term 'National Government' gradually fell into disuse.

To some extent the massive majorities — in terms both of seats and votes — which the Conservative party registered in 1931 and 1935 were obtained by default. In 1929 Labour had won no less than 118 seats on a minority vote. But now that the old Liberal Party was a spent force many of these Labour seats became exceedingly vulnerable in straight fights with Conservative opponents. In 1931 Labour was in evident disarray. What else could the electorate do but vote for the Conservative Party? However, to offer this explanation would be less than just to the party which Baldwin led. The 1930s were characterised by a broad consensus that eschewed the politics of extremes. A moderately-led TUC presided over a moderate trade-union movement; compared with the 1920s, the 1930s were years of marked industrial tranquillity. The Communist Party tried to exploit the miseries of the socially deprived but could only claim one parliamentary success, that of Willie Gallagher at West Fife (1935). The British Union of Fascists picked up some support at the London County Council elections of 1937, but failed to secure any seats at County Hall; it did not contest the 1935 general election and its membership never exceeded about 40,000. In returning Conservative majorities at Westminster the nation demonstrated its confidence in the moderation — in both foreign and domestic fields — that Baldwin personified. But Baldwin's charisma was gradually overshadowed by that of Neville Chamberlain, the true hero of inter-war Toryism. The folk-memory of Neville Chamberlain has been distorted by his disastrous three years as Prime Minister (May 1937-May 1940), dominated as they were by the apparent triumph but ultimate failure of his policy of appeasing Nazi Germany. Had Chamberlain died in 1937 he would have been remembered as a great social reformer.

The younger son of Joseph Chamberlain, and half-brother to Austen, Neville had not entered Parliament until 1918, when he was nearly 50 years old. He had followed a career in business and local government, becoming Lord Mayor of Birmingham in 1915. He represented a Birmingham constituency throughout his parliamentary career. He was a meticulous administrator and a keen advocate of technological innovation; he grasped at once the potential of the talking-cinema newsreel, which he used to excellent effect to explain his budgets when Chancellor of the Exchequer between 1931 and 1937. Above all, he identified with that broad, sympathetic outlook towards the victims of social distress that had once characterised the Conservative party, and he brought it to life once more.

Between 1922 and 1923 Chamberlain held successively the offices of Postmaster General, Paymaster General, Minister of Health and Chancellor of the Exchequer. In 1924 Baldwin reappointed him to the Health portfolio. He at once mapped out a programme of 25 Bills; 21 reached the statute book. Of these the most significant was the Widows', Orphans' and Old Age Contributory Pensions Bill, enacted in 1925. There had been pressure to bring health and pensions insurance within one scheme. For the time being this proved impracticable (though it was achieved, by Labour, in 1948, when the approved societies which administered health insurance were superseded). Chamberlain did, however, succeed in linking the two types of provision: all those covered by National Health Insurance were entitled to benefits under his Bill: a pension of 10s a week for widows (plus allowances for their dependent children), 7s 6d for orphan children, and 10s for insured workers and their wives payable at 65 years of age. The 1908 scheme of non-contributory old-age pensions payable at 70 continued in force. The new scheme started almost at once; in his 1925 budget Churchill announced that although income tax was to be reduced by 6d, death duties were to be increased, and an annual subsidy was to be paid by the Treasury to finance Chamberlain's legislation.

The record of the approved societies was mixed; some were inefficient, others used their powers to block reform. Labour was grudging in its approval of the 1925 Act. Lansbury claimed that it represented a reversion to the Elizabethan Poor Law because, he told the Commons, the principle of contributory insurance had shifted the burden from society as a whole back to the individual. This was arrant nonsense. At 9d a week, half of which was paid by the employer, Chamberlain's scheme was very good value for money, and amounted to a real transfer of wealth from the rich to those of more modest means. But Chamberlain had not forgotten the Poor Law. In November 1928 he introduced a mammoth Bill to reform the administration of poor relief. Under the terms of what became the Local Government Act of 1929, the 635 Poor Law Unions, along with their associated Boards of Guardians, were swept away. Their powers, and the institutions they administered (including hospitals), were transferred to the counties and county boroughs; local authorities were also empowered to co-operate with the voluntary hospitals in developing a co-ordinated hospital service. The Poor Law remained, but, under its new name of Public Assistance, it was now more efficiently administered by Public Assistance Committees; the unemployed were henceforth the responsibility of these committees or, if they were still 'in benefit', of the Ministry of Labour.

The 1929 Act also wrought profound changes in the organisation and powers of local authorities. The legislation instituted a ten-yearly review of urban and rural district councils. By 1939 the number of urban districts had been reduced from 783 to 572, and of rural districts from 652 to 475; during the same period 33 new municipal boroughs were created. The county councils were given new areas of responsibility covering roads, town and country planning, public health (including hospital provision), maternity and child welfare. In Scotland, separate but parallel legislation transferred most of the powers of local government, including education, to the county authorities. Although, in 1928, Winston Churchill had announced a substantial measure of derating, to help industrial recovery (agricultural land and farm buildings were entirely exempted from the payment of rates, and industrial property and the railways received three-quarters relief), the Treasury instituted a system of 'block grants' to make good to local authorities the money lost thereby. The payment of block grants, calculated according to the rateable wealth and social needs of each authority, replaced the old system of percentage grants, whereby the Treasury had contributed a proportion of total expenditure. The old system had favoured the prosperous, high-spending areas; the new system gave most money where it was most needed. Here, too, therefore, the Conservatives instituted a measure of wealth-redistribution.

During the period of office of the second Labour government Chamberlain consolidated his position within the Conservative party as the champion of tariff reform, the bearer of the torch kindled by his father at the beginning of the century. As chairman of the party's research department he helped organise the carefully worded 'Home and Empire' campaign to promote the idea of 'safeguarding' the domestic economy through the adoption of imperial preference. At the same time Lords Beaverbrook and Rothermere (proprietors, respectively, of the *Daily Express* and the *Daily Mail*) launched the United Empire Party to pursue the cause of 'Empire Free Trade'. Baldwin was forced to agree to the resignation of J.C.C. Davidson as chairman of the party organisation, a post to which Chamberlain at once succeeded.

The defeat of the official Conservative by an Empire Free Trade candidate at the South Paddington by-election on 30 October 1930 inaugurated a furious struggle between the press barons and Baldwin, in which the latter fought for his political life. In a rare display of measured statesmanship, Baldwin appealed to the good sense of the Conservative public (17 March 1931) to choose between him and 'the engines of propaganda for the constantly changing policies, desires, personal wishes, personal likes and personal dislikes of two men. . . . What the proprietorship of these papers is aiming at is power, but power without responsibility — the prerogative of the harlot throughout the ages.' Baldwin survived, and his leadership of the party was never again seriously challenged. But he owed his survival in no small measure to Chamberlain's sense of loyalty, and it was Chamberlain who became his heir apparent. Winston Churchill, at odds with the party because of his support for free trade and his opposition to Dominion status for India, entered the political wilderness, from where his criticisms of appeasement and his calls for rearmament against the dictators of Europe failed to make much impact. On 27 January 1931 Churchill resigned from the 'shadow cabinet'; he did not hold public office again until the formation of Chamberlain's War Cabinet in September 1939.

During the lifetime of the ill-fated Labour government there were other signs that the battle against free trade was being won. Chambers of Commerce, the Federation of British Industries, William Morris, the manufacturer of motor cars, all added their weight to demands for 'safeguards' within a system of imperial preference. In March 1931 Keynes announced his support for a temporary revenue tariff. Later that year Keynes, McKenna and Bevin joined three other members of the Macmillan Committee on Finance and Industry in signing an addendum to the committee's report, urging the adoption of a tariff. The Mosley Memorandum was rejected by the Labour Cabinet, but widely applauded outside government circles. The fall of the government accelerated the collapse of the old economic order. As Chancellor in the National Government Philip Snowden did what he had previously said could not be done: payments into the Sinking Fund were reduced by £20 millions; income tax was raised to 5s in the pound; and, on 21 September, the Gold Standard was suspended. By the end of 1931 the pound had stabilised at $3.40.

Following the National Government's landslide election victory Chamberlain became Chancellor and Walter Runciman, another enthusiastic advocate of tariffs, was put in charge of the Board of Trade. In November 1931 Parliament approved Runciman's Abnormal Importations Bill, which imposed a duty of 50 per cent on a wide range of imports. Early the following year Chamberlain introduced an Import Duties Bill. When it became law, in March 1932, a general duty of 10 per cent was placed upon almost all imports not covered by the earlier measure, but goods originating from within the Empire were exempted. At the same time an Import Duties Advisory Committee was established, to recommend to the Treasury the imposition of additional tariffs.

Later that year an Imperial Conference was held at Ottawa. The dominions (except the Irish Free State) agreed to a series of bilateral trade agreements with the United Kingdom, and to a raising of tariffs against foreign goods. To the disappointment of the Empire Free Traders, the already high tariffs against British goods were not lowered. None the less, if Empire Free Trade was unattainable *laissez-faire* had been killed off and, as Chamberlain told the Commons, the policies of his father had been vindicated. Herbert Samuel, with three other Liberals, resigned from the government, in public acknowledgement of Joseph Chamberlain's posthumous victory.

Thus, although the National Government had come into being as the instrument of existing economic orthodoxies, it had within a year been obliged to repudiate the policies of its begetters. Philip Snowden (then Lord Privy Seal) resigned along with the Liberals; the Cabinet thus lost the sternest advocate of the balanced budget. Neville Chamberlain professed to a desire to balance the books, but did not take the philosophy very seriously. His budgets were frankly inflationary. The first, in 1932, was meant to be orthodox, but was wrongly calculated, and led to an excess of expenditure over revenue of some £32 millions. Chamberlain did not seek to make good this loss, but simply added it to the National Debt. In 1933 the Sinking Fund was suspended; debt repayments were met by borrowing. The War Loan was converted from 5 per cent to 3.5 per cent, a rate of return which seemed to satisfy the investing public; by 1936, through this conversion and the lowering of the bank rate from 6 to 2 per cent, Chamberlain was managing to save the nation about £86 millions per annum in interest charges. In 1934 the cuts in unemployment pay were rescinded, and the following year the reductions in the pay of public servants were also fully removed; income tax was lowered from 5s to 4s 6d. When the need to pay for rearmament forced Chamberlain to restore the 5s rate, in two stages in 1936 and 1937, he balanced the higher direct tax by an impost of 2d per pound on tea, the appropriation of the Road Fund revenue (£5.25 millions) and (April 1937) a tax on business profits (the so-called National Defence Contribution) which delighted the socialists and caused a short-lived panic on the Stock Exchange.

Neville Chamberlain deserves his place as one of the country's great Chancellors. But we should exaggerate neither the motives which underlay his policies nor the extent to which they contributed to the national recovery. Chamberlain believed in 'good house-keeping', but not in economic planning. He was not a disciple of Keynes. In the *Treatise on Money* (1930) and the *General Theory of Employment, Interest and Money* (1936), Keynes set forth a blueprint for state intervention to stimulate the economy and create employment. The idea of economic planning aroused some interest within the Conservative party. In 1933 the young Harold Macmillan published *Reconstruction: a plea for a national policy*, and the organisation Political and Economic Planning (PEP), founded two years earlier, brought together Labour, Liberal and Conservative politicians as well as businessmen, academics and civil servants who were interested in finding solutions to the country's economic and social problems. But even within the Labour movement economic planning was regarded with suspicion. To many trade unionists it signified only greater state direction of labour, and to many moderate socialists it smacked of Bolshevik 'Five Year Plans'. Ironically, Keynes found a much more enthusiastic audience for his ideas in the United States of America: President F.D. Roosevelt's 'New Deal' owed something to Keynesian philosophy.

Chamberlain's policy of 'cheap money' certainly aided economic recovery, particularly in the house-building sector. The government did take some very modest initiatives to stimulate economic growth. In 1935 it agreed to guarantee the payment of interest on capital sums needed for railway reconstruction, and it gave similar guarantees for the building of the liner *Queen Mary*. The Bank of England was encouraged to advance monies for the construction of new steelworks. The Treasury advanced some money to local authorities to build roads, bridges, schools and houses. But these sums were never large (capital expenditure on roads and bridges actually fell from £10 millions in 1933 to £8 millions in 1936), and the lower interest rates which Chamberlain brought about were not as important in stimulating the economy as cheap labour (reinforced by the large pool of unemployed) and cheap raw materials (a product of the slump in world trade). The government's most significant contribution to economic recovery was its implementation of a rearmament programme after 1935.

However, the single most important factor in stimulating economic growth was the rise in real incomes of those in work. Between 1930 and 1935 weekly wage rates fell by about 2 per cent, but the fall in retail prices was of the order of 10 per cent. The difference between these two figures represented a major increase in real wages. For those who were employed — the majority of the working population — the 1930s were years of affluence, which may be measured in a variety of ways. In spite of record taxation levels, the volume of trade in — for example — clothing, furniture, electrical and other durable goods, cars and motor cycles increased practically without respite during the entire inter-war period. How were these purchases financed? Partly, no doubt, from savings but partly, too, by borrowing, which was not restricted to the acquisition of the more costly items. George Orwell remarked that 'the youth who leaves school at fourteen and gets a blind-alley job is out of work at twenty, probably for life; but for two pounds ten on hire-purchase he can buy himself a suit which, for a little while and at a little distance, looks as though it had been tailored in Saville Row'. Investments in building societies rose from £88 millions in 1920 to £711 millions in 1939; much of this money was made available to house-purchasers on very easy terms. A semi-detached house, complete with bathroom and garage, typically located in the suburbs of London, could be bought for as little as £450; mortgages, at around 4.5 per cent, were well within the means of most middle-class and some working-class families. These houses invariably incorporated electric lighting systems. In 1920 there had been only 730,000 electricity consumers in Britain, and only one house in seventeen had been wired to the national grid; by 1939 there were some nine million electricity consumers, and two out of every three houses were 'wired up'.

The provision of domestic electricity stimulated the growth of industries manufacturing household appliances such as refrigerators, vacuum cleaners and radios; the number of radio licences issued rose from 1.7 millions in 1925 to 8.9 millions in 1940. The development of the electricity industry also assisted in the electrification of suburban railways, while the completion of the national grid (1933) facilitated the siting of industries away from the coalfields. For some industries, in particular, the 1930s were years of unparalleled growth. By 1937 Britain was producing over half a million motor vehicles a year. A major new industrial activity, employing roughly 400,000 people, had thus come into being, located not in the areas of the old staples but in Birmingham, Coventry, Oxford, Luton and London. Mass production and falling prices stimulated car sales; the number of private cars registered in the United Kingdom stood at about one million in 1930, but had risen to over 1.8 millions by 1937. Progress in engineering technology was reflected not merely in the building of motor vehicles, but also in the growth of the aircraft industry and the development of more efficient methods of building construction. Progress in petro-chemical technology was responsible for the increasing use of plastics ('bakelite') in consumer goods, and of man-made fibres (such as 'rayon') in the clothing industry, and led to the development of synthetic dyes and cheaper chemicals and fertilisers.

The 1930s were years of great paradox. For those in work they were years of plenty, of more money to spend on a greater variety of convenience foods and consumer durables, on newspapers and radio sets, on better clothes, on outings to the cinema and holidays by the sea. For those out of work they were years of misery and humiliation. In 1934 the government officially designated four areas (parts of Scotland and of South Wales, West Cumberland, and Tyneside with most of County Durham) as 'Depressed' (renamed by the House of Lords as 'Special') Areas, over which commissioners were appointed and given £2 millions to spend to attract new industries. The scheme was a conspicuous failure.

Those who could, simply moved away from the Special Areas to find work in the Midlands and the South. Those who could not joined the ranks of the long-term unemployed.

When these unfortunates had exhausted the benefits to which their contributions had entitled them, they became eligible for grants from the Exchequer, known first as 'uncovenanted benefit' (1921–4), then as 'extended benefit' (1924–8), later as 'transitional benefit' (1928–31) and 'transitional payment' (1931–4) and finally as 'unemployment assistance'. In 1931 the National Government imposed a test of means upon all those claiming transitional benefit. At first the 'means test' was administered by the Public Assistance Committees of the local authorities, but in 1934 Chamberlain's Unemployment Act transferred these functions to a 'non-political' Unemployment Assistance Board, which continued to function (as the Assistance Board) until 1948. The intimate investigations carried out by those who applied the means test, the visits of 'relieving officers' to the homes of the unemployed, perhaps to suggest that furniture be sold, or that fathers rely on the income of their sons, became a greater source of bitterness than the fact of unemployment; the gnawing resentment to which it gave rise extended beyond the unemployed themselves and outlived the Second World War.

Life on 'the dole' was unpleasant, demoralising and a waste of human resources. But people did not starve. Between 1931 and 1935 a husband, his wife and three children at school would normally receive about 29s 3d a week; in 1936 they could expect to receive about 36s. Contemporary observers differed as to the real worth of such an income. In *The Road to Wigan Pier* (1937) George Orwell referred to the view given in one newspaper that a single person could afford a balanced diet on less than 4s a week. In *Poverty and Progress* (1941) Seebohm Rowntree placed the threshold of absolute subsistence (for a family with three dependent children) at 30s 7d a week, excluding rent; the minimum income necessary for a healthy life he put at 43s 6d, or 53s with rent. He found that one-third of the working-class population of York was living below this level.

'To keep a family of five in health on 53s. a week, [Rowntree wrote] even when income is guaranteed for fifty-two weeks in the year, needs constant watchfulness and a high degree of skill on the part of the housewife' (*The Human Needs of Labour*, 1937). Yet the writings of Orwell, of Walter Greenwood (*Love on the Dole*,

1933) and of J.B. Priestley (*English Journey*, 1934), though they paint a picture of boredom, frustration and helplessness, also reveal a capacity for survival and — on the part of the young at any rate — an ability to make the most of small luxuries. 'It is quite likely', observed Orwell, 'that fish-and-chips, art-silk stockings, tinned salmon, cut-price chocolate . . . the movies, the radio, strong tea and the football pools have between them averted revolution.' And, though it shocked some contemporaries, couples did marry and raise families on the dole, the income from which might be higher than that which could be obtained in low-paid employment.

How far the experience of the 1930s was reflected in the politics of the 1940s must remain (in the absence of detailed survey evidence) a matter of conjecture. The decade that separated the general elections of 1935 and 1945 was dominated by a 'total' war which, through the common suffering and privation which it brought to the nation, swept away a great many assumptions which had been widely believed but a few years previously. The evacuation of children from urban areas to middle-class homes in the countryside demonstrated the effects of deprivation in a way that could not otherwise have been achieved in an age before television. The owner of one country house explained,

> I had little dreamt that English children could be so completely ignorant of the simplest rules of hygiene, and that they would regard the floors and carpets as suitable places upon which to relieve themselves.

Instances of head lice and scabies were commonplace; the clothes of evacuee children had often to be destroyed on account of the vermin harboured within them. But if the condition of these children shocked their hosts, the condition of the hosts impressed itself on their guests. The children of the urban poor experienced a standard of living that would ordinarily have been totally beyond their grasp. They, and their parents, now knew that there was more to life than they had been led to believe.

The experiences of the Blitz, of conscription, of rationing as well as of evacuation no doubt had a cumulative corrosive effect upon the barriers of class. The demands of the war effort upon manpower (and womanpower) solved the problem of unemployment; by 1944 the total number of registered unemployed in Great

Britain had fallen to a monthly average of 75,000. Since, as Rowntree had demonstrated, unemployment had been the commonest cause of poverty, the war had an effect here too. When Rowntree again surveyed York, in 1951, he found that less than 3 per cent of the working-class population were living below the subsistence level. The war also brought about the demise of the household means test; supplementary pensions were introduced in 1940, and the means test was abolished the following year. A national scheme of reduced price or, if necessary, free milk was introduced (1940) for mothers and young children. At the moment when the very existence of the nation was at issue, money was found to improve the lot of its citizens.

In April 1941 the Chancellor, Howard Kingsley Wood, agreed to the continuation of emergency subsidies on food (and, if necessary, on other commodities) so as to stabilise the cost of living at around 25-30 per cent above its 1939 level. By 1941 personal consumption had fallen by 14 per cent of its pre-war volume; the nation was spending 20 per cent less on food, 38 per cent less on clothes and 43 per cent less on household goods. Private motoring all but ceased, as petrol was unobtainable for non-essential purposes. Yet, in spite of the bombing and the longer hours of work, the standard of living actually increased. As Prime Minister of a coalition government (May 1940-May 1945) Churchill concerned himself almost exclusively with the direction of the war; it was Attlee, first as Lord Privy Seal and later (1942) as Deputy Prime Minister, who was left to preside over the 'home front'. But Churchill had had the foresight to include in his government Ernie Bevin, who became Minister of Labour. Under emergency legislation Bevin made all strikes illegal and set up a National Arbitration Tribunal to settle wage disputes. In March 1941 all skilled workers were made subject to direction of labour. But in agriculture a Wages Board was established to fix national minimum wages (1940), a Catering Wages Commission was set up in 1943, and in 1945 all trades boards were converted into wages boards and given increased powers.

During the war wage rates tended to rise slightly less than the cost of living (which increased by 50 per cent between 1939 and 1944), but, because of more regular employment, overtime and weekend working, actual earnings grew none the less by over 81 per cent compared with 1938. The freezing of house rents in 1939 undoubtedly helped to bolster living standards, and the general provision of subsidised school meals (1941) also did something to maintain the level of real wages. One indicator of improvement in the standard of life is provided by the infant mortality rate, which declined from 56 per thousand live births in England in the period 1936–8 to 45 per thousand in 1944–6. It is also worth noting that although nearly four million homes were destroyed by bombing (which accounted for 60,000 civilian deaths), many of these dwellings were back-to-back gardenless and insanitary slum properties in decaying city centres. People made homeless in this way were later rehoused in neat prefabricated one-storey dwellings before being moved into local-authority housing estates built in the suburbs.

There was, therefore, a very substantial amount of social improvement even though the nation was at war — indeed, the war alone had made it possible. Scarcely less significant was the fact of government intervention at all levels of society, from the control of all basic industries and industrial output and the direction of manpower, to the provision of food and clothing, and fixing of wages and the control of rents and mortgage repayments. Civil servants administered a policy of 'war socialism' in co-operation with business managers and trade-union officials. The power and ability of the state to enforce change was amply demonstrated, and a climate of opinion emerged which made it quite unthinkable to return to pre-war habits. In one of his popular Sunday radio broadcasts J.B. Priestley put the matter thus:

> Now the war, because it demands a huge collective effort, is impelling us to change not only our ordinary social and economic habits, but also our habits of thought. We're actually changing over from a property view to a sense of community, which simply means that we're all in the same boat.

In two famous reports, *Social Insurance and Allied Services* (1942) and *Full Employment in a Free Society* (1944) Sir William Beveridge, the Chairman of the Unemployment Insurance Statutory Committee (which had since 1934 supervised the administration of the unemployment insurance scheme), caught the mood to which Priestley had given expression. 'The purpose of victory [Beveridge wrote in his December 1942 report] is to live in a better world than the old world . . . each individual is more likely to concentrate upon his war effort if he feels that his government will be ready with plans for that better world.'

Beveridge added that, 'if these plans are to be ready in time, they must be made now'. Churchill allowed the Beveridge blueprints for a welfare state to be published (after a clumsy attempt had been made in December 1942 to prevent details of the *Social Insurance* report reaching the troops) less because he actually supported them than because he felt their publication was good for national morale: the country had something to fight for as well as an enemy to fight against. In February 1943 the government accepted in principle Beveridge's ideas for family allowances, the avoidance of mass unemployment and a national health service, as well as for a universal contributory insurance scheme covering sickness, unemployment, old-age and widows' pensions and funeral grants. But the acceptance was not enthusiastic. In a broadcast delivered in March, Churchill warned against 'fairy tales', and the Coalition Government refused to implement any of the proposals until after the end of hostilities.

However, the government took a different view of the need for educational reform. In his broadcast Churchill laid great stress on the need for such reform, so that 'the path to the highest functions throughout our society and Empire is really open to the children of every family'. The following year the government permitted the President of the Board of Education, R.A. Butler, to introduce the most fundamental reform of the organisation of education in England and Wales since Balfour's Act of 1902. Indeed, the Butler Act of 1944 was more far-reaching, since it provided the framework for a general system of education under the direction of a Minister whose duty it would be to map out 'a national policy for providing a varied and comprehensive educational service in every area'. The provision of a progressive system of primary, secondary and further education was to be in the hands of local authorities, and the school-leaving age was to be raised to 15 (a reform not actually implemented until 1947). There was, therefore, to be 'secondary education for all', the break between the primary and secondary stages coming (in practice) at 'eleven-plus'.

The Act itself did not specify what forms secondary education might take. However, following the lines of a government White Paper (1943) three types of secondary school emerged: the grammar, the secondary technical and the secondary modern. This tripartite division was quite artificial, and the institution of the eleven-plus examination probably did more harm than good:

children whose performance in the examination did not warrant their admission to grammar schools were written off as failures. But if these concepts have now gone out of fashion, we should remember that it was society that wrote off the eleven-plus 'failures', not the Butler Act, and that the grammar schools were the means by which hundreds of thousands of children from working-class homes received an education, free of charge, of a standard easily comparable with that offered by the most prestigious fee-paying establishments.

When, in May 1945, the war in Europe came to an end, the Labour Party, then in conference at Blackpool, determined to pull out of the Coalition. On 23 May Churchill became head of a caretaker government while a general election was held. Polling took place on 5 July but owing to the necessity of counting servicemen's votes the result was not known for another three weeks. On the night of 25 July it became clear that Labour had won a sweeping victory. The following day Churchill resigned and Attlee became head of a Labour administration with a majority of 146 seats in the House of Commons. The Labour Party had polled 47.8 per cent of the total votes cast, but if we confine ourselves to those constituencies which Labour fought (604 out of 640) the average Labour vote was actually 50.4 per cent.

At no general election before or since has Labour achieved such a result. The 1945 victory was a famous one: with the support of nearly 12 million voters as against the Conservative total of just under 10 millions, Labour could rightly claim to have become a, and perhaps the, national party. It is not difficult to understand why. During the 1930s, and particularly after Attlee had taken over as Leader, the party had rehabilitated itself with a series of constructive proposals which may have seemed almost revolutionary at the time but which, in the light of 'war socialism', now seemed both reasonable and practicable. People will accept in war forms of state action and state intervention which they will not accept in peace, and the experience of the Second World War had taught the British electorate that the powers of the state could indeed be harnessed to bring about social and economic change while avoiding a dictatorship of the left or the right. There was to be no return to the drift of the 1930s. More importantly, the Conservative party, as it was then constituted, could not be trusted to consolidate and build upon the advances that had been made during the war. Churchill had been a great war leader. But the

Conservative Party he led was tainted with the triple stigmas of mass unemployment, social deprivation and appeasement. During the war some of the key posts in government had been held by Labour men: Attlee, Arthur Greenwood and later Bevin, Cripps (Lord Privy Seal, 1942) and Morrison (Home Secretary, 1942) had all entered the War Cabinet, Albert Alexander had been in charge of the Admiralty, Hugh Dalton of the Board of Trade and William Jowitt had been Solicitor-General. Labour had proved itself as an experienced party of government. It was now given the chance to govern.

Those who believed that the advent of the first Labour government to command its own majority in the Commons would inaugurate a social and economic revolution were to be cruelly disappointed. The legislative achievement of the Attlee administrations of 1945–51 was massive, but it did not amount to the birth of a socialist or egalitarian society. True, the basic utility industries were put under state ownership. The Civil Aviation Act of 1946 brought two public corporations into existence, British European Airways and the British Overseas Airways Corporation. In the same year the Bank of England was nationalised and the National Coal Board was set up to manage all the coal mines and a host of ancilliary activities, such as coking plants. The creation of the British Transport Commission, in 1947, brought under public control all the railways and canals, most road-haulage companies, and a miscellany of enterprises (such as docks, ferries and hotels) which the railway companies had come to operate; the Commission also acquired the formal direction of London Transport. The generation and retail distribution of electricity were also taken over by the state. In 1948 came the nationalisation of the gas industry, and in 1949 the British Iron and Steel Corporation was set up as a holding company to manage the nationalised iron and steel undertakings.

What did the government hope to achieve by these measures? Formally, their passage into law was in fulfilment of Labour Party policy. Actually, most of them were made necessary by post-war conditions. The state of the coal-mining and railway and canal industries was such that many owners and shareholders were only too pleased to be rid of confirmed loss-makers. Of course, a ritual fuss was made over the terms of compensation. Owners of railway, canal and dock shares received £1,065 millions of British Transport 3 per cent stock, redeemable by 1988; each individual stock allocation was made on the basis of Stock Exchange valuations between February 1945 and November 1946. While interest at the rate of 3 per cent was not as high as some stockholders had been receiving during the most profitable years of the 1930s, it was significantly higher than railway shareholders had received in bad years (such as 1932 and 1938), and was probably higher than the return which the private railway companies would have achieved once exposed to the full force of road-traffic competition in the 1950s and 1960s.

As for the other nationalised undertakings, some of these (such as gas and electricity) were already under substantial municipal ownership; the wholesale distribution of electricity had, in any case, been under the control of the state-owned Central Electricity Board since 1926. The reorganisation of civil aviation actually set up two corporations where only one had existed before (the British Overseas Airways Corporation, established through the compulsory amalgamation in 1939 of Imperial Airways and British Airways). The nationalisation of the mines had, as we have seen, been recommended by the Sankey Royal Commission in 1919. Its enactment now was regarded as a debt of honour owed to the miners, just as the repeal of the 1927 Trade Disputes Act was an acknowledgement of the sanctity of Labour's trade-union roots.

There was, of course, nothing particularly 'socialist' about public ownership *per se*. Nor are we justified in concluding that Labour's method of nationalisation served socialist ends. There were, for example, no concessions to 'workers' control': public ownership was not used as a means of shifting power within industrial concerns. The adoption of the public corporation as the model for running the nationalised industries meant that there was — in effect — a board of directors for each enterprise, nominated by the government but with virtually complete freedom in matters of day-to-day management. The rights of trade unions to engage in meaningful collective bargaining were indeed considerably strengthened; but the unions were given no managerial status. A handful of trade-union officials were appointed to the boards of the nationalised undertakings, but on a purely personal basis. By 1951 only 16 of the 95 full- and part-time members of these boards were trade unionists. In the main, those who were appointed to the boards were, like Lord Hyndley (a leading private colliery owner, appointed to head the National Coal Board) those who had previous experience of owning and running large industrial concerns: that is, they were capitalists.

The aim of Labour's nationalisation programme was, simply put, efficiency. In its 1945 election manifesto, *Let Us Face The Future*, Labour had expressed the hope that 'amalgamation under public ownership' of the coal mines would bring about 'great economies in operation and make it possible to modernise production methods and to raise safety standards'. Morrison had declared bluntly that the nationalised undertakings were 'not ends in themselves' but that the object was 'to make possible organisation of a more efficient industry, rendering more public service'. Moreover, only 20 per cent of the economy, encompassing some of the most under-capitalised and worn-out sectors, were taken under public control. The remaining 80 per cent were left in private hands.

In this connection Labour inherited an armoury of wartime controls, which it could have used to implement a programme of planned economic recovery, by — for example — directing investment into certain areas and restricting growth in others. Some use was made of this machinery. Through the Capital Issues Committee the government blocked investment in the distributive trades, entertainment, insurance, banking and hire-purchase, but encouraged new issues to finance industries that manufactured for export or that saved on imports. But the only significant exercise in planning that the government ever undertook was its *Economic Survey for 1947*; this document set out manpower and output targets in a variety of industries, but omitted any discussion of how such targets were to be reached. Even in those areas of public finance where there was control machinery, such as restrictions on the movement of capital out of the country, this machinery did not work well; between 1946 and 1949 about £2,000,000,000 of private capital was exported illegally.

The basis of Labour's economic policy was not state direction of private enterprise, but state assistance to help the recovery of the private sector; in practice, therefore, there was not much difference between Attlee's approach and that of MacDonald 16 years earlier. The 1947 *Survey* declared in unambiguous terms that 'controls cannot by themselves bring very rapid changes or make fine adjustments in the economic structure. . . under democracy the execution of the economic plan must be much more a matter for co-operation between the Government, industry and the people than of rigid application by the State of controls and compulsions'. Thus, just as 'workers' control' was rejected in the sphere of nationalisation, so the task of planning economic recovery was entrusted to those who already managed British industry and commerce. In 1947 a Central Economic Planning Staff was appointed, headed by a Chief Planning Officer (a leading industrialist and a director of British Aluminium); the most important planning functionaries attached to the Whitehall departments were likewise drawn from the ranks of big business. This guaranteed that such controls as the government did possess were not used for any socialist end. In any case, after 1948 (when Harold Wilson took over from Stafford Cripps as President of the Board of Trade) the government embarked upon a deliberate policy of doing away with controls over the private sector. By 1950 it no longer had access to the mechanisms necessary to implement state direction of the economy.

We may explain this lack of socialist commitment by reference to the conservatism of most members of the government, to the inertia of the senior civil service, to the influence wielded by the captains of industry. We may refer to the opprobrium in which planning was held following the unexpected fuel and sterling crises of 1947. We must, however, bear in mind the economic background to Labour's tenure of office in the immediate post-war period. Put briefly, in 1945 the United Kingdom was — as near as any nation can be — bankrupt. During the war the national wealth of the country had declined by a fifth; the economy had been kept going only because of generous 'Lend-Lease' arrangements which Churchill had negotiated with President Franklin Roosevelt of the United States. By the spring of 1941, when Lend-Lease began, Britain's gold and dollar reserves had fallen from £864 millions (1939) to just £3 millions. This potentially disastrous situation had been redeemed somewhat by the end of the war because of purchases by American forces in the sterling area; by the autumn of 1945 the gold and dollar reserves had risen to £453 millions. Still, the country's overseas debt now stood at £3,355 millions (over four times its 1939 value), and with the end of the war the free-spending American forces began to depart.

The need to negotiate new American loans was therefore paramount, and the Americans were willing to grant them, but only under strict conditions, some of which were explicit (for instance, the removal of restrictions on the convertibility of sterling into other currencies) and some of which were not (such as support for American policy towards Stalin's Russia, and the maintenance of a military presence in Europe). When convertibility came (15 July-20 August 1947) the drain on Britain's gold and dollar reserves amounted to $150,000,000. Covertibility was suspended, and was not fully restored until 1958. The implementation of the American Marshall Aid Program in 1948 also had domestic implications for the Labour government. Aid was given on condition that grandiose plans of social reform were watered down or shelved altogether; indeed, the Americans appointed a supervisor of their own ('The Chief of the Special Mission of the European Co-operation Administration to the United Kingdom') to make sure that this was so. He was able to reassure the American Congress (1948) that the British 'housing programme has been quite seriously cut back. So has the health programme, and so has the programme for education'.

Given these unprecedented limitations on the freedom of action of a British government, the achievements of the Attlee administration in the field of welfare provision can be more accurately appreciated. The National Insurance Act of 1946 implemented the Beveridge proposals for comprehensive social insurance. In 1948 the National Assistance Board was set up 'to assist persons in Great Britain who are without resources to meet their requirements or whose resources . . . must be supplemented in order to meet their requirements'; the concept of a locally administered poor law was thus finally laid to rest. Housing Acts of 1946 and 1948 resulted in the construction of over 800,000 dwellings and the conversion of 333,000 others. Above all there was Aneurin Bevan's 1946 National Health Service Act, designed to provide free medical care for every inhabitant of the country, with finance derived partly from insurance contributions and partly from national taxation; although private health care remained, the hospitals were nationalised and their services were henceforth provided without charge.

It is undoubtedly true that the persistence of austerity, the stringent limits placed upon personal consumption, the rationing and the drabness of immediate post-war Britain contributed to the decline in popularity of the Labour administration. At the general election of 23 February 1950 the government's vote increased by over a million, but Conservative support rose by well over two millions; the Labour majority slumped to just five seats, hardly sufficient to permit another five-year term. With the onset of the Korean War the new Labour Chancellor, Hugh Gaitskell, budgeted for increased military expenditure by cutting back on social-service spending. Each prescription for medicines under the Health Service now cost one shilling; Bevan, Wilson and John Freeman, a junior minister, resigned from the government in protest. Yet between the elections of 1950 and 25 October 1951 the government did not lose a single by-election. And at the 1951 poll the Labour vote (13.9 millions) was actually greater than that of the Conservatives (13.7 millions). Only the vagaries of the electoral system permitted the Conservatives to emerge with a larger number of parliamentary seats than Labour and an overall majority of 17.

The electorate had clearly not 'rejected socialism', partly because (as Hugh Dalton later admitted in his memoirs), socialism had not been tried: 'we weren't really beginning our socialist programme until we had gone past all the public utilities. . . which were publicly owned in nearly every capitalist country in the world' (*High Tide and After*, 1962). Moreover, the 1951 election result showed that Labour was more popular than the Conservatives and, indeed, was only marginally less popular (in terms of the share of the vote) than in 1945. Labour had not engineered a social transformation or a significant transfer of wealth. It had sustained capitalism, not destroyed it. But it had created a caring society, it had transferred control of some industries to the state, and it had broken with the divisive class politics of the inter-war period. Perhaps, therefore, the message of the electorate in 1951 was that it approved of all this, and that a future Conservative government would need to move carefully if it chose to tamper with the post-war consensus.

7 A NEW BRITAIN?

The 1950s, rather than the late 1940s, marked the transition from a wartime to a peacetime society in Britain. The period of office of the Attlee governments had been marked by the persistence of rationing, consumer credit restrictions, and other remembrances of a society at war. Vast areas of the major inner cities remained as derelict 'bombed sites', the redevelopment of which awaited the easing of financial constraints. City centres themselves had been permanently depopulated, and the need to demolish housing stocks that remained, in order to rebuild and redevelop in a comprehensive manner, led to a further movement of population into the suburbs. The population of Greater London ceased to grow; from a record 8.7 millions in 1939, the number of persons living in the nation's capital fell by 150,000 during the 1950s and contracted still further in the following two decades. A new 'urban region' arose in the south-east of England, where people who worked in the old County of London lived — if they were fortunate — in less crowded if rather drab two-storey council and private 'semi-detached' dwellings, comfortable but lacking in individuality and — if they were not — in 'high-rise' flats, the designs of which served as tributes to architectural insensitivity.

The wider ownership and use of motor cars greatly assisted in the suburbanisation of Britain. There are a variety of ways in which this trend may be measured. The number of cars (and motor cycles) licensed for use rose from 2.2 millions in 1946 to 4.8 millions in 1955. Over the following 15 years the number leapt to 12.7 millions; in 1970 the number of driving licences held stood at 17.5 millions, or roughly one for every three persons then living in the United Kingdom. At that time about 36 per cent of the working population motored to work, either as a driver or as a passenger in a private car. In 1981 the proportion had risen to more than 50 per cent. By then more than 60 per cent of households in Britain possessed one car; 16 per cent boasted two or more. But the fateful twist in the upward spiral of motor car use came in the 1950s. Petrol rationing was brought to an end in 1953. Its demise coincided with increases in real earnings; motor manufacturers cashed in on a rapidly expanding home market, and amalgamated to produce economies of scale; the firms of Austin and Morris merged in 1951 to become the British Motor Corporation, and in 1960 Leyland Motors took over Standard-Triumph. To cope with the demands of a new motoring public a powerful lobby, led by the Road Haulage Association and the motoring organisations (the Automobile Association and the Royal Automobile Club) campaigned for greater public expenditure on the nation's road system.

In its 1953 publication *No Road*, the British Road Federation condemned the existing road network as an amalgam of 'bottlenecks, sharp turns, blind bends, inadequate sight lines, narrow and often humped-back bridges, low bridges, congested built up areas and a carriageway for the most part only wide enough for one line of traffic in each direction'. But the nation had to wait until November 1959 for the inauguration of its first substantial motorway (the initial stage of the M1, from London to Birmingham), a road of several lanes from which all pedestrians and cyclists were banned. By 1982 over 1,600 miles of motorway had been constructed in Great Britain, linking all the major centres of population. The social as well as the economic effects have been profound. Released from the physical constraints of conventional roads, the road haulage industry (denationalised in stages by Conservative governments between 1953 and 1956) experienced a renaissance; the number of goods vehicles in use rose from about one million in 1955 to over two million by 1980 and the size of individual vehicles also increased. It became possible to carry by road even the bulkiest commodities, which had previously been carried by rail, but with virtually no sacrifice of speed, and as part of a door-to-door service which the railways could not match.

The construction of motorways also affected patterns of passenger travel. Immediately the M1 was opened the journey time by express coach from London to Birmingham was reduced from over five hours to under three; although this still compared unfavourably with the time taken by fast trains, coach operators were able to offer much lower fares. Market towns which had previously suffered heavy traffic congestion were liberated, so to speak, by the provision of motorways and of by-passes. At the same time the greater freedom of travel now available served to dissolve still further the division between town and country. Because they operated between fixed points, the railways had only had this effect to a limited extent. The effects of the growth of private motor transport were more pervasive. In 1962 the sociologist Ruth Glass explained these results as follows:

> The cities draw workers from suburbs, from exurbia, and from even more remote hinterlands. Holidays with pay and greatly increased speed and provision of public and private transport have resulted in frequent exchanges of visits between town and country. The same media of communication reach everywhere . . . The same chain stores which serve urban customers have become accessible to rural customers.
>   (in A. T. Welford *et al.*, *Society* (1962))

In the early 1950s horses were still to be seen at work in the cities of Britain, pulling milk and bread delivery carts and mobile grocery and greengrocery vans. By the time the Conservatives went out of office (1964) these sights were rare indeed. Instead, once empty streets were filled with parked cars and, increasingly, with parking meters. 'For personal and family use', Professor Colin Buchanan wrote in his celebrated report *Traffic in Towns* (1963), 'for the movement of people in mass, and for use in business, commerce and industry, the motor vehicle has become indispensable'. Inevitably, the railways suffered a desperate contraction as a result of these changes. The deficits experienced after 1955 derived much less from falls in passenger traffic than from very heavy losses in receipts from the carriage of freight. In 1952 the nationalised railways carried 24 per cent by tonnage of all freight transport in Great Britain. By 1970 the figure was as low as 10 per cent and most freight (85 per cent by tonnage) was carried by road. In 1952 the railways managed to show an overall return of £3.6 millions, but thereafter annual deficits were the order of the day; in 1962 alone a deficit of £156.1 millions was recorded.

   It is easy to blame the decline of the railways on poor productivity and, in particular, on over-manning. The realities were more complex. The Victorian railway system had been constructed when road competition was virtually non-existent. To serve small communities many branch lines had been built in the knowledge that they would never, by themselves, be profitable, but that they would generate traffic for the major parts of the network. The growth of motor transport dealt this arrangement a fatal blow. In its 1961 *Annual Report* the British Transport Commission explained how 'on the passenger side, enormous train mileages are run to provide local stopping services between stations which are still spaced with little regard to the competition from buses or the ever-growing availability of private transport'.

In 1962 the Conservative government reorganised the nationalised transport undertakings. The Transport Act of that year swept away the Transport Commission and replaced it with separate, independent Boards covering British Waterways, British Transport Docks, London Transport and British Railways, with residual road transport, hotel and other assets being managed by a Transport Holding Company. A Nationalised Transport Advisory Council was also established, but without any executive powers. The avowed purpose of the new arrangement was to give the various parts of the publicly owned transport system a greater degree of independence, and to endow them with responsibility for their financial affairs; they, in turn, were given more commercial freedom than hitherto.

To head the British Railways Board the Conservatives appointed Dr Richard Beeching, who had previously been on the board of Imperial Chemical Industries and had (briefly) served as chairman of the Transport Commission. In 1963 Beeching published a report on *The Reshaping of British Railways*. Written with meticulous attention to running costs, the report demonstrated how one-third of the route mileage of the railways carried only 1 per cent of the total passenger miles and only 1½ per cent of the freight ton-miles. The remedy could not be simpler: shut down over 5,000 route miles, and close about one-third of the stations to passenger traffic. Although Beeching did acknowledge that the implementation of such a policy would incur social costs (for instance, congestion of roads and road injuries and deaths) these matters were not the concern of the Board over which he presided. Within four years 84 per cent of the passenger-train withdrawals that he had proposed, and 72 per cent of the station withdrawals, had been carried out.

Beeching had also turned his attention to the operating efficiency of the railway system. In this connection it is clear that the years immediately following nationalisation had witnessed a number of policy decisions taken on grounds which not even the 'social costs' argument could justify. Foremost among these was the failure to implement an immediate policy of replacing steam with diesel and electric traction. A steam locomotive is a wonderful sight, but it is a notoriously inefficient machine; coal can be burnt much more efficiently in power stations, and the electricity generated thereby can drive electric locomotives at speeds no steam engine can match. But because of the existence of a powerful steam lobby in the old Railway Executive (abolished 1954), new steam locomotives were built throughout the 1950s.

Towards the end of the decade this mistake was recognised, but a new policy of replacing steam with diesel locomotives was carried out with undue haste: half the diesel locomotives bought from the North British Locomotive Company were of such poor quality that they had to be scrapped within a short time of delivery; the company itself was soon bankrupted. The electrification of the main lines from London to Birmingham, Liverpool, Manchester and Glasgow was too long delayed, though its desirability was obvious. The completion of the London-Manchester-Liverpool electrification (April 1966) witnessed an increase of 50 per cent in passenger receipts.

By then Beeching had returned to ICI. By drastic pruning of the workforce (which decreased from 641,000 to 273,000 between 1948 and 1963), modernisation of the wagon fleet and of freight yards, and increases in the speed and quality of passenger services, he had achieved some dramatic improvements in the productivity of the nation's railway system, particularly in regard to freight charges. But he was not able to make the railways run at a profit. Deficits of between £123 and £153 millions continued to be recorded in the period 1963–68, mainly due to the decline in coal and coke traffic. Nor was he, or any of his successors, able to convince governments that the railways must be regarded as a social service, in respect of which more rather than less government investment is necessary. Sir Peter Parker, chairman of British Rail from 1975 to 1983, warned in his annual report for 1979 that 'the results of under-investment are now showing through the deteriorating quality of service in parts of the system. We are replacing our assets at a slower rate than any other European railway.'

We noted earlier how the triumph of road over rail helped bring about important social transformations in Britain after the end of the Second World War. In particular, town and country have been brought closer together. The population of the United Kingdom has continued to grow, but the rate has moderated appreciably compared with the early twentieth century. In 1951 the total population stood at 50.2 millions; by 1971 it had reached 55.5

millions — an increase of 10.5 per cent, but at a rate of not much more than 0.5 per cent per annum. Much of this increase was due to high birth-rates in Northern Ireland. In the 1960s the Northern Irish birth rate stood at over 22 births per thousand of the population. In England the immediate post-1945 'baby boom' (when the rate reached 18 per thousand) was over by 1950, and though there was a boom of similar proportions in the early 1960s, by the late 1970s the rate had fallen as low as 12.1 per thousand, a figure never before reached since the systematic recording of births was begun. While the population of Northern Ireland increased by about one-eighth (or 166,000) between 1951 and 1971, that of Scotland stagnated at around 5.1 millions, and that of Wales grew by only 200,000 (i.e. less than 4 per cent) over the same twenty-year period.

A greater proportion than ever before of the total population of the United Kingdom (46.8 millions in 1981, or 83.1 per cent) now lives in England. But the percentage living in city centres has declined. The 1951 census found that 44.7 per cent of the population of England and Wales lived in urban areas; by 1981 the figure stood at 36.4 per cent. The population of Greater London at the end of the 1970s stood at 7 millions, having fallen by well over a million since 1951; the population of Manchester fell by 30 per cent between 1951 and 1977, of Liverpool by 32 per cent, of Glasgow by 24 per cent, of Bristol by 8 per cent and of Birmingham by 6 per cent. Those towns which have experienced population growth (such as Leeds and Bradford) have done so largely because of special factors, pre-eminently the settlement of immigrants from the New Commonwealth and Pakistan.

Post-war Britain has therefore been witness not merely to an intensification of the pre-war trend, to work in the city but to live in the suburbs, but to a new trend, to work in the city but live in the country, and even to live and work in rural surroundings, perhaps in one of the 'new towns' created following the passage of the New Towns Act of 1946, such as Stevenage and Peterlee. As a consequence of this, and of the effective spread of existing towns over their administrative borders, the crisp Victorian divide between the shire and the municipality broke down. The realisation that this was so led to a drastic re-ordering of local administration, the effect (intended or not) of which has been to kill off local self-government throughout the country.

The first stage in this process occurred as an inevitable by-product of the Labour reforms of the late 1940s. The passage of the 1948 National Assistance Act deprived local authorities of responsibility for the poor law; the counties and county boroughs were left with the obligation to provide residential accommodation for the elderly and the infirm, and to look after the handicapped. The nationalisation of electricity and gas undertakings took away from local authorities their powers in these spheres. The Water Act of 1945 imposed upon Whitehall (first the Ministry of Health, later the Ministry of Housing and Local Government) the obligation to formulate and execute a national water policy. Initially this involved nothing more than the amalgamation of small units. But in 1974 the various water functions — the supply of fresh water, the provision of sewers and the treatment and disposal of sewage, and the responsibility for rivers and land drainage, were all concentrated in the hands of Regional Water Authorities, upon which the last vestiges of local authority representation ceased as a result of Conservative legislation in 1983.

In respect of the two major functions of local authorities, housing and education, there has been a fundamental shift away from local control. Again, this has happened under both Labour and Conservative governments. During the 1950s and 1960s many local education authorities took advantage of their powers under the 1944 Education Act to abolish the grammar and secondary modern schools under their control, and to institute instead a system of comprehensive secondary schools catering for pupils of mixed ability. This policy had historically been a Labour preserve, but in fact it found favour also with a radical wing of the Conservative party, led by Sir Edward Boyle, who became Minister of Education in 1962. Boyle applauded the decision of the London County Council to end the eleven-plus examination, and publicly attacked the grammar-secondary modern divide as socially undesirable. Sir Robin Williams, of the Tory reformist Bow Group, condemned the public schools 'as at present organised' because they attracted 'a degree of envy and resentment which is unhealthy in a stable democracy'(*Whose Public Schools?* 1957).

In 1965 the Labour government took steps to end the eleven-plus examination and 'separatism' in the organisation of secondary schooling. A great deal of pressure — short of actual compulsion — was put on local authorities, so that by 1970 over a third of children in the secondary-age group were in comprehensive schools. Mainstream Conservatives, however, though generally favouring a broader base of recruitment to the public schools, could not bring themselves to force comprehensive education upon local authorities. But when Labour resumed office an Act to achieve just this objective was passed in 1976. This legislation was repealed by Mrs Thatcher's Conservative administration four years later. However, the Education Act of 1980 obliged local authorities to take account of parents' choice of school for their children, and gave parents the right to be represented on school governing bodies. At the same time, an Assisted Places scheme was instituted to enable parents of modest means to opt out of the state system, and send their able children to independent schools. These reforms proved generally popular. Yet one of their effects has been to erode the discretion and authority of elected local government so far as the provision of education is concerned.

Conservative housing policies have had an even more dramatic impact on the Victorian concept of local autonomy and permissiveness. After 1945 the Conservative party committed itself to the development of a 'home-owning democracy' and post-war Conservative administrations have consistently stressed the importance of home-ownership, on both social and political grounds. Believing that the establishment of a home-owning electorate would damage the future prospects of the Labour Party, the Thatcher government legislated (1980) to endow the tenants of local authorities with the right to buy the council houses in which they lived. In this way, by 1983 over half a million council houses and flats had been sold to the people living in them, and the proportion of people living in owner-occupied homes was increased from 55 to 60 per cent.

Successive Conservative administrations since the 1950s have also mounted complex operations to reduce the number of local authorities, and to deprive them of the last vestiges of financial autonomy. The London Government Act passed by Sir Alec Douglas-Home's administration in 1963 abolished the London County Council and the County of Middlesex, and instituted instead a Greater London Council, under which functioned 32 London Boroughs (instead of the 85 Metropolitan Boroughs, Boroughs and Urban Districts that had existed hitherto). Labour politicians declared that the legislation was politically motivated: the Conservatives had not been able to wrest control of the LCC from Labour, but there was a possibility (realised between 1967 and 1973 and again between 1977 and 1981) that they would be able to command a majority on the GLC. On administrative grounds the reform had much to commend it. But the suspicion of ulterior motives remained, particularly since the square mile of the City of London was left out of the new arrangements, and retained its medieval system of rule by a self-perpetuating oligarchy.

As a matter of fact many Conservatives remained unconvinced that larger units of local government really were in the national interest. In 1972 the Conservative administration of Edward Heath carried into effect the first comprehensive reorganisation of the structure of local government in England and Wales since 1888. Following the report of a Royal Commission headed by Lord Redcliffe-Maud (1966–69), the Local Government Act of 1972 dismantled the entire system of local authorities in England and Wales (excluding Greater London). In the 'conurbations' six metropolitan counties were established (Greater Manchester, Merseyside, South Yorkshire, Tyne and Wear, West Midlands and West Yorkshire), within which 36 metropolitan district councils operated; elsewhere 47 non-metropolitan counties (and, within them, 333 district councils) replaced the old shires.

Again, there were very sound administrative and societal reasons for undertaking such a fundamental reform, in particular the recognition of the reality of the 'region', embracing urban, suburban and rural areas, and the total anachronism of administering town and country units as distinct entities. But the new metropolitan counties proved to be bastions of Labour rule, and their large budgets a source of independence from Treasury control. The inequity — not to say iniquity — of the rating system was universally recognised. In 1948 the responsibility for fixing rateable values had been transferred from local authorities to the Board of Inland Revenue. Rates are a regressive form of taxation (in that the burden is not related to the ability to pay); the poorest local authorities, where social deprivation is greatest, are usually those with the lowest domestic rateable values; these authorities tend to look to business ratepayers and central government to make good inevitable shortfalls in resources matched against needs.

When the Attlee government abolished (1948) the university and business votes (that is, the remaining forms of plural voting) at parliamentary elections, and at the same time did away with the residence qualification for the parliamentary franchise, it enacted that all voters qualified to vote at parliamentary elections would henceforth be entitled to vote also in elections for the local authorities (for example, the LCC and one London Borough) in which they reside. As a concession to occupiers of business premises, the 1948 Act additionally permitted a local-government vote to the occupier of any rateable land or premises of a yearly value of not less than £10, but with the proviso that no person may vote more than once in an election for the same local authority. This right has proved of very little value to occupiers of business premises; their rates are invariably higher than those of domestic ratepayers, and the votes of the former are swamped by those of the latter. Conservative promises to restore the business vote at local level have not been kept. Instead, in redemption of a 1983 manifesto commitment, the Conservatives legislated to give the Secretary of State for the Environment the power (which already existed in Scotland) to limit the rate increases of all local authorities. In 1985 the legislation was passed to abolish the GLC and the six metropolitan counties.

Labour opposition to these far-reaching reforms was passionate and sincere. The tradition of local self-government had been destroyed. But it is worth recalling that, although the final blows were delivered by Conservative administrations, Labour had played an active part in the destructive process. Education is one example, the police another. No Labour government has ever proposed to give Londoners the same democratic control over the Metropolitan Police that other counties have over their police forces. In 1966 the Labour Home Secretary, Roy Jenkins, compulsorily amalgamated the police forces of England and Wales, reducing their number from 117 to 49 (now 43); this reform, justifiable on the grounds of police efficiency and the fight against crime, has brought the effective existence of one national police force much closer to realisation.

To say that local self-government has been destroyed is to make a statement of fact, not a value-judgement. Perhaps all that has happened is that the inevitable has come to pass. Modern forms of communication have (effectively) contracted the size of the British state. 'Whitehall' is not as distant as it once was. In any case, many government departments have been moved out of London; the Driver and Vehicle Licensing Centre is in Swansea; pensions and other social security benefits are calculated at Newcastle-upon-Tyne; the headquarters of the National Savings movement are located in Durham; the tax affairs of many Londoners are dealt

with from offices in Edinburgh. Developments in electronic communications promise to bring still closer the centre and the
periphery of Great Britain.

In the 1960s and 1970s the relationship between the two was a
subject of public discussion and governmental concern. In the
Carmarthen by-election of July 1966 a political party hardly
noticed outside Wales, Plaid Cymru (founded 1925) won, from
Labour, its first parliamentary seat. Carmarthen was lost in 1970,
but at the general election of February 1974 the Plaid captured
Caernarvon and Merioneth, and at the October 1974 election both
these seats were retained, and Carmarthen was won back. Scottish
nationalism also appeared to be on the march. The Scottish
National Party (formed by amalgamation in 1934) had had a
short-lived by-election success at Motherwell in April 1945. In the
early 1960s it began to contest by-elections with increasingly
creditable results. In 1967 it won the Lanarkshire seat of Hamilton
from Labour. This seat was lost in 1970, but that of the Western
Isles was gained. In November 1973 a second seat was won, that
of Glasgow Govan. In February 1974 the SNP lost Govan but
retained the Western Isles and won no less than six other seats,
two from Labour and four from the Conservatives. All seven seats
were retained the following October; in addition, four more seats
were captured from the Conservatives.

The nationalist upsurge perplexed many Englishmen and
worried the major political parties. It was caused by the conjunction of a number of different factors. In Wales there is some
justification for viewing it, in part at least, as the protest of rural,
Welsh-speaking areas against neglect from London, a cultural
movement as much as a political one, based on a species of
populist radicalism which had strong roots in Welsh politics. It was
also a protest against the complacency (and corruption?) to be
observed within local Labour parties that had controlled Welsh
politics for more than half a century. In Scotland nationalism also
fed upon high unemployment rates, bad housing, the economic
decline of rural areas and the plight of small farmers. Plaid Cymru
asked merely for some devolution of power from London to
Cardiff. The SNP, exploiting the discovery of North Sea
Oil — 'Scottish Oil ' — demanded complete separation.

A Royal Commission on the Constitution, established by the
Labour government in 1969, reported in 1973 in favour only of
such devolution of authority as would permit the retention of the

economic and political integrity of the whole of the United Kingdom. When the October 1974 election returned Labour to power with an overall majority of only three seats (a majority which for all practical purposes disappeared with the loss of West Woolwich to the Conservatives in 1975), it seemed prudent for the Labour party to make some accommodation with the Scottish and Welsh nationalist movements, which now commanded 14 votes in the House of Commons. Proposals were therefore brought forward to establish representative assemblies in Cardiff and Edinburgh. The necessary Acts were passed, with a great deal of ill will from both Conservative and Labour backbenches, in 1978, but were not to take effect until after consultative referendums had been held.

In Wales the referendum (March 1979) resulted in only 11.9 per cent of the electorate (20.3 per cent of those who voted) indicating their support for the proposals. In Scotland 51.6 per cent of those who voted favoured the devolution plan, but since this was less than the 40 per cent of the electorate stipulated in the legislation (it was actually only 32.9 per cent), the Scottish proposals, too, fell by the wayside. Mrs Thatcher's government quietly repealed the Acts in 1979. The plans they contained have not since been resurrected.

Only in Northern Ireland has the integrity of the United Kingdom seemed in genuine doubt. Following the Treaty of 1921, and the establishment of the Stormont parliament in Belfast (an act of devolution which most Englishmen were delighted to witness), Northern Ireland had been left to run its own internal affairs. The twelve Northern Irish MPs at Westminster could, for all practical British purposes, be regarded as an adjunct of the Conservative party. In 1949 the Irish Free State severed all its remaining constitutional links with Great Britain, and became the Republic of Eire. Though the Republic laid (and lays) claim to 'the north of Ireland', it eschewed violence as a means of achieving this goal. Bombing campaigns by the Irish Republican Army, which repudiated the 1921 Treaty and those of its number who had signed it, were contained; the IRA was suppressed on both sides of the border.

In reality, however, a cauldron of troubles was brewing in Northern Ireland. The Unionist (i.e. Protestant) majority, which comprised roughly two-thirds of the population of the province, developed a siege mentality, based partly on the knowledge that high birth-rates among the Catholic minority might one day lead to a Nationalist takeover at Stormont, and reunion with the Republic. In some areas (especially Armagh and Omagh Urban Districts, County Fermanagh and Londonderry County Borough) there were already Catholic majorities among the voters. By a process of blatant gerrymandering, these majorities were denied their rights; in Londonderry, for instance, in 1967, Catholics numbered 14,429 voters and Protestants only 8,781, but the local authority was controlled by 12 Unionists, the Nationalists having only eight seats. There was similar discrimination against Catholics in housing and recruitment to the public service.

On 5 October 1968 a vicious attack by the police upon a march organised by the Northern Ireland Civil Rights Association in Londonderry marked the commencement of serious disorders and escalating violence, with which it eventually proved beyond the capacity of the Stormont government to cope. In August 1969 the Labour Home Secretary, James Callaghan, sent British troops to Northern Ireland, initially to protect Catholics from Protestant violence while reforms were discussed. But so long as the Protestants formed a majority of the Northern Irish community, these reforms stood little chance of being implemented. If majority rule was good enough at Westminster, why not at Stormont? Edward Heath's administration solved this problem by abolishing (30 March 1972) the entire Northern Ireland constitution; Northern Ireland was to be ruled from London, just like Scotland and Wales, with a Secretary of State who is a British MP and sits in the British Cabinet.

The establishment of 'direct rule' ought to have pleased the Protestants, for it emphasised the 'Britishness' of the province, and the Catholics, for it removed the Protestant veto on long-overdue reforms: Catholics in Northern Ireland were to be governed in exactly the same way as Catholics in Liverpool or Kilburn (north London). But politics in Northern Ireland are never that logical. The religious labels of the two communities in the province are just that — labels. The two communities comprise two competing nationalisms, one British, the other Irish. Northern Ireland is the only part of the United Kingdom policed by the military, and where fundamental rights (in particular, the right not to be detained without trial) have been breached. To afford some guarantee against the tyranny of the majority, proportional representation has been forced upon Northern Ireland, especially for local government and Common Market elections, although both the Labour and Conservative parties are adamant that this system is not appropriate for Westminster elections. The IRA continues to enjoy the sympathy and support of the Catholic minority. The Protestant majority harbours in its midst paramilitary forces in defiance of United Kingdom law. Constitutionally Northern Ireland is still a part of the United Kingdom. Practically it is a totally separate entity, where consensus has evaporated and very special considerations apply.

The troubles in Northern Ireland have had two effects upon the domestic life of Great Britain. The first has been the spilling over into English cities of the violence of Ulster, and the periodic bombing sorties carried out by active service units of the IRA on the mainland. On 21 November 1974 explosions in some Birmingham public houses resulted in twenty deaths. One week later Parliament was panicked into passing a Prevention of Terrorism Act which declared the IRA an illegal organisation in Great Britain (as if this proscription would lead its members to see the errors of their ways); gave the Home Secretary power to 'exclude' suspected persons from the mainland (thus interfering, upon mere suspicion, with the right of a citizen of the United Kingdom to move freely about the country); and gave the British police the right to detain suspects for seven days without any charge being brought.

The Act, uncomfortably reminiscent of the restrictions upon personal liberty imposed after the end of the Napoleonic Wars, has not prevented further terrorist outrages, whether by the IRA, the even more extreme Irish National Liberation Army, Libyan gunmen or Palestinian Arab or Bulgarian assassins, all of whom have been active on the streets of Britain since 1974. Perhaps the enactment of the legislation salved the consciences of both Conservative and Labour MPs who had voted for and supported the abolition (by a private member's Bill in 1965) of capital punishment for murder. This reform, laudable on humanitarian grounds, had been prompted also by publicity given to serious miscarriages of justice, which had almost certainly resulted in the execution by hanging of innocent persons. Yet the abolition of capital punishment was, on the evidence of numerous opinion polls, opposed by a clear majority of the British electorate. In democratic terms, its enactment was inexcusable.

The other impact of the Northern Irish imbroglio was a political one. The Unionists of the province split into (broadly speaking) a moderate Official Unionist Party and a more extreme Democratic Unionist Party (led, both in the province and at Westminster, by a talented demagogue, the Reverend Ian Paisley). The demise of the old Unionist entity, with which Bonar Law had been happy to make common cause, led to the rapid dissolution of the Unionist-Conservative alliance. By 1970 most Conservatives were eager that this divorce should take place; for, as the troubles in Northern Ireland escalated, the marriage had proved a decided embarrassment. Not only did the Unionists no longer control the twelve Northern Irish seats, but the Northern Irish MPs (whose number had been increased to 17 by the time of the 1983 general election) formed an independent voting bloc in the House of Commons. The SNP and Plaid Cymru members constituted other independent elements. After the June 1983 poll, the House of Commons contained no less than 44 MPs who did not take the Labour or Conservative whip; of these, 17 were Liberals. A greater number of minor-party MPs had not been seen at Westminster since 1931, and the Liberal total was higher than at any time since the dissolution of 1945.

The emergence of 'third parties' in British national politics and, in particular, the resurrection of Liberalism, forms one of the most distinctive and original themes in the political history of Britain after the end of the Second World War. The Liberal revival was, indeed, more dramatic than numbers of MPs might suggest. It is a feature of the single-member constituency, first past the post electoral system that minor parties may accumulate many millions of votes nationally although, in terms of individual constituency results, their victories may be very thinly spread. In the 1966 election the Liberals gained twelve seats, but their total vote was over two millions, or 8.5 per cent of the poll. In October 1974, with over 6.3 million votes (the largest Liberal poll ever, amounting to 18.3 per cent of the total votes cast), only 13 Liberal candidates were successful.

Two features of the Liberal revival stand out; these features, in turn, act as markers of a far more profound shift in the political sociology of Great Britain. First, the electoral base of Liberalism was broadened. Between 1945 and 1970 this base resided in Scotland and Wales, the Celtic fringe which provided the majority of Liberal victories. In the quarter-century after 1945, even the English successes of the Liberal Party were in areas remote from London, such as Devon, Cornwall and Berwick. But since 1970 an increasing number of Liberal successes have come in English urban constituencies, such as Sutton and Cheam, Ripon, Rochdale, Colne Valley, Liverpool Edge Hill, Croydon North-West, and Southwark and Bermondsey. In 1983, the Liberal-Social Democratic Alliance recorded 13 of its 23 victories in England; six of these were in the metropolitan counties and Greater London.

Secondly, Liberal support has been spread remarkably evenly among different social classes in the electorate, a fact reflected in the results of numerous opinion surveys. The growth and growing sophistication of opinion polling in Britain since the 1950s is itself a feature worthy of note. An offshoot of the advertising industry, the opinion polls, sponsored by newspapers and television, have become one of the major channels through which the general public has followed political events. If the result has been to portray the political process (especially general elections) as a horserace, this has at least captured the popular imagination and stimulated interest in current affairs. The Institute of Practitioners in Advertising uses the following categories to describe the socio-economic status of the population:

A — Professional and higher managerial
B — Administrative and lower managerial
C1 — Supervisory, clerical and skilled non-manual
C2 — Skilled manual
D — Semi-skilled and unskilled manual
E — State pensioners and casual workers

Using poll data collected on this basis, the 'classless' image of the Liberal party since its revival in the 1960s can be easily appreciated:

Table 7.1: Liberal Party Preference by Class, 1964–1983[a]

	AB	C1	C2	DE
		(percentage of voters)		
1964	15	14	11	9
1966	11	11	8	7
1970	10	9	7	6
1974(F)	20	25	20	17
1974(0)	22	21	20	16
1979	15	20	11	14
1983[b]	27	24	27	28

Notes: a. Data for 1964-February 1974 from National Opinion Polls; for October 1974 from Louis Harris; for 1979 and 1983 from Gallup.
b. Liberal-SDP Alliance.

Since support for the Liberal party has been growing over the past twenty-five years, these findings have a deeper significance. In the decades that followed the collapse of the old Liberal party British politics was completely dominated by Conservatism and Labourism. At each of the three general elections of 1951, 1955 and 1959, the Labour and Conservative parties together attracted well over 90 per cent of the votes cast, and could claim to have the support of well over 70 per cent of the electorate. Moreover, this support was undeniably class-based. Data collected by the Gallup poll showed that at no time between 1945 and 1964 did middle- class support for the Conservative Party average less than 68.5 per cent; working-class support for the Labour party averaged not less than 55.5 per cent.

As these statistics indicate, not all middle-class voters supported the Conservatives, and not all working-class electors voted Labour. Middle-class Labourism has been an invariable component of Labour support, and working-class Conservatism is even older; two investigators of working-class deference in the 1960s were able to record the following tribute voiced by a working-class Tory supporter:

[The Conservative Party] have some of the best brains in the country. They are altogether more successful and brainy than the Labour, and they have a great deal of experience behind them. They've a tradition of governing and leadership behind them for generations.
(quoted in R.T. McKenzie and A. Silver, *Angels in Marble* (1968), p. 109)

None the less, until the mid-1960s it could be said that manual workers in general voted Labour and that non-manual workers in general voted Conservative. The hallmark of electoral behaviour was a marked lack of volatility, with the two major parties, each with solid class support, gathering up the lion's share of the votes. There were very good grounds for declaring that 'Class is the basis of British party politics; all else is embellishment and detail' (P.G.J. Pulzer, *Political Representation and Elections in Britain*, 3rd edn, 1975), and for asserting that 'the most significant division in electoral loyalties is that the well-to-do . . . predominantly vote Conservative, while those of a lower social status and a lower income group tend to vote Labour' (R.M. Punnett, *British Government and Politics*, 3rd edn, 1976).

By the late 1960s the era of stable class-based partisanship within the British electorate was drawing to a close. Table 7.2 charts the extent of class support for the Labour and Conservative parties in the six general elections from and including 1966:

Table 7.2: Conservative and Labour Party Preference by Class, 1966–1983[a]

	AB	C1	C2	DE
percentage of voters supporting the Conservative Party				
1966	72	59	32	26
1970	79	59	35	33
1974(F)	67	51	30	25
1974(O)	63	51	26	22
1979	67	58	46	32
1983	62	55	39	29
percentage of voters supporting the Labour Party				
1966	15	30	58	65
1970	10	30	55	57
1974(F)	10	21	47	54
1974(O)	12	24	49	57
1979	18	21	47	55
1983	12	21	35	44

Note:a. Derivation of data as in Table 7.1.

By 1983 Conservative support among the professional and managerial groups had fallen, steadily but without respite, to just over half, while, among manual workers, it had risen to over a third. Within the same period, manual-worker support for Labour had declined to less than a half, but this loss was in no way balanced by a rise in middle-class Labour identification.

Behind these percentages there lay a complex warp and weft of sociological and political transformations. According to survey evidence collected by the British Election Study at the University of Essex, in 1964 no less than 81 per cent of the electorate identified themselves with the Labour or Conservative parties; 40 per cent had a 'very strong' identification. In October 1974 only 24 per cent identified 'very strongly'. Until 1970 this erosion among the strong identifiers was hardly noticeable. Thereafter it proceeded so rapidly that the Essex researchers have likened the election of February 1974 to a 'critical' or 'realigning' election, as those of 1923 and 1924 had been in relation to support for the Labour Party. Even among those electors who have continued to vote Conservative or Labour, 'secularism' has been on the increase — that is, the motivation for such support has been pragmatic rather than dogmatic; the electorate has come to reflect the habits of the consumer society from which it is drawn, choosing a political party as it might choose a car or a refrigerator, and putting perceived needs above loyalty to a brand label.

One important component of the diminution of class-based partisanship has been the attitude of young voters. The hardening of partisanship with age is a well-established phenomenon. It is among the young electors that party attachments are weakest. The influence of the family and the home are less pervasive than formerly, the mass media provide alternative standards, there are more opportunities for travel. 1970 was the first election in which the voting age was lowered to 18 (a reform enacted by the Labour government the previous year). It is therefore possible that the newest generations of electors have repudiated the two-party system.

Survey evidence collected at Essex supports this thesis, but also points to a weakening of partisan commitment within all age-groups. Thanks to the broadening of educational opportunities consequent upon the passage of the 1944 Education Act, the acceptance by the Conservative government in 1963 of the major recommendations of the Robbins Committee on Higher Education (which had called for a doubling of university places, to 218,000, within ten years and an expansion of opportunities generally in higher education), and the raising of the school-leaving age, to 16, in 1973 (another Conservative reform), the electorate is better educated now than it has ever been. One consequence has been a growing refusal on the part of electors to believe in or take much notice of the shibboleths of class politics.

Another, the result also of a growth in the habit of discernment among electors, has been an increasingly volatile — and unpredictable — electorate. At the general elections of 1950, 1951, 1955 and 1959 the 'swing' to the party which formed the government (the average of the change in Labour's share of the United Kingdom vote and the change in the Conservative share) varied only between 0.9 per cent and 2.9 per cent. At the 1964 election the swing (to Labour) was 3.0 per cent, and in 1966 2.7 per cent. In 1970 there was a 4.7 per cent swing to the Conservatives. Much lower swings (of, respectively, 1.3 per cent and 2.1 per cent to Labour) were recorded at the polls of February and October 1974, but at the election of 1979 there was a swing to the Conservatives of 5.2 per cent and in 1983 of 5.5 per cent, though in this election the Conservative and Labour parties suffered losses of support, both in absolute terms and relative to their showing in 1979.

At the election of 1983 Margaret Thatcher obtained a parliamentary majority of 144 seats, only two fewer than Clement Attlee had had in 1945. But whereas Labour had achieved its 1945 victory with 47.8 per cent of the total votes cast, in 1983 the Conservatives only had 42.4 per cent (slightly higher, at 43.5 per cent, if we confine the calculation to Great Britain); in 1945 Labour won the support of 35.4 per cent of the electors, but in 1983 the Conservatives could claim the support of only 30.8 per cent. Yet, although the 1983 result was not a particularly impressive one for the Conservative Party, it was a severe reverse for Labour. At no general election between 1951 and 1970 (inclusive) had the Labour vote fallen below twelve millions, nor had its share of the votes cast dropped below 43 per cent. Table 7.3 charts its downward progress since then:

Table 7.3: Labour's Electoral Performance, 1974–1983

	Total Vote	% of total vote	% of electorate
1974(F)	11,646,391	37.1	29.2
1974(O)	11,457,079	39.2	28.6
1979	11,532,218	37.0	28.1
1983	8,456,934	27.6	20.0

During the 1970s support for Labour fell by about 10 per cent, but from a base which was already low. Its 1983 result was the worst that Labour had recorded since 1918. Although, therefore, it continued to fill the role of Her Majesty's Opposition, and although its support in the north of England had not been eroded as deeply as in the south, its status in the country as a whole was almost that of a minor party. Some reasons for this are contained in Table 7.2, namely the failure to attract middle-class voters and, much more significantly, the marked contraction in manual-worker support. Using evidence collected by the Gallup organisation, Professor Ivor Crewe, of Essex University, has been able to demonstrate that nearly a third of all those who voted Labour in 1979 deserted the party in 1983, and that some of the severest losses were among working-class home owners (more than two-fifths of whom defected) and skilled manual workers; among trade unionists, support for Labour was only 7 per cent ahead of that given to the Conservatives. 'The Labour vote', commented Professor Crewe, 'remains largely working class; but the working class has ceased to be largely Labour' (*The Guardian*, 13 June 1983).

How has this come about? We can point to the creeping affluence among manual workers, the growth in home ownership and car ownership, to which reference has already been made, to the fact that over 96 per cent of households in the country possess a television, over 75 per cent a telephone, over 70 per cent a refrigerator, and over 62 per cent enjoy some form of central heating. Many of these luxuries (if, indeed, they may any longer be considered as such) have come within the reach of the masses through the growth of hire-purchase. The amount of credit obtained in this way stood at only £68 millions in 1947; however, with the easing of credit restrictions in the 1950s, it had grown to £1,115 millions by 1964, and by a further £1,000 millions over the following decade. But the fundamental basis for all this newfound wealth was the growth in real wages, which increased by 19 per cent between 1955 and 1970, and which in 1979 stood at 52 per cent above their 1955 level.

There is, therefore, a great deal of circumstantial evidence for the *embourgeoisement* thesis. But can it be seriously argued that anything as deep-rooted as class consciousness can be overturned through the purchase of a range of consumer durables by a prosperous workforce? Affluence has not turned the manual workers into Conservative supporters (see Table 7.2). What it has achieved, however, is the rejection of the socialist ethic of class warfare. The Labour Party developed upon the foundations of the heavy industries — coal, engineering, shipbuilding, the railways, and so on — in which the workforce struggled to make ends meet. This is no longer the case. The trade unions have, in the main, won the fight for recognition. The working classes no longer live at subsistence level. The hard grind that characterised the life of many working people before 1939, and which sustained their support for the Labour Party, has gone.

It is not a socialist society which has given the working classes the life they enjoy; it is a capitalist society, or at least a 'mixed economy'. In 1983, when registered unemployment stood at a monthly average of over three millions (an unprecedented figure, even if it represented a mere 11 per cent of the total civilian workforce, as opposed to the 15 per cent of 1932), the Labour

Party attracted the support of only 45 per cent of those unemployed electors who voted for the Conservative, Labour and
Alliance parties. This — astonishingly — actually amounted to a
fall of 4 per cent compared with 1979. Over a quarter of the
unemployed vote went to the Alliance, which had been born out of
a rebellion against the socialism of the Labour left. Again, in 1983
only 39 per cent of trade unionists voted Labour, a drop of 14 per
cent compared with 1979; here too the Alliance was the chief
beneficiary, but even the Conservatives registered a 1 per cent
increase in trade-union support. In 1983 more trade unionists
supported the Conservative and Alliance parties than Labour:
working-class politics had been stood on its head.

When Labour went out of office in 1951, such a situation could
scarcely have been envisaged. In 1951, the Labour government
was exhausted, but party members were not unduly worried about
their technical defeat at the hands of Churchill. A return to power
after a few years of Conservative rule seemed entirely feasible.
Indeed, there were those in the Labour movement who argued
that five years of a Tory administration might be a positive long-
term benefit, for it seemed to them unlikely that Churchill's government would support the continuation of the welfare state and
of full-employment policies. 'It is a fact', Aneurin Bevan told the
Labour Party Conference in 1952, 'and even Keynesians have to
admit it, that there is no means of preventing unemployment in
capitalist society.' Unemployment would return, and at the next
general election Labour would be swept back into power.
Meanwhile, Labour's priorities would be to defend the reforms of
1945–51 against Tory attacks, and to settle the question of the
leadership; Attlee was already in his late sixties, and had several
heirs apparent, including Bevan (the hero of the Left), Morrison
(a moderate) and Gaitskell (Attlee's own protégé).

In fact, the expected Conservative assault upon the welfare state
and the nationalised industries never materialised. In 1951
Churchill was 77 years of age, too old, perhaps, to engineer a
radical change of direction in social and economic policy, but with
sufficient authority in the party to prevent others from travelling
down this road. In any case, the small majority in the Commons
would permit no such thing, and the election result could not be
interpreted as a mandate for change of this sort. Churchill appointed to his Cabinet men of moderate outlook, such as Butler
(at the Exchequer), Macmillan (at the Ministry of Housing) and

Walter Monckton (Ministry of Labour); the Foreign Office went to Anthony Eden and Churchill himself held the Defence portfolio.

Churchill's major interests were in foreign affairs, and his prime concern was the preservation of Britain's world role in the face of the superpowers, the USA and the USSR. This policy was a continuation of that pursued by Attlee; Britain's nuclear bomb was unveiled by Churchill (1952), but the building of it had been a Labour decision, a revelation which the left of the Labour Party greeted with shock and initial disbelief. There was some de-nationalisation, of iron and steel and road haulage, but there was also one important extension of public control, when the United Kingdom Atomic Energy Authority was set up in 1954. Conservative budgets implemented cutbacks in government spending and a reduction of food subsidies. But to balance these unpopular measures Butler imposed an excess profits tax, and the Treasury agreed to increase its subsidy to local authorities from £22 to £35 per home to help fund Macmillan's ambitious programme (actually fulfilled) to build 300,000 houses a year.

The government demonstrated its susceptibility to business pressure by agreeing to the establishment of commercial television (1954). This was opposed by Labour, the TUC, the Archbishops of Canterbury and York, and professional educationalists, but it was genuinely popular; the campaign against it was an early sign that the organised Labour movement was no longer on quite the same wavelength as ordinary working people. In April 1955 Churchill stepped down in favour of Eden. A general election was not due until the following year, but Eden called one almost at once, hoping to capitalise upon a reduction in the standard rate of income tax two weeks after he took office. In a premiership of less than two years, marred by his own ill health and the fiasco of the Suez adventure (October-November 1956), the decision to go to the country in May 1955 was Eden's one act of political acumen as Prime Minister. The Conservatives obtained a greater share (49.7 per cent) of a lower turnout than in 1951, and picked up seats in the Midlands and the north of England as well as in the south. In terms of seats the Labour losses (18 seats net) were small; but the Labour Party had attracted the votes of over 1.5 million voters less than in 1951, and the Conservatives now had a comfortable overall majority of 58 in the Commons.

This majority, and the fact that the next election was now clearly some years away, helped sustain the Conservative Party over the Suez troubles, so that when Macmillan took over as Prime Minister, on 10 January 1957, he had plenty of time in which to repair whatever damage had been done by the ill-fated attempt (virtually vetoed by the United States) to reverse by military intervention the Egyptian nationalisation of the Suez Canal. As a matter of fact there is little evidence that Suez harmed the domestic popularity of the government. Labour's vociferous attacks upon the morality of Eden's policy make good reading, but they cut little ice with the general public. Immediately prior to Suez Labour had been ahead of the Conservatives in the Gallup Poll; but in November 1956 this lead temporarily disappeared.

Labour might have been able to exploit Suez to greater permanent effect had it not been rent by deep divisions over policies and personalities. Because he wished neither Dalton nor Bevan nor Morrison to succeed him, Attlee had decided to retain the leadership until Gaitskell's succession had been assured. Bevan seized upon a number of foreign-policy and defence issues with which to drum up support against Attlee and his followers. In 1954, when the Parliamentary Labour Party had voted, by 113 votes to 104, in favour of the principle of German rearmament, Bevan resigned from the shadow cabinet, though the decision of the party conference later that year to endorse this policy (albeit by a very small majority) showed that Bevan's views were not those of the movement as a whole; at that conference Bevan stood against Gaitskell for the post of Party Treasurer, and lost. In February 1955 Bevan led a revolt of some 60 Labour MPs against Attlee's endorsement of the Conservative decision to build a hydrogen bomb; the Parliamentary Party decided by 141 votes to 112 that Bevan should have the whip withdrawn — generally regarded as a prelude to expulsion.

Labour thus entered the 1955 election as a party divided. Its hastily devised and under-organised election campaign could not mask these divisions, and the campaign itself was marred by a newspaper strike, a dock strike caused by inter-union rivalry, and a rail strike (fought over the issue of pay differentials) that was anticipated during the campaign and actually commenced two days after the election had been held. Public opinion began to turn against what was regarded as the indiscriminate use of the strike weapon, often over issues that had little connection with the welfare of union members and less still with the well-being of the community as a whole. After the election defeat, Attlee was prevailed upon to resign. Dalton had already retired from the shadow cabinet. Gaitskell had an easy victory, obtaining the votes of 157 Labour MPs to Bevan's 70; Morrison, with 40 votes, came bottom of the poll.

In a number of ways Hugh Gaitskell closely resembled Clement Attlee. He came from a well-to-do middle class family and had been educated at a public school (Winchester) and Oxford; later he became a teacher of economics in London University, and during the war had served under Dalton at the Ministry of Economic Warfare. When he became Labour leader Gaitskell had been in Parliament less than ten years. A greater handicap, in communicating with the party rank and file, was his aloof manner and his lack of oratorical powers. Much more serious, however, was the fact that though he understood the changing nature of the British electorate, and had come to believe what was undoubtedly true — that the mixed economy was here to stay — he lacked the argumentative ability to convince his party of this view, and he proved extraordinarily insensitive to party feeling. We have only to contrast his failure, in this regard, with Harold Wilson's success (discussed below) to appreciate the sheer mediocrity of Gaitskell's political craftsmanship.

For the moment these shortcomings were not generally apparent. Bevan learned the lesson of his defeat in the leadership contest and accepted the position of Shadow Foreign Secretary. He also abandoned his faith in unilateral nuclear disarmament, warning the 1957 Party Conference that the implementation of such a policy by a future Labour government would send the Foreign Secretary 'naked into the conference chamber'. Having thus succeeded in neutering the leader of the Left, Gaitskell set about steering the party in a new direction which, he hoped, would bring it electoral success.

Gaitskell was by no means alone in this task. During the mid-1950s a number of younger party thinkers — the Revisionists — prominent among whom were Anthony Crosland, Douglas Jay, Roy Jenkins and Dennis Healey — examined the relevance of traditional socialist policies, and especially of public ownership, to contemporary British society. The most exquisite — and erudite — synthesis of their views came in 1956, with the publication of Crosland's *The Future of Socialism*. Crosland methodically demonstrated how radical had been the changes in

British society since the dark days of the early 1930s; how, in particular, the achievement of full employment and the popularity of the welfare state had banished the primary poverty that had so scarred that landscape; and how the public ownership of basic utilities had had so little to do with the prosperity that the nation now enjoyed. Was nationalisation an end in itself, or simply a means to an end? Crosland had no hesitation in answering that it was merely a device, a way of achieving greater social equality and of distributing national wealth more evenly. Moreover, the experience of Conservative rule since 1951 had shown that the advances made under Attlee could be retained side by side with a formidable private sector in the nation's economy. Crosland concluded that the prescriptions advocated by the early socialists had been formulated in a society which no longer existed. 'The much-thumbed guide-books of the past', he wrote, 'must now be thrown away.' And in a later work, *The Conservative Enemy* (1962) he declared of the Labour Party:

> The trouble is that some of its leaders are radical, but not contemporary — they are discontented, but with a society which no longer exists; while others are contemporary but not radical — they realise that the society has changed, but quite enjoy the present one.

The Revisionists believed that the wider, almost ethical aims of socialism could be achieved without a great deal of public ownership, simply through the wise planning and regulation of the mixed economy which the country seemed to favour, assisted, certainly, by further reform of the nation's educational system. They pointed, moreover, to the sombre lesson of the Soviet economy, where 'private capitalists and landlords have been eliminated, but so have free labour movements' (*Twentieth Century Socialism*, published by the revisionist Socialist Union, 1956), and they noted that, in any case, further nationalisation seemed now to occupy a very low priority in the thinking of the British working classes.

The revisionist attack upon nationalisation struck many in the Labour Party — not just within the left — as rank heresy. At the 1957 party conference E. Shinwell declared nationalisation to be 'the vital principle on which this party was founded'. Clause 4 of the party constitution gave formal expression to this view. Moderates did not believe that a future Labour government would be able or would really wish to implement Clause 4 to the letter. At the 1957 conference the party adopted a policy document, *Industry and Society* (introduced by Harold Wilson on behalf of the National Executive Committee) which called for the renationalisation of the road haulage and steel industries, but beyond that simply marked down as possibilities for public ownership those industries which had 'failed the nation' in some way, such as the abuse of a monopolistic position, or a poor export record or a history of bad labour relations. A wiser leader than Gaitskell would have left the matter there; *Industry and Society* had been approved by 5.3 million votes to 1.4 millions; a left-wing resolution calling for the nationalisation of all basic industries was defeated by the same margin.

The prospects for Labour at the end of 1957 seemed rosy. The Conservatives had not been able to find solutions to the country's underlying economic problems. As the post-war economies of Europe and Japan grew stronger, Britain's share of world trade diminished (between 1951 and 1959 from 22 to 17 per cent). It is true that in the late 1950s Britain experienced a net balance of payments surplus (of about £132 millions per annum), but this was entirely due to 'invisible' trade — banking, insurance etc. Throughout the 1950s the value of imports, both of raw materials and of manufactured goods, far outstripped the value of goods exported. A particular source of concern was the rising volume of imported semi- and finished manufactures; in 1954 these accounted for 20 per cent of total imports, but by 1964 the proportion had risen to 36 per cent (and by 1976 to 54 per cent). Britain had long since ceased to be the workshop of the world. Now, it seemed, she could not even manufacture for her own domestic needs.

Some of the country's economic ills derived from the imperial legacy. There was clearly too much investment abroad and not enough at home and, apart from the United States, Britain in the 1950s spent more on defence than any of her allies in the North Atlantic Treaty Organisation. But other causes of economic weakness were domestic in origin. There were too many trade unions, and they were too often engaged in conflicts with each other. There were many unofficial stoppages. Yet, as the Conservatives themselves admitted in 1964, the record of days lost through industrial action over the previous decade was much better in Britain than in any major industrialised nation of the free world, West Germany alone excepted. More damaging was the poor quality of British management, a circumstance caused in turn by inadequate technical and managerial training and lack of opportunity to progress from the shop-floor to supervisory positions. Even where training was given (a Ministry of Labour Committee reported in 1962), some of it was 'inadequate, superficial and sporadic'.

Because the overall stability of the economy depended so obviously upon invisible earnings, it was necessary at all times to reassure foreign investors that their money was safe in London. Continued international pressure on sterling had been accelerated by the events at Suez; to retain confidence and prevent massive withdrawals of investments it became necessary, in September 1957, to raise the Bank Rate from 5 to 7 per cent (an unprecedented increase) and to reduce public spending. Additional public protests stemmed from the passage of the 1957 Rent Act, which de-restricted the rents on many properties. Had a general election been held in the autumn, Labour would have won a handsome victory. But this was not to be. Ever the showman, Macmillan brushed aside the long-term view, declaring, in a speech at Bedford on 20 July 1957 that 'most of our people have never had it so good' — which was true. In 1958 he adopted an expansionist strategy. Bank Rate was reduced to 4 per cent, the credit squeeze was brought to an end, and the public investment programme increased by £50 millions. The following year the Chancellor, Heathcoat Amory, reduced income tax and purchase tax, and restored investment allowances. In October 1959 Macmillan went to the country on the slogan 'Life's better with the Conservatives; don't let Labour ruin it.' He was returned with a majority of one hundred.

The election result was in fact less impressive than the parliamentary outcome might suggest. In terms of their share of the total vote the Conservatives did marginally less well (at 49.4 per cent) than in 1955. But the result was a bad one for Labour. Labour's share of the vote fell from 46.4 to 43.8 per cent. At the 1959 party conference, which turned inevitably into a post-mortem on this defeat, Gaitskell made use of sociological research into the erosion of Labour support. This research had identified the rise in real incomes as a prime source of the alienation of working-class voters from the Labour Party. Rightly or wrongly, this newfound affluence was linked to the fact of Conservative rule.

The stark fact is [Gaitskell told the conference] that this is the third General Election we have lost and the fourth in which we have lost seats . . . What has caused this adverse trend? It is, I believe, a significant change in the economic and social background of politics. . . . insofar as Labour appears to be doctrinaire on the subject of ownership, it saddles itself with a liability. . . . [Clause 4] implies that we propose to nationalise everything, but do we? Everything? — the whole of light industry, the whole of agriculture, all the shops — every little pub and garage? Of course not. We have long ago come to accept, we know very well, for the foreseeable future, at least in some form, a mixed economy.

Gaitskell's attempt to persuade the party to alter Clause 4 did not succeed. Worse still, he roused the left to one of its periodic attacks of self-righteousness. The left now cast itself in the role of guardian of the fundamental tenets of Labourism, and it rediscovered its pacifist past. For some time the anti-nuclear movement had been gaining strength among party activists. In 1957 the Campaign for Nuclear Disarmament (CND) had been formed 'to demand a British initiative to reduce the nuclear peril and to stop the armaments race, if need be by unilateral action by Great Britain'. CND was not a truly mass movement and it was certainly not a working-class movement. Its supporters were, in the main, middle-class intellectuals and university students. But it also had support within the trade unions (pre-eminently from Frank Cousins, who had in 1956 become secretary of the largest union, the Transport and General Workers) and from constituency activists. Its Easter marches from the Atomic Weapons Research Establishment at Aldermaston attracted only a few thousand walkers, but a great deal of media attention. At the 1960 party conference, Cousins swung the massive block vote of his union (over 1.2 millions) behind a resolution completely rejecting 'any defence policy based on the threat of the use of strategic or tactical nuclear weapons'. Gaitskell fought hard to have the resolution defeated. However, Bevan's death, in July, had deprived him of his most valuable ally. The resolution was carried by a small majority.

This great schism within Labour ranks had a significance that went far beyond arguments over defence policy and the morality of nuclear deterrence. Moderates began to question the justification of the block vote, and even of the continued wisdom of formal links between Labour and the trade-union movement. Labour MPs — most of whom were not of the left — did not relish having to defend, in Parliament, a unilateralist policy in which they did not believe; equally, however, they did not relish the consequences of acting contrary to that policy. In 1961 Gaitskell succeeded in persuading conference to adopt his defence policy: abandonment of Britain's attempt to become or remain an independent nuclear power, but retention of American nuclear bases in Britain; this left the way clear for a future Labour government to participate in a NATO nuclear defence policy.

However, Gaitskell's victory was made possible by the strenuous lobbying of the Campaign for Democratic Socialism (CDS), formed in November 1960 by William Rodgers, General Secretary of the Fabian Society, and Anthony Crosland. In January 1981 a Special Conference of the Labour Party at Wembley decided to establish a new mechanism for the election of the party Leader, namely an Electoral College in which affiliated trade unions were to have 40 per cent of the votes, and the constituency parties and the Labour MPs 30 per cent each. The deliberations at that conference, and its outcome, expressed the long-felt tensions — clearly visible in the debates of 1960–1 — between those who championed the cause of intra-party democracy and those who stood by the doctrine of parliamentary sovereignty and the independence of MPs. William Rodgers left the Labour Party to become a founder of the Social Democratic Party, as did Roy Jenkins, another CDS member; other MPs who joined CDS were Christopher Mayhew, who later defected to the Liberal Party, and Reg Prentice, who served in Labour governments from 1966 to 1970 and between 1974 and 1976, but who later joined the Conservatives and was given ministerial office by Mrs Thatcher in 1979. We are, therefore, justified in seeing in CDS, and in the circumstances which gave rise to its formation, evidence of much deeper and more permanent rifts within the Labour movement, and of growing suspicion by moderates that the influence of the left was pushing the Labour Party in directions that were, at best, irrelevant to the needs of the moment and to the wishes of the public.

At the time, however, it appeared that Labour was on the road to recovery, united as it was behind a defence policy of sorts, an understanding that Clause 4 was inviolate, and a commitment

(October 1962) to approve British entry into the European Economic Community (EEC) only if there were stringent safeguards for British economic interests and ties with the Commonwealth. In October 1961 Edward Heath, the Lord Privy Seal, had begun negotiations on Britain's application to join the EEC, of which Macmillan had refused to become a founder four years earlier. The change of policy, which had the support of the Foreign Office, the Treasury and most sections of the business community, was political in origin. With the gradual ending of Empire, it was unlikely that newly emergent nations would allow British industry the same access to cheap raw materials that had been enjoyed hitherto, and it seemed inevitable that British goods would face fierce competition from other industrialised nations. Nor could British manufacturers afford to be excluded by high tariff barriers from the markets of Europe. But Macmillan was also concerned about Britain's international influence; this, it was argued, could best be preserved through a strong Europe rather than a weak, ever looser Commonwealth of Nations.

The application to join the EEC made sense. At home, however, it appeared as an act of weakness, a public admission of Britain's reduced circumstances, a betrayal of the Commonwealth. It did not have the support of a united Conservative Party. As measured by the Gallup Poll, the unpopularity of Macmillan's government dated almost exactly from the commencement of the negotiations. Their veto (by President de Gaulle of France) and their termination (August 1962) were widely applauded in the British press. By then the country was experiencing serious economic difficulties. Renewed pressure on the pound had led the Chancellor, Selwyn Lloyd, to introduce a series of deflationary measures (April-July 1961), including increases in national health charges, raising the Bank Rate back to 7 per cent, an increase in purchase tax and — most unpopular of all — a 'pay pause' followed (February 1962) by a 'guiding light' of 2-2.5 per cent for pay settlements.

The country was back in recession, the Conservative image seriously damaged. In March 1962 the Liberals won a spectacular by-election victory at Orpington; in June the Conservatives lost another seat, Middlesborough West, this time to Labour. The following month, more as an act of desperation than of statesmanship, Macmillan dismissed seven Cabinet ministers, some of whom (especially Selwyn Lloyd) had been among his most loyal colleagues, and who had done nothing more than carry out his policies. In a comment that was widely applauded the Liberal MP Jeremy Thorpe (who succeeded Jo Grimond as Liberal leader in 1967) declared of Macmillan's action 'Greater love hath no man than this, that he lay down his friends for his life'.

Macmillan's premiership never recovered from this episode. It ended in the mud of the Profumo affair (June 1963), a scandal involving a relationship between John Profumo, Secretary of State for War, and Christine Keeler, a model who also enjoyed the attentions of Captain Eugene Ivanov, a naval attaché at the Soviet Embassy. Profumo was imprudent to have engaged in such a liaison; he was stupid to have denied it in the House of Commons. In a report which Lord Denning was asked to compile, the Prime Minister was criticised. 'It was [wrote Denning] the responsibility of the Prime Minister and his colleagues, and of them only, to deal with this situation: and they did not succeed in doing so.' In the autumn Macmillan became ill; he resigned in October.

But the Conservative government survived. The party demonstrated, not for the first time, an ability to pull together in a crisis. 'A great party', Lord Hailsham had declared on BBC Television on 11 June, 'is not to be brought down because of a squalid affair between a woman of easy virtue and a proven liar.' True, there was an unseemly public squabble for the leadership, involving Reginald Maudling, Iain Macleod, Quintin Hogg (the former Lord Hailsham, who took advantage of the Peerage Act of 1963 and disclaimed his hereditary title) and Edward Heath. R.A. Butler was regarded with suspicion by traditionalists in the party; Hogg was disliked by the progressives. Aloof from the battle stood the fourteenth Earl of Home, a wealthy Scottish landowner who had last sat in the Commons in 1951, whose only administrative experience of home affairs had been as a junior minister in the Scottish Office (1951–55) and whose elevation to the Foreign Office (1960) had been greeted with incredulity in party circles (Home had served as Parliamentary Private Secretary to Neville Chamberlain, 1937–9).

Butler, under whom Hogg and Maudling agreed to serve, might have snatched the premiership for himself had he been willing to fight Home for it. He was not, thereby proving that he was not the stuff of which Prime Ministers are made. In the interests of the unity of the party he made way for the Scottish Earl, who thus became (18 October) the first peer to hold the office of Prime

Minister since the retirement of Lord Salisbury in 1902. He at once disclaimed his peerage. A Commons seat was found for him at Kinross and West Perthshire. Sir Alec Douglas-Home (as he became) was clearly a caretaker party leader. A general election could not be delayed beyond one year, and Sir Alec used this period to rebuild the party image. He did a remarkably good job. At the Board of Trade Edward Heath enacted (1964) a very popular reform, the abolition of resale price maintenance, the system whereby manufacturers and wholesalers required retailers to abide by minimum price levels for the sale of their products. During the summer party morale improved. In September the Gallup Poll put the Labour lead over the Conservatives at less than 2 per cent; National Opinion Polls actually gave the Conservatives a slight edge over Labour. When the election came (18 October), the difference between the Conservative and Labour shares of the total vote was less than 1 per cent. In the Commons Labour had an overall majority of just four seats. After 13 years the Conservative party was out of office; but its defeat could have been much worse.

Hugh Gaitskell did not live to witness this narrow Labour victory. At the beginning of 1963 he had become unexpectedly ill, and died, prematurely, on 18 January, in his fifty-eighth year. The Parliamentary Labour Party elected to succeed him Harold Wilson, then aged 46. A former university teacher of economics who had once been a Liberal, Wilson had been in Parliament since 1945, and had the reputation of a man of the left, having resigned from Attlee's government, along with Bevan and Freeman, in 1951. But he had been careful to distance himself from the dogmatism of the Bevanites, and had not been afraid to enter the Shadow Cabinet in place of Bevan in 1954.

By 1963 Wilson had moved to occupy a more centrist position in the spectrum of opinions in the Labour movement. He had also developed considerable skills as a parliamentary debater and a television performer. Wilson's critique of capitalism was entirely pragmatic. He attacked the Conservatives, not for presiding over a capitalist society, but for their incompetent management of it. In urging his party to 'unite on policy, not divide on theology', he turned attention right away from unilateralism ('defence policy', he said, '. . . by the very nature of things changes from year to year and even from month to month'), and, without for one moment suggesting that Clause 4 was somehow not quite right, he focused the mind of the party, and of the nation, upon the 'scientific revolution'. *Labour and the Scientific Revolution*, a policy document issued by the National Executive in 1963, called for 'A new deal for the scientist and technologist in higher education, a new status for scientists in Government, and a new role for Government-sponsored science in industrial development'. Did this new role for Government-sponsored science mean more public ownership? No-one really knew. But in putting forward these ideas Wilson trumped the Conservatives and gave back to Labour the aura of a governing party; the left trusted him.

The Wilson governments of 1964–70 were reformist, up to a point, but they were in no sense socialist. In 1964 Gaitskellites were given important Cabinet positions: Patrick Gordon Walker went to the Foreign Office, George Brown to the newly created Department of Economic Affairs, James Callaghan to the Exchequer (to be succeeded in 1967 by Roy Jenkins, who became Home Secretary in 1965), Douglas Jay to the Board of Trade (to be succeeded, in 1967, by Anthony Crosland), and the Defence portfolio was given to Dennis Healey. Left-wingers were relegated to positions from which their impact on domestic policy was bound to be minimal: Barbara Castle to the Ministry of Overseas Development, Anthony Greenwood to the Colonial Office, Arthur Bottomley to Commonwealth Affairs and Frank Cousins to the new Ministry of Technology. The one Bevanite to be given an important home ministry was Richard Crossman, who took charge of Housing and Local Government.

However, the composition of the Cabinet (which contained eight working-class members out of a total of 23) mattered far less than the knife-edge position of the government in the Commons. A majority of four (reduced, at one stage, to one) was not viable. It was widely believed that another election would have to be held after a decent interval. Some promises had to be redeemed. Prescription charges were abolished and retirement pensions were increased. Wilson dutifully introduced a Bill to renationalise iron and steel; it was vetoed by two right-wing Labour backbenchers (May 1965). In dealing with the balance of payments deficit inherited from the Conservatives, the Cabinet — or rather, a few selected members thereof, with subsequent rubber-stamping by the full Cabinet — decided against devaluation, but in favour of an emergency package that included higher national insurance contributions, more petrol duty, an increase in income tax and the introduction of a capital gains tax. A surcharge of 15 per cent was placed on imports. The surcharge had already been planned by the Conservatives.

Indeed, there was little to distinguish Labour's economic policy from that of the Macmillan-Home administrations, except that Labour executed orthodox Treasury remedies of deflation with more panache. For instance, in the spring of 1965, in order to impress the international banking fraternity, tough restrictions were put on hire-purchase and on local-authority borrowing. But the *Joint Statement of Intent on Productivity, Prices and Incomes*, signed in December by the government, the TUC and representatives of the employers, seemed to promise a new partnership based on equality of sacrifice, even if the National Board for Prices and Incomes (established in March and given statutory authority later in the year) was headed by Aubrey Jones, a former Conservative MP and minister. On 16 September 1965 George Brown published a *National Economic Plan* which envisaged an annual rate of growth of 3.8 per cent (higher than Britain was then achieving, but modest by comparison with Britain's major competitors); unfortunately, the government's recent deflationary measures rendered the *Plan* obsolete at birth.

In February 1966 Wilson announced that Parliament would be dissolved on 31 March. The decision seems to have been prompted by a Labour comeback in the opinion polls and by continued disunity in the Conservative camp. Alec Douglas-Home had clearly outstayed his welcome as a stopgap leader, but there was to be no repetition of 'the customary processes of consultation' (Macmillan's phrase in 1963). Instead, the election of a Conservative leader was, to some extent at least, democratised. In a poll (26 July 1965) of all Conservative MPs, Edward Heath emerged victorious. Enoch Powell, by far the ablest of the candidates, had stood in the contest in order to see how much support there might be for good old-fashioned *laissez-faire* economics. There was — palpably — very little. Powell obtained only 15 votes, and turned his attention thereafter to exploiting popular prejudice against coloured immigrants, large numbers of whom had come to Britain to do the jobs nobody else seemed to want to undertake.

In Edward Heath, who as Chief Whip had maintained the unity of the party during the Suez crisis, the Conservatives hoped they had chosen a match for Harold Wilson. They had done no such thing. 'He is', the press baron Cecil King confided to his diary, 'essentially an able civil servant, but the Tories have no one better' (*The Cecil King Diaries*, 1965–1970, p. 326). The Conservatives had chosen a disciple of Macmillan to preside over a party still associated, in the popular mind, with the Macmillan era. Wilson capitalised on his good fortune, and won a splendid victory at the polls. For the first time since 1951 the Labour vote exceeded 13 millions. For the first time since 1945 the Conservative vote fell below 12 millions. For the first time ever a Labour government had been returned with an increased majority (96 seats).

We should note, however, that this result was achieved on a low turnout (75.8 per cent). Several million voters seem to have decided that party differences were bound to have little impact on economic performance; so they did not bother to cast their votes. Between 1966 and 1970 the Labour administration pursued an orthodox economic strategy, but with certain refinements which few Conservatives at that time would have dared propose had they been in office. Iron and steel were renationalised in 1967 and the National Freight Corporation was established in 1968, but the major intervention in industry had come with the establishment of the Industrial Reorganisation Corporation (1966), which, under the chairmanship of Frank Kearton (the head of Courtaulds), provided government money to fund mergers between private corporations. The takeover of AEI and English Electric by GEC, and the merger of the British Motor Corporation with British Leyland, were facilitated in this way.

The introduction of a Selective Employment Tax, designed to hit employment in the service industries and foster a move back to the manufacturing sector, was unpopular with employers and trade unions alike; it was also ineffective, and added to the cost of living. When the National Union of Seamen struck (16 May–2 July 1966) in support of a pay increase beyond the government's 'norm' of 3–3.5 per cent, Wilson used an old Tory trick (the allegation that the union was being manipulated by the Communists) to turn public opinion against it and force the union leadership to call it off. This victory was followed almost immediately by a further dose of deflation (yet tighter hire-purchase restrictions, yet another increase in purchase and petrol taxes) and a six-month freeze on wages and salaries.

These measures were taken, as Richard Crossman recorded, 'horribly inefficiently, at the last moment' (R.H.S. Crossman, *The*

Diaries of a Cabinet Minister, vol. I, p. 578). Wilson did have a long-term strategy, the three planks of which were (i) admission into the Common Market, (ii) drastic pruning of the defence budget and (iii) state regulation of industrial relations. Neither the first nor the last of these was in the traditions of the Labour Party, and neither found favour with Labour's paymasters, the trade unions. The British trade-union movement, famed for its insularity and aversion to socialist internationalism, did not share the enthusiasm of its continental comrades for the EEC, which it, and the left of the Labour Party, regarded as a club to further the interests of multinational corporations. The decision to reapply to join the EEC found much opposition among Labour MPs; the application was vetoed — again by de Gaulle — on 27 November 1967.

The pruning of defence commitments was clearly more popular with the party, which had never been happy in administering Britain's imperial legacy. In February 1966 the government had decided to evacuate the British base in Aden; the closure of the Suez Canal following the Six Day War between Israel and Egypt (1967) pointed to the logic of withdrawing altogether from the Persian Gulf. Early in 1967 the government had already determined to evacuate Singapore by the mid-1970s. But it was the economic crisis of November 1967, and the devaluation of the pound by 14.3 per cent, that forced the Cabinet to decide upon evacuating both the Gulf and Singapore by 1971, and to abandon any capability to mount military operations east of Suez. Only the stubbornness of a minority white regime in southern Rhodesia, and the need (on economic grounds) to support the federal side in the Nigerian civil war, prevented a complete disengagement from Africa as well. These blemishes aside, however, the Labour government did bring the Empire more or less to an end. After 1971 all that remained were scattered remnants, principally Hong Kong, Gibraltar and the Falkland Islands.

The ending of Empire was entirely appropriate and utterly realistic. However, though popular with the party it did not strike voters as particularly exciting. Apart from the economy, the major focus of domestic interest in 1967–8 was Enoch Powell's attack on continued black immigration, especially from east Africa. Here the Labour Party was in a genuine dilemma. Should it act in what it conceived to be an enlightened manner — as Labour MPs had done in their private capacities in voting for the abolition of capital

punishment for murder, and for the Abortion and Homosexual
Law Reform Acts of 1967? Or should it give the voters what they
wanted, regardless of moral considerations? In 1968 the government placed on the statute book the most racially motivated
piece of legislation ever passed by a British government, an Immigration Act designed unashamedly to exclude would-be Kenyan
Asian immigrants.

If this enactment, accompanied though it was by a Race Relations Act, did not square with socialist principles, it did at least
please the trade-union rank and file. Wilson's third plank, a
thorough reform of industrial relations, most certainly did not. In
January 1969, following the report of a Royal Commission,
Barbara Castle (now Secretary of State for Employment and Productivity) published *In Place of Strife*, a White Paper which proposed to give the unions many new rights, but which also proposed
a compulsory 'cooling off' period of 28 days before strikes or lock-
outs could take legal effect; the White Paper further proposed to
endow the government with the authority to order a ballot where
an official strike was to take place, and to remove the legal
immunity enjoyed by unofficial strikers. Though approved by the
House of Commons, these proposals were rejected by the
National Executive Committee and the TUC. The legislation was
abandoned in March.

In June 1970 Wilson went to the country. The Conservatives
polled fewer votes than they had done in their victorious
campaigns of 1951, 1955 or 1959 but, against the background of
the lowest turnout since 1935, the support they obtained was
enough to give them an overall majority of 30 seats. The experience of 1964–70 had a profound effect on the mass Labour
movement. It distanced the party from the trade-union movement,
and led trade unionists to become disenchanted with
parliamentary politics. This mood led inexorably to outright defiance by the TUC of the Conservative's 1971 Industrial Relations
Act and contributed, in some measure, to the worsening record of
labour disputes during Edward Heath's period as Prime Minister
(June 1970-February 1974). Trade unionists ceased to have much
confidence in politicians; they relied instead on their industrial
muscle. The lesson which the left drew was not dissimilar: Labour
Cabinets could not be trusted to pursue socialist policies, and
Labour MPs could not, except under extreme duress, be trusted to
oppose Labour Cabinets intent on ignoring party policy.

The voting public seems to have reached a different conclusion. The four years of Conservative rule under Edward Heath had elements of the farcical as well as of the tragic. The 1970 Conservative manifesto, *A Better Tomorrow*, had stated: 'We will stop further nationalisation'; yet Rolls-Royce was nationalised by the government after only eight months in office. The manifesto had also stated: 'We utterly reject the philosophy of compulsory wage control'; such a philosophy was implemented in November 1972. Attempts to hold down inflation foundered when, in the aftermath of renewed conflict in the Middle East (October 1973), much higher charges for imported food, raw materials and oil had a devastating impact on the cost of living. Heath succeeded at last in negotiating the United Kingdom's entry into the Common Market (1 January 1973), but he split his own party in the process, and the benefits of entry, overtaken as it was by the great inflation later in the year, were not immediately apparent. The reorganisation of local government, already discussed, and of the National Health Service (1973) did not grip the public imagination; like Heath himself they exuded dullness.

Heath's government was terminated not, as is often supposed, by the miners' strike of February 1974, but by the government's own lack of realism in confronting it. Had the Conservatives been returned with their majority trebled, that would not have made one miner go down his pit to dig one sackful of coal. Perhaps the Cabinet thought that an increased majority would restore its status and authority. At all events, a generous offer by the TUC not to treat any pay settlement in the mining industry as a precedent was, foolishly, turned down. A general election was held on 28 February. Heath lost, but no party won. Instead, the country was to be governed for the next five years by minority Labour administrations propped up, towards the end of the period, by Liberal support.

Reference was made earlier in this chapter to the ways in which the election of February 1974 might be regarded as a watershed. With a historical perspective that only the passage of time can bestow, it may well be that the entire period 1974–9 will be seen in this light. The minority Labour governments negotiated an end to the miner's strike, repealed the 1971 Industrial Relations Act, and settled (by referendum) the dispute about the country's membership of the EEC. But inflation reached double figures (26 per cent by July 1975) and unemployment continued to grow (5.9

per cent of the workforce were unemployed in the winter of 1977–8). Nor had there been any noticeable redistribution of the country's wealth; nearly one-third of all personal wealth was owned by 1 per cent of the population.

The government's alibi appeared sound enough: it was in office but not in power. To the left, however, this excuse rang hollow. Socialists within the Labour movement have always put a greater premium upon loyalty to principles than upon the art of the possible. The economic policy pursued by James Callaghan, who had succeeded to the premiership on Wilson's resignation early in 1976, was full of pragmatic compromise; there were no import controls, and there was more than a suspicion that too much of the profit from North Sea oil was being left in private hands. Even before the election of June 1979 swept Labour from government, plans were being laid for much greater grass-roots participation in the election of future Labour leaders, and for the compulsory annual reselection of Labour parliamentary candidates (a device obviously aimed at weeding out the over-moderate). The road to Wembley was, so to speak, already under construction; it led, at least in the short term, to much greater socialist influence over the party, but also to the exit of some leading moderates, inheritors, for the most part, of the revisionism of the 1960s, to form the Social Democratic Party.

On the Conservative side, too, there was a return to fundamentalism of a kind. The turnabouts in policy practised by the Heath government, the resort to nationalisation, the rescue of 'lame ducks', the failure of statutory wage control to halt inflation, the capitulation to union power, all combined to oust Heath from the leadership. In February 1975 Mrs Margaret Thatcher was elected in his place, the first woman to lead a British political party, and also the first scientist (she had read chemistry at Oxford before turning to law and embarking upon a political career). The forces which brought her to the head of the Conservative Party were those which rejected the politics of consensus, doubted the wisdom of the welfare state, were hostile to the power of the trade-union movement, and — above all — broke with the commitment to full employment that had characterised post-1945 Conservatism hitherto. Unemployment was to be allowed to rise, and the public knowledge that a Conservative government would permit it to do so was to be used to neutralise the unions (a process that was to be aided by depriving them of many of the immunities they had enjoyed since 1906) and curb what were deemed to be excessive wage demands. The marketplace was to rule.

This new Conservatism was but old Liberalism writ large. It did not have majority support in the country, but in 1979 it offered a kind of positive approach (whether one liked it or not) which was totally lacking on the Labour side. The centre-ground came to be occupied by the Liberal-SDP Alliance, formed in the autumn of 1981 and celebrated in the Liberal victory at Croydon North-West that October. Early in 1982 the opinion polls gave the Alliance a lead of 2 per cent over Labour and 3.5 per cent over the Conservatives. Mrs Thatcher's government was saved by the Argentinian invasion of the Falklands. The general election of June 1983 was by no means a 'khaki' election, as that of 1900 had been. But public approval of the successful military action in the south Atlantic enabled the government to stage a recovery. It did not 'win' the 1983 election, but it did, by default, emerge with a very large majority in the Commons.

In terms of political sociology the mould of British politics has been broken. In terms of party politics the future is far from clear. Beyond purely political considerations, however, other fundamental changes have, since 1945, affected the functioning of the machinery of government, and the relationship between government and society. During the 1970s it became fashionable in the media to ponder on whether the United Kingdom had become 'ungovernable'. There was a great deal of talk of 'overload' — of Whitehall trying to do too much and not succeeding in achieving anything — and there was a great deal of pressure-group activity, which, it was said, signified a national rejection of parliamentary politics.

There is probably more than a grain of truth in such observations, but we can make this admission without in any way denying the power of the British state to adapt, as it has done on numerous occasions over the past two hundred years. There has certainly been a revolution in values, particularly in relation to the position of women in society, and a technological revolution, brought about by the microprocessor, is clearly under way. Change is always painful in itself and usually has unpleasant side-effects. The necessity for change is not denied. But it remains to be seen whether change can be achieved without any loss of compassion.

GUIDE TO FURTHER READING

(Unless otherwise stated, the place of publication is London)

Works of Reference

The standard collections of economic statistics are those of B.R. Mitchell and P. Deane, *Abstract of British Historical Statistics* (1962) and B.R. Mitchell and H.G. Jones, *Second Abstract of British Historical Statistics* (Cambridge, 1971). Economic, political and social statistics and chronologies appear in C. Cook and J. Stevenson, *The Longman Handbook of Modern British History 1714–1980* (1983). D.E. Butler and A. Sloman, *British Political Facts 1900–1975* (1975) should be read alongside F.W.S. Craig, *British Electoral Facts 1885–1975* (3rd edn, 1976) and M. Kinnear, *The British Voter: An Atlas and Survey since 1885* (2nd edn, 1981). The standard compilation of twentieth-century social statistics is by A.H. Halsey, *Trends in British Society since 1900* (1972).

Two very compact works of biographical reference, which also contain more general historical entries, are by J.P. Kenyon (ed), *A Dictionary of British History* (1981) and A.W. Palmer, *A Dictionary of Modern History 1789–1945* (1962).

General Surveys

Four general histories offer, between them, a most comprehensive survey of British history since the Glorious Revolution: in the Oxford 'History of England', the volumes by B. Williams, *The Whig Supremacy 1714–1760* (2nd edn, Oxford, 1962), J. Steven Watson, *The Reign of George III 1760–1815* (Oxford, 1960), E.L. Woodward, *The Age of Reform 1815–1870* (2nd edn, Oxford 1962), R.C.K. Ensor, *England 1870–1914* (Oxford, 1936) and A.J.P. Taylor, *English History 1914–1945* (Oxford, 1965); in the

Nelson 'History of England', the works by J.B. Owen, *The Eighteenth Century, 1714–1815* (1974), D. Beales, '*From Castlereagh to Gladstone 1815–1885* (1969) and H. Pelling, *Modern Britain 1885–1955* (1960); in the Longman 'Foundations of Modern Britain' series, the volumes by E.J. Evans, *The Forging of the Modern State: Early Industrial Britain 1783–1870* (1983) and K. Robbins, *The Eclipse of a Great Power: Modern Britain 1870–1975* (1983); and in 'The New History of England' (Arnold) the works by W.A. Speck, *Stability and Strife: England 1714–1760* (1977), I.R. Christie, *Wars and Revolutions: Britain 1760–1815* (1982), N. Gash, *Aristocracy and People: Britain 1815–1865* (1979) and M. Beloff, *Wars and Welfare: Britain 1914–1945*).

These works may be supplemented, for the later period, by C.J. Bartlett, *A History of Postwar Britain 1945–74* (1977), D. Childs, *Britain since 1945* (1979) and P. Calvacoressi, *The British Experience 1945–75* (1978).

The recent history of Scotland is surveyed in W. Ferguson, *Scotland 1689 to the Present* (1968) and J.G. Kellas, *Modern Scotland* (1980). Modern Welsh history has been admirably chronicled in K. Morgan, *Wales in British Politics, 1868–1922* (3rd edn, Cardiff, 1980) and the same author's *Rebirth of a Nation: Wales, 1880–1980* (Oxford, 1981). Of the many general histories of Ireland I would recommend J.C. Beckett, *The Making of Modern Ireland, 1603–1923* (1966) and E. Norman, *A History of Modern Ireland 1800–1969* (1971).

The Constitution

Some editions of constitutional documents suffer from the almost total absence of commentary and explanation, which makes them virtually useless to the non-specialist. The volumes edited by E.N. Williams, *The Eighteenth-Century Constitution 1688–1815* (Cambridge, 1960) and H.J. Hanham, *The Nineteenth-Century Constitution, 1815–1914* (Cambridge, 1969) do not fall into this trap. For the twentieth century the most useful collection is that edited by M. Minogue, *Documents on Contemporary British Government* (2 vols, Cambridge, 1977), the second volume of which is devoted entirely to local government (this should be read in conjunction with B. Keith-Lucas and P.G. Richards, *A History of Local Government in the Twentieth Century* (1978)). P.A. Bromhead provides a survey of constitutional developments in *Britain's Developing Constitution* (1974), and of the House of Lords in *The House of Lords and Contemporary Politics* (1958). For an examination of the role and work of the Commons the reader should consult S.A. Walkland (ed), *The House of Commons in the Twentieth Century* (Oxford, 1970). A lively discussion of the problems of 'overload' in British government since 1945 is provided in A. King (ed), *Why is Britain becoming harder to Govern?* (1976).

Party Politics

Many general histories tend to concentrate heavily on political developments. Lord (R.) Blake's *The Conservative Party from Peel to Churchill* is worth reading, together with T.F. Lindsay and M. Harrington, *The Conservative Party 1918–1979* (2nd edn, 1979). The Liberal Party is provided for in R. Douglas, *History of the Liberal Party 1895–1970* (1971) and V. Bogdanor (ed), *Liberal Party Politics* (Oxford, 1983). The most stimulating account of the formation of the Social Democratic Party is that written by I. Bradley, *Breaking the Mould* (Oxford, 1981). H. Pelling's *Short History of the Labour Party* (5th edn, 1976) remains a standard work. E.H. Hunt's *British Labour History 1815–1914* (1981) and J. Hinton's *Labour and Socialism: A History of the British Labour Movement 1867–1974* (Brighton, 1983) combine political narrative and analysis with examinations of the interaction between the Labour and trade-union movements. The societal implications of political debate are examined superbly in K. Middlemas, *Politics in an Industrial Society: The Experience of the British System since 1911* (1979). The decline of the two-party system since the Second World War forms the subject of S.E. Finer, *The Changing British Party System 1945–79* (Washington DC, 1980) and V. Bogdanor, *Multi-Party Politics and the Constitution* (Cambridge, 1983).

Economic Development

The best one-volume introduction to the growth of the British economy in the eighteenth and nineteenth centuries is by P. Mathias, *The First Industrial Nation: An Economic History of Britain 1700–1914* (2nd edn, 1983). For more specialised treatment

of agricultural and industrial aspects the reader should consult
J.D. Chambers and G.E. Mingay, *The Agricultural Revolution
1750–1880* (1966) and A.E. Musson, *The Growth of British Industry* (1978). The vicissitudes of British economic performance
after 1914 are examined in S. Pollard, *The Development of the
British Economy 1914–1967* (1969) and M.W. Kirby, *The Decline
of British Economic Power* (1981). In understanding the evolution
and impact of different forms of transport H.J. Dyos and D.H.
Aldcroft, *British Transport* (Leicester, 1969) and P.S. Bagwell,
The Transport Revolution from 1770 (1974) are invaluable.

Society and Social Policy

R. Porter, *English Society in the Eighteenth Century* (1982) provides a stimulating and detailed overview for the pre-industrial
period. E.P. Thompson's *The Making of the English Working
Class* (1968 edn) remains the classic statement of the Marxist
viewpoint; a longer time-perspective is provided in E. Hopkins, *A
Social History of the English Working Classes 1815–1945* (1979).
Two very different analyses of social change in the nineteenth and
twentieth centuries are presented in A. Bédarida, *A Social History
of England 1851–1975* (1979) and J. Ryder and H. Silver, *Modern
English Society: History and Structure 1850–1970* (1970). J.
Stevenson, *British Society 1914–45* (1984) deals in much greater
detail with the early twentieth century, and usefully complements
D.C. Marsh, *The Changing Social Structure of England and Wales
1871–1961* (1965). H.M. Pelling, *A History of British Trade Unionism* (1963) remains the best one-volume survey of this subject,
but a more microscopic examination is presented in the Oxford
University Press's *History of British Trade Unionism since 1889*;
volume I, covering the years 1889–1910 (1964) is by H.A. Clegg,
A. Fox and A.F. Thompson and volume II, 1911–1933 (1985) is by
H.A. Clegg alone.

Two standard and authoritative accounts of social policy in the
nineteenth and twentieth centuries are by D. Fraser, *The
Evolution of the British Welfare State* (1973) and M. Bruce, *The
Coming of the Welfare State* (4th edn, 1968). E. Evans has edited a
useful collection of documents as *Social Policy 1830–1914* (1978).
The history of educational provision is traced in J. Lawson and H.
Silver, *A Social History of Education in England* (1977) and S.J.

Curtis and M.E.A. Boultwood, *An Introductory History of English Education since 1800* (4th edn, 1966). Religious issues are examined in E.R. Norman, *Church and State in England, 1770–1970* (Oxford, 1976). The best introduction to the political aspects of the female suffrage controversy is by C. Rover, *Women's Suffrage and Party Politics in Britain, 1866–1914* (1967). But for a sensitive account of the position of women generally in Victorian society the reader can do no better than consult the collection of essays edited by M. Vicinus, *Suffer and be Still: Women in the Victorian Age* (1980).

NAME INDEX

SUBJECT INDEX

289